Visual Basic.Net
Developer's Headstart

About the Author

Jeffrey Shapiro has been a practicing software engineer, software architect, and technology expert for more than 13 years. He has written numerous articles and books on software development and technology, and is the author of *SQL Server 2000: The Complete Reference*. Jeffrey also writes the *Java for the Enterprise* newsletter, published by *Network World*.

A frequent speaker at software development conferences, Jeffrey has worked with hundreds of companies such as Microsoft and IBM, a number of public institutions, and several governments.

Visual Basic.Net
Developer's Headstart

Jeffrey Shapiro

Osborne/**McGraw-Hill**

New York Chicago San Francisco
Lisbon London Madrid Mexico City Milan
New Delhi San Juan Seoul Singapore Sydney Toronto

Osborne/**McGraw-Hill**
2600 Tenth Street
Berkeley, California 94710
U.S.A.

To arrange bulk purchase discounts for sales promotions, premiums, or fund-raisers, please contact Osborne/**McGraw-Hill** at the above address. For information on translations or book distributors outside the U.S.A., please see the International Contact Information page immediately following the index of this book.

Visual Basic.Net Developer's Headstart

1234567890 FGR FGR 01987654321

ISBN 0-07-219581-9

Publisher	Brandon A. Nordin
Vice President & Associate Publisher	Scott Rogers
Acquisitions Editor	Ann Sellers
Project Editor	Mark Karmendy
Acquisitions Coordinator	Tim Madrid
Technical Editors	Amir Liberman, MCSD; Lou Boni, Jr.
Copy Editor	Lisa Theobald
Proofreader	Paul Tyler
Indexer	Rebecca Plunkett
Computer Designers	Lucie Ericksen, Jean Butterfield
Illustrators	Michael Mueller, Greg Scott
Series Designer	Roberta Steele
Cover Designer	Greg Scott
Cover Illustration	Eliot Bergman

This book was composed with Corel VENTURA™ Publisher.

Contents

Acknowledgments . . . . *xi*

Introduction . . . . *xiii*

Chapter 1   **An Introduction to the .NET Framework and VB.NET**   1

Casting the .NET   2

 Divide and Rule   5

 The First COMing   6

 The Elements of COM   8

 COM Unbecoming   11

The Second COMing   12

 What Is the .NET Framework?   13

 The Common Type System   13

 Why .NET Is Better   14

 Is .NET Another Java?   15

 Why .NET Depends of Visual Basic   17

The Legacy of Visual Basic   17

 Don't Mind Us: We're Making Moolah   18

 Componentware Arrives with OLE and COM   19

 Death of a C++ Programmer   20

 The Legacy of ASP   20

And the VB Machine Rolls On   21

 And then Along Came a Cpider?   21

Entering VB Nirvana   23

 True Object Orientation   23

 Structured Exception Handling   26

 Delegates   27

 Interfaces   27

Multithreading 27

Managed Execution 28

ADO.NET 28

ASP.NET 29

Observations 30

Chapter 2   **Introduction to the Common Language Runtime** **33**

The CLR Is More, by Far 34

A Hosted Execution Environment 35

An Execution Manager 36

Assembly Basics 37

Assemblies Exposed 41

The Elements of the Assembly 42

Generating MSIL 43

The Common Language Specification 44

Language Interoperability 44

Metadata 46

Down to Executable Code 48

"JIT'er" Bugs Beware 48

Managed Execution 49

Side-by-Side Execution 49

Application Domains 50

Garbage Collection 51

The .NET Security Model 53

Just-in-Time (for Tea) Deployment 54

Observations 56

Chapter 3   **VB.NET Building Blocks** **57**

Let the Mission Begin 58

Goodbye World, Hello VB.NET 60

Option Compare, Explicit, and Strict 63

Data Type Conversion 63

VB.NET Operators 64

The Value of True Is −1 64

Operator Precedence 65

Unary Operators 66

Assignment Operators 66

Relational Operators 67

Concatenation Operator 69

Bitwise Operators 69

Arithmetic Operators 70

Execution Control Statements 71

Branching 71

Decision-making and Switches 73

Iteration Statements 76

Do...Loop 76

For...Next 77

For Each...Next 78

While 78

Arrays 79

Declaring and Initializing Arrays 79

Working with Arrays 80

Working with the Array's Upper Boundary 82

The Erase Statement 84

The IsArray Function 85

Collections 85

The Collections Namespace 86

Strings 87

Working with Strings 88

The Methods of System.String 88

Methods 104

Sub-procedures and Functions 106

Observations 106

Chapter 4   **Object-Oriented Software Development Using VB.NET** **107**

Types 109

The .NET Value Type Reference Model 109

The .NET Object Reference Model 110

Inheritance, Encapsulation, and Polymorphism in VB.NET 114

Inheritance 114

Encapsulation 119

Polymorphism 121

A "Real-World" Scenario 123

Designing the Application 124
    Modeling 125
Creating Classes 127
    Class Visibility and Role 128
    Encapsulation at Work 128
    Creating a Class Others Can Use 129
    Inheritance at Work 132
Implementation in the Parent Class 134
    Adding the Methods 134
Object-Oriented Development at Work 138
    Inheriting the Implementation 138
    Using the Classes 141
    Instantiation 143
Observations 145

Chapter 5   **VB.NET in Action** **147**
.NET Exception Handling 148
    The Exception Handler 151
    Exit Try and Finally 153
    Nesting Exception Handlers 154
    Creating Your Own Exception Classes 155
Extending the Base Class 157
Object Serialization and .NET I/O 160
    Serialization Part I 162
    I/O Support in .NET 163
    Serialization Part II 167
    Serialization Part III 170
ADO.NET 173
    ADO Revisited 173
    Enter ADO.NET 174
    Connection Architecture 176
    XML 177
    Implementing Database Integration with ADO.NET 178
Interfaces 180
Forms 182
    Windows Forms and Web Forms 184
    The Graphical Login 185

ASP.NET 187

    ASP.NET in Action 188

Creating a Simple Web Service 191

Observations 194

Chapter 6   Migration to and Interoperability of VB.NET **195**

Protecting Your Investment in Existing Code 197

    Stay in Classic VB 198

    Migrate Code to VB.NET 198

    Rewrite 199

Is It Worth Porting? 201

Using the Visual Basic Upgrade Wizard 202

    Understanding the Upgrade Process 203

    Upgrading COM and COM+ Services Using the Wizard 206

    Upgrade Tools for Interop 206

Accessing COM Components from VB.NET Clients 207

    Using the TLBIMP Utility 208

Calling .NET Objects from COM or Standard VB Clients 209

Understanding Object Lifetime and Deterministic Finalization 211

Moving from ASP to ASP.NET 211

Observations 212

Chapter 7   Making the Move to VB.NET **213**

What Makes a Software Development Language 214

    The Way It Was 216

    The Way It Is 216

Syntax and Idioms 217

Managed Execution, Managed Code . . . and Java 219

User Interfaces 220

VB.NET: The Best RAD Tool 220

    Late Binding 220

    VB.NET With Blocks 221

Market Demand 222

Observations 223

Index **225**

Acknowledgments

This book was conceived at Tech Ed 2001, June 23, and had to be finished before the July 31, Beta 2 "time bomb" Microsoft had so "inadvertently" dropped in the Beta 2 release. This could not have been achieved without a great deal of effort and coordination by a team of committed individuals, every one of which had to find the time in their busy schedules to tackle a project that "came out of the blue."

The first person I need to thank is my editor, Ann Sellers, for believing me when I said it was both "doable" and that I could do it . . . and for then making it happen.

This book would also not have happened without the effort of my two technical editors, Amir Liberman and Lou Boni, of Ziphex Consulting, Inc. Both did a lot more than edit and check for technical accuracy; they were also responsible for the Migration and Interoperability discussion and code in Chapter 6, and the ASP.NET and Web services examples in Chapter 5 . . . and a ton of fact-checking and code verification. Thanks guys; without your quick response to my plea for help to get the project to the press, we would not be reading these words. Lou and Amir are highly committed VB/VB.NET experts (with answers for everything) and you can contact them at **http:\\www.ziphex.com**.

I also owe a lot of gratitude to the production team, in particular Mark Karmendy, the project editor, for keeping everything together, and for those late nights and weekend office visits waiting for last minutes changes and the like. This book was also brilliantly edited by copyedit ace, Lisa Theobald, whose excellent insight to some highly technical (and often befuddled) writing saved more than my proverbial bacon.

Lastly, but of no lesser importance, I owe tons of gratitude to my wife, Kim, who kept me continuously supplied with the motivational, emotional, and physical fuel (such as tea, coffee, meals, vitamins, love, etc.) to keep on churning out the words. And of course to my eight-year-old Kevin for his incessant reminders about what I was doing and who I was doing it for.

Introduction

There has been a lot of fur and fingernails flying in the Visual Basic community, with some debates not unlike the opening to the movie *Gladiator*. There are clear divisions in the ranks. You might be one of the many developers who believe that Visual Basic.NET is too radical a departure from classic VB. Or you may be in the camp that is ready for the new VB.NET that—with its new features such as pure OOP, structured error handling, and free threading—gives VB developers extraordinary power. I believe that with VB.NET you have the ability to compete equally for the most complex software development solutions waiting for us in the years to come.

Like it or not, Visual Basic.NET is here to stay. Microsoft has bet the farm on the .NET Framework, and VB is going to be the leading tool to develop .NET software for a long time. Amid all the anticipation and anxiety surrounding both .NET and VB.NET, and a lot of controversial opinion—some of it mine—this little book was created.

The Mission

With a lot of uncertainly about VB.NET in the air, I also wrote this book for as wide an audience as possible. It is aimed at software architects and development project managers who need to get the skinny on .NET software development as quickly as possible. If you are puzzled about the advent of the Common Language Runtime and what it's intended to replace on the Windows operating system, then the first two chapters are for you.

And if you are a software engineer looking to quickly get up to speed understanding how writing software for the Windows operating systems is going to change, then the first two chapters are also for you.

The book is also aimed at the new members joining our ranks who have some basic, and not so "basic," programming skills. Yes, that means that you need to have some prior knowledge of programming in general to get the most out of this book—so much the better if you are a VB programmer. But prior knowledge of VB is not necessary to grasp the concepts discussed.

On the other hand, if you are an experienced, professional VB programmer, you'll want to get directly to the parts that matter the most for you. Chapter 3 covers VB.NET building blocks and deliberately steers clear of the OOP discussion. It takes a look at working with arrays, strings, flow control, and so on. My approach is not to *tell* you what's different or new or unchanged, but rather *show* you what's different or new or unchanged, while providing some foundation and insight into the language, its syntax and its idioms.

Chapters 4 and 5 are *all* about object-oriented programming in Visual Basic.NET. These chapters have targeted not only hard-core VB programmers, but also the followers of any mainstream OOP language. The chapters also show you database, Web applications, and XML Web services development using VB.NET.

Chapter 6 is aimed at anyone wondering exactly how portable classic VB code is, and how VB.NET fits into their current development environment. Chapter 7 places VB.NET alongside software languages like C#, Delphi, and Java, and provides some food for thought if you are unsure whether to move to VB.NET or learn C# or Java instead. It also allays fears you might have about losing your current investment in VB 6 skills.

What You Need to Get a Headstart

To get into the driver's seat and feel the G-forces of VB.NET, you will need to install the .NET Framework SDK Beta 2 or later and Visual Studio.NET with Visual Basic.NET. While .NET is supported on Windows 9*x*, Windows ME, and Windows NT, I recommend using Windows 2000 or Windows XP.

Code on the Web

For your convenience, the code written for this book is available at its page on the Osborne Web site at **http://www.osborne.com**. But I strongly recommend you create the classes and *write* the code demonstrated in Chapters 3, 4, and 5. Just downloading and running the examples will not give you a full taste of either the marvelous development environment that Visual Studio.NET offers or the true power of VB.NET.

Write Me

This book is exactly what it claims to be, a head start for Visual Basic.NET. This is such an exhaustive and complex subject that you should not expect to find all the answers to your questions on these pages. Rather than employing microdot technology to do that, I would like to give you a heads up to a bigger reference due from Osborne/McGraw-Hill by the time of Microsoft's final release date of Visual Basic.NET and the .NET Framework. This book will be *Visual Basic.NET: The Complete Reference*. It greatly expands on all the topics discussed here, plus a whole lot more. From time to time in this book, I have referenced material that will be covered or further expanded upon in the Complete Reference. If you would like to see something given special treatment in the upcoming title, please do not hesitate to let me know.

I appreciate any feedback you want to give: bouquets, brickbats, or otherwise. You can write me at **jshapiro@codetimes.com**. You can also contact Amir Liberman and Lou Boni at **amir@ziphex.com** and **lou@ziphex.com**, respectively, for anything related to VB.

An Introduction to the .NET Framework and VB.NET

IN THIS CHAPTER:

The Origins of .NET

Placing COM in Context

Reviewing the Past Decade of Visual Basic

Introducing Visual Basic.NET

Computers are meant to solve problems, make our lives easier, allow us to communicate over long distances, save lives, and make life fun. But before they can do any of these things, computers have to be programmed. Unfortunately, except for a few gifted individuals, programming computers is a difficult thing to do.

Without question, the computer's ability to solve business problems and make companies more competitive has been the plutonium that has powered workstations and servers into permanent fixtures in tens of millions of offices around the world. For more than a decade, the demand for business software to run on these machines has continued unabated, and this demand will continue to grow for as long as profit remains king.

Since the advent of the personal computer, Microsoft has owned the operating system space uncountable times over. Perhaps no single business strategy can account more for the success of Bill Gates and his team than providing programmers with the tools they need to create software to run on these machines. No operating system or computer platform (hardware) stands a chance if applications and software solutions do not support it. This is the first rule, and Microsoft has never broken it.

Casting the .NET

The first question most people have for all this new stuff is: "What is .NET?" At Tech-Ed 2000, Microsoft *usurped* this popular Internet root name and made it the official label for what was once known as the Next Generation Windows Services (NGWS).

While the entire company, most of the world's developers, and a global industry is now banking on .NET, the birth of the so-called initiative goes back a number of years. This section will examine what it has taken to get to this point. Many of you will probably say, "Why do I care? I just want to get cracking with code." However, recapping will help you appreciate many of the revolutionary features the .NET Framework introduces and why it will change the way you develop and deploy applications for years to come.

Some like to think the .NET initiative started circa 1995, at about the same time that Sun released Java. But in many respects, .NET started when DOS was the reason we existed.

It is pretty easy to plot the life of .NET: Figure 1-1 tracks its progress from the early years to the present. First, we had the DOS era, and much has been written about the sweaty-palms-clutching-ice-picks days of the marriage and divorce between Microsoft and IBM.

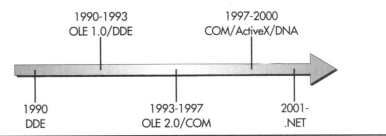

Figure 1-1   *.NET is less a new technology and more the result of a lengthy iteration of solutions that began with DOS in the 1970s.*

Next came the Windows 16-bit era in the late 1980s, which almost ended in turmoil by about 1995 when the world, fixated on the graphical user interface, struggled to be productive with its various slothlike implementations. We were given a 16-bit processing command stack, multitasking too terrible to trust, and fault protection so bad that the term *GPF* is still too dastardly to include as an acronym in Webster's Dictionary.

Windows 95 was a great improvement (despite the problem that DOS still lurked underneath the colorful desktop and the pretty icons). Windows NT changed a lot of things, along with the new user/kernel mode abstraction layers, the 32-bit kernel, the hardware abstraction layer, a revamped driver model, and better use of the processor, which greatly improved sharing, fault tolerance, and threading.

Then came Windows DNA (which, among other things, stands for *Windows Distributed interNet Applications Architecture*), the fourth era. This era for Microsoft might not have been, had the software company not stopped to gawk at the Internet parade crashing through its backyard (as so many believe). After that party, Gates signed a couple of billion-dollar checks, which brings us to today, the next era, with .NET and the Common Language Runtime (CLR).

Windows DNA, as an initiative, was really nothing more than the stopgap to a better deal. But it is clear that OLE 1.1 and dynamic data exchange (DDE), and then OLE 2.0 on COM and DCOM (Component Object Model and Distributed COM), set the scene for what we now experience as software developers. When you look back at those earlier eras, you will see that sharing memory, hardware, devices, and processing space and time was the major cause of our problems as application developers.

Once the operating system settled the conflicts with new abstraction layers, new issues arose—*at* the various application layers. At this point, a plethora of excellent development tools hit the market, and it became easier to develop some sophisticated software for the Windows operating system. By the time Windows 2000 was announced, everyone was creating their own services, interfaces, and little hellholes.

While we were desperately trying to share everything, we ended up sharing only chaos. The only stable machines were those dedicated to a single service or application. The IT people who had to install and manage the *dreck* we created can vouch for the problems created by installing too many applications. To put the picture into brutal context, managing a server of applications has up to now been much like managing a group of overcommitted individuals trying to share one bar stool.

During the years of the Windows DNA initiative, Microsoft set in motion a plan to fix the problems of who was doing what on the operating systems, who was doing what with the hardware, and so on. At the same time, it became as clear as angel breath that the Internet would become the fuel for computing for the next few decades. After all, we all became really productive when we could write books on computers instead of typewriters and do our bookkeeping in spreadsheets instead of ledger sheets. We became even more productive when we could wire our computers together and share common folder hierarchies, printers, and other devices.

Then we discovered how useful and cheap it was to send e-mail instead of faxes or telexes. As for the World Wide Web—we are still trying to figure out what we can use it for, other than online banking.

Windows DNA was founded on an impressive collection of guiding principles. Briefly, here is what Microsoft, and their loving competitors, envisaged in the run-up towards Y2K (let's dub this the "Bold Six-Principle Plan"):

▶ **Internet Enabled**   The operating system is to attach to the Internet invisibly and seamlessly. The Internet protocols, TCP/IP, FTP, HTTP, and so on, should make it so that every application and service can fully integrate with the Internet and consume whatever remote services are needed.

▶ **Interoperability**   Open standards and protocols must allow applications on various platforms to interoperate and communicate. Barriers to interoperation should be removed.

▶ **Integration**   The shared services and facilities of the operating system, or those supported by it, should be simple enough to implement and integrate by multiple vendors. It should also be easier to maintain software, especially binaries, interfaces, and libraries. Version control must be simple to implement and the installation of new software and functionality by vendors should not break existing functionality.

▶ **Language Agnostic**   Software developers should be able to use the language of choice that is both suitable for the job at hand and within the expertise and knowledge base of the developers. In other words, developers should not have to learn new languages to compete with the latest features that are lighting up the marketplace.

▶ **Less Time to Market**   The plumbing must be in place. Developers should not have to reinvent the wheel or try and build a better mousetrap. It must be a simple matter of "insert-and-turn" to release a new version or a new product.

▶ **Total Cost of Ownership**   Companies should not have to spend vast amounts of money on administration, change control, and support. Installation of new applications or versions should not be viewed as something akin to the effort of sending centurions into battle.

The objectives of Windows DNA were rather lofty. Implementing the vision was another matter. And this brings us to a question: How many of the six principles were fully implemented by 2001? If you read on, you should be able to answer the question before the end of the chapter.

Divide and Rule

The next phase in this evolution (or revolution) was building the architecture. The subject of separating interfaces from implementation has been hotly debated since the earliest times, and this book also gets in its two-cents worth. Windows DNA, on the other hand, needed to implement a tiered architecture on several levels. *Tier* is a rather abstract term, but it adequately describes the process of separating functionality spaces from one another, essential in a computing environment that had become network-centric (wide area) rather than machine- or processor-centric.

The Windows DNA model, hardly a new idea, proposed that the tiers could be divided logically in three ways: presentation, logic, and data. But this system needed some ether that would provide space for each tier to interact and communicate one with the other. Presentation services need access to logic and the logic needs access to data. (Presentation services actually supply and consume the data, and they should be largely ignorant of the logic required to satisfy these duties.)

At about the same time as the engineers in Redmond thought they had reinvented breakfast, a similar distributed movement was afoot in the software development world. It became widely accepted that software services and applications should and could no longer be Sasquatchian, leaving huge footprints on our hard drives. Software needed to be broken down into smaller interlocking modules or components.

Database engines were one of the first of the excess weight to be dropped out of single application binaries and relegated to the duties of operating systems services and servers. Network access, device management, and presentation services were pulled at about the same time. Developers needed a way to upgrade, fix, and improve software without having to ship the product to the consumer in a five-pound box. (It was fun to receive a big box of software, but the joy ended soon after the polystyrene peanuts ended up in the trash, to help pollute our planet.)

The agent that was slated to make this happen for both services and applications in the world of Microsoft Windows is a technology called *COM*, the *Component Object Model*.

NOTE

COM's competitor in the Java world is CORBA (the Common Object Request Broker Architecture), its principal component object model.

The First COMing

COM is essentially a binary standard that enables two algorithms to talk to each other and negotiate an exchange of information. It defines an interface between a consumer of a component and a provider. As such, Microsoft has aggressively promoted COM as the silver bullet of distributed computing. To understand .NET, you need to understand (basically) what COM is and what it sets out to achieve… and where it succeeded and where it failed.

A COM *object* or component implementation cannot become useful without the publication of a COM *interface*. This interface is a distributed piece of information— a specification—that provides a *"global positioning system"* for an application to access implementation somewhere. When an application consumer or client consumes a COM component, it should consume only the interface. The implementation is kept entirely separate, in a dynamic-link library (DLL) or an executable file somewhere.

NOTE

Many component developers provide both interface and component in the same module. And for classic VB, this was the default.

COM interfaces can be designed in any capable language, but they are best designed using object-oriented (OO) languages. C++ has, for a variety of reasons, been the number one choice among COM developers. For example, C++ lets you design a COM interface using a pure abstract base class, and the ability to inherit the base class has powerful object-oriented benefits for COM programmers. When the interface is inherited, the blueprint or map of the memory required by the interface is inherited as well. This is a design trait of C++, which is one of the reasons for its extensive use for component work.

The interface comprises a pointer to a collection of virtual functions, which is known as a *virtual functions table* or *vtable*. The vtable (see Figure 1-2) then points to the actual implementation of the virtual functions listed in the vtable. The vtable is platform independent and as such it can reside on any operating system or platform, although the memory layout of the vtable varies from operating system to operating system.

NOTE

Virtual functions are definitions of functions and thus are not implemented in the COM interface. Virtual methods in a base class follow the same implementation principles. They are implemented in the derived or extended class.

The implementation of a COM object is binary, and while the COM implementation can be developed in just about any modern language, it *is* platform specific, which means it can only run when the COM runtime is present.

NOTE

That Microsoft would let you develop COM components in Visual J++ was one of the issues that irked the Sun gods. This kind of skewed VJ++ toward Windows development.

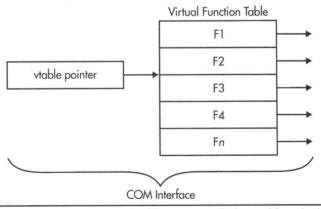

Figure 1-2   *A pointer points to an array of functions called a vtable, which in turn points to the implementation of the functions in dynamic link libraries or executables called COM servers.*

The Elements of COM

The COM specification and purpose—as an object model for components—reflected the shot in the arm that Windows software development and distributed computing was looking for. Component-based software development demands adherence to several specific tenets (or philosophies), and these tenets have carried over into the .NET initiative, which you shall soon see. Here are the four most important tenets, in no particular order:

▶ Language independence

▶ Encapsulation

▶ Dynamic linking

▶ Versioning

Language Independence

Many of you might not think this is important, until you discover that you cannot support a popular platform or idea in the language you *principally* write code in. Both the proponents of COM and Java have to some extent failed this requirement. For a component-based architecture to succeed, one should be able to write components of equal (or almost) functionality in any language. This has not been the case with COM, because Microsoft's most popular language, Visual Basic, has not been truly up to the task.

 NOTE

While most good programmers today can write software in more than one language, it is not the most productive habit. Specializing in one language, like VB.NET, allows you to be more productive by an order of magnitude.

The Java world is also not language agnostic. Despite claims that the Java Virtual Machine can support bytecode generated from other language compilers, the JVM has been around for more than five years and someone has yet to make a go of this.

Encapsulation

We have gone into encapsulation in Chapter 4 in some depth, so we will not dwell on the subject too long here. In the world of software components and services, you have *consumers* and *providers*—or clients and servers (*client* is the more popular term, but I believe that *consumer* says a lot more). Consumers consume components on an as-needed basis. When a consumer is done with one component, it should be able to shed the component, unlink from it, and consume a new component as seamlessly as possible.

Encapsulation helps achieve this by hiding the implementation of components. A consumer need only know how to consume a component, and it does this through an *interface*. The uncoupled implementation could thus be situated anywhere—on the same machine as the consumer or on a server somewhere else. As long as the interface to the implementation never changes, the software can easily be upgraded and enhanced.

The consumer does not always need to know that the implementation has changed. Think of the ignition system in a car: you insert the key and turn, and off you go. Imagine the public outcry if one day the manufacturer decided to replace the key with a combination lock mechanism. As long as the interface remains unchanged, the consumer can carry out the action with his or her eyes closed—or while talking on a cell phone.

What does it take to achieve optimum encapsulation? First, language independence is a big step in the right direction. It should be that if you decide to implement in Yorick because Yorick is all you have coded in since you left the cradle, and Yorick is supported by the runtime, then Yorick it should be. Many COM-based implementations have actually achieved this today. For the most part, while VB may have not always made an ideal component language, it did make an ideal consumer language for components used in client applications, user interfaces, and frontends. As for C++, the reverse is the case. You don't get worshipped for creating a killer GUI in C++. You get fired for missing deadlines.

Next, the implementation of components should be locatable anywhere. A component's implementation should be accessible from the same address and processing space as the consumer, or it should be possible to utilize the implementation from remote processes, running on remote machines. In other words, the consumer should generally be completely ignorant of the location of the implementation. If it were any other way, the consumer would have to be recompiled so that the new libraries could be compiled into the monolithic application and redistributed if the implementation changed.

NOTE

COM largely succeeded in implementing "trans-network" instantiation through DCOM; however, DCOM has had its own share of problems, and trying to connect through firewalls was one problem that was impossible to resolve with binary code.

Components, by being language independent and omnipresent, should thus be deployed in binary form. This allows them to be dynamically linked, without needing compilation to be used, and to be secure. You will see that any component implemented in a .NET application can be serialized as an XML stream.

Finally, if all the above conditions are met, it should (*should* is the watchword here) be possible to dynamically link and upgrade the components without the consumer needing to know about it, even while the consumer application is still running. That brings us to dynamic linking and versioning.

Dynamic Linking

Dynamic linking is a critical feature for all software systems. It allows a consumer to link to the functionality of a component without having to be recompiled every time the component is changed. We use dynamic linking to loosely couple consumer applications to their components.

Dynamic linking while the application is still running (the ability to overwrite the DLL with a new DLL while the consumer is still up) seems to be a big step up from linking after an application has restarted. Actually, it isn't really such a big deal. If we were able to get the versioning story down, the dynamic linking during runtime would follow in a heartbeat.

The idea of upgrading implementation, or consuming new and improved implementation dynamically, during runtime over the Internet is a desirable feature to master. And it has been the force driving the Java applet and bean industry for some years now. It also presents its own issues, of which security is one, as we will touch upon in Chapter 5.

Versioning

It's debatable which is more important: the ability to install new versions of components without breaking the consumer, or the ability for the consumer to assume the new implementation while still running. The latter is impressive, if achievable by the implementers, but version control has caused more pain for software developers than just about anything else that brings those little blades twirling in our heads to a squealing halt.

Call it DLL hell, or whatever else you want, but applications should not break every time a new version of a component is installed on a machine. What would be the purpose of an interface in that case? Here we are, 40 years later, still yapping on about why we write interfaces—and we are still hosing apps, thanks to version-control problems.

In a nutshell, here's the versioning problem: Say that you have an application that uses the November release of Smee's component. Along comes a user and installs another application that also uses Smee's component. (After all, Smee won the "Greatest Visual Component" award and just about every developer in the world uses it. Smee released a new version of his component every month.) The problem is that user A was happy with his Smee-infested application until user B decided to install a December version of the Smee DLL on the server. Now user A's application is broken because Smee changed something in the component's December version.

COM Unbecoming

Despite the lofty hopes of Windows DNA in general and COM in particular, it has not been an easy fix to get to where we are now. Let's review COM's progress to date.

Plumbers Required

Creating COM components is hard work. COM requires a lot of plumbing. Consumers have the easy part: they link to the interface in a DLL and that's about the entire extent of the coupling they need to perform, and the process is mostly automated. But all the real work lies in the rest of the plumbing in the COM interfaces and implementation.

COM DLLs, for starters, need to report to the registry when they show up for work for the first time. Even installing COM components is an elaborate process. Plus, the attributes and elements of a COM implementation must be further identified with globally unique identifiers (GUIDs), class IDs (CLSIDs), and so on. The coupling of interfaces and implementation is also tedious and tricky.

Make that C++ Plumbers Only

Language independence turned out to be a stopped-up idea in the Windows DNA era. While it is certainly possible to build COM interfaces and implementation in languages like Java and VB, it was neither easy nor flexible. And without a doubt, few languages could match the power of C++ when it came to creating COM components. Even consuming COM components in Visual Basic 6.0 and Visual J++ applications needs additional layers and interfaces that C++ classes do not need.

A COM interface is more than a simple interface. It is also a structure that lays out a specific memory configuration for the array of function pointers—the vtable. While you can create the interface in any language, even with a Unified Modeling

Language (UML) editor, C++ makes the whole tedious process much easier, thanks to its ability to create and inherit classes in its specialized object-oriented framework.

Versioning? What Versioning?

Once distributed, the COM interfaces cannot change, which means that it is difficult to be creative with when it comes to versioning. Current versioning in the COM world relies on maintaining current interfaces and trying to ensure backward compatibility. In other words, new versions of the implementations need to maintain backward compatibility with older versions, or else the entire version hierarchy comes crashing down. The code is designed and implemented such that only one version of it can exist on a computer at any given time. This version problem requires a lot of extra work on the part of the developers, and it is thus easy to screw up the process.

Dynamic Link...Straight to Hell

It's remarkably easy to break a working application because a new version of a DLL is not 100-percent backward compatible with an old DLL that your application is using. DLL conflicts are almost impossible to repair and usually require that the old application and DLL be completely removed and reinstalled.

Getting software off a machine can be hellish—particularly one that has more entries in the registry than there are telephones in the Pentagon. Sometimes the uninstall procedure breaks the registry, and with remnant DLL entries hiding out in the hives, you have to either remove them manually or reinstall the operating system.

If you look back at the COM years, almost a decade now, it goes without saying that for the most part COM has been successful. After all, we created a lot of components with it and many services in the operating systems would not have been possible without COM. But for many, working with COM has been more difficult than finding a cure for the common cold.

The Second COMing

Now imagine that one day you wake up and discover that all the problems described up to now are about to go away. Versioning is no longer an issue. Creating components is a cinch because all the plumbing has been created and is being handled, and you can write your software in your favorite language.

What's more, you also find that your favorite language is fully enabled as a pure object-oriented development environment, so you don't have to compete with C++ masochists any more, and application developer apartheid has been abolished. What are we talking about? This is the .NET Framework, a new era in software development that will change the way you develop applications for many years to come.

What Is the .NET Framework?

The .NET Framework is many things, but two parts make up the significant extent of it: the CLR and the .NET Class Library. The CLR manages the execution of code, and it manages memory, code compliance, threading, remote invocation, code safety, security, and so on. *Managed* code is code that you write that targets the runtime. Code you write that does not target the runtime is *unmanaged* code.

The .NET Class Library (also known as the Base Class Library or BCL) is a vast collection of interfaces and classes, more than 6000 as of this writing. These classes are object-oriented and consist of classes that let you reuse implementation through implementation inheritance, dynamic linking, and instantiation, and classes that provide interface definitions that you can implement in your own custom, extendible classes. Using the .NET Class Library, you can create your own reusable classes, interfaces, and components.

This class library comprises many classes that you can also use to instantiate objects that provide a specific service, such as database access (using the Active Data Objects (ADO.NET) collections), graphics programming (using the Graphic Device Interface (GDI+) classes), and so forth.

The .NET Framework also includes a selection of runtime hosts that can load the CLR into their processing spaces. These hosts operate in a number of places. They can run on base operating systems that are not .NET compliant out of the box, such as Windows NT and Windows 2000, Internet Explorer, and Internet Information Server (IIS). The CLR will, however, be built into the operating systems of the new enterprise .NET servers that ship in 2002.

The .NET Framework software development kit (SDK) lets you create your own custom hosts, and hosts for mobile and even non-Windows platforms are currently being developed by several companies.

The Common Type System

The CLR makes sure that code targeted to the runtime can be easily managed and safely executed. You can think of the CLR as the host master that makes sure that if you join the club, other club members will get along with you, and you will get along with them. The CLR does this by enforcing a specification called the Common Type System (CTS). The CTS makes sure that all managed code is CLR compliant. It checks that code conforms to a standard so that once it is compiled to a common intermediate language (similar to the idea of Java bytecode), all managed code, no matter the language that produced it, can integrate with and consume any other managed class. The CTS makes sure that a class that says it is a *struct,* is really a *struct,* or that an *enum* is really an *enum,* and so on.

The CTS also enforces code for class safety, which makes sure that classes are not incorrectly used (such as incorrect typecasting). It also ensures type fidelity or conformity.

Why .NET Is Better

You can do a lot more in the managed world of .NET than you could in the unmanaged world, especially as a Visual Basic developer. The framework lets you create console applications, scripted or hosted applications, thin clients and browser-hosted applications, Windows classical GUI applications, system services, ASP.NET applications, Web services, and, of course, componentware.

.NET attempts to solve the fundamental problems of the Windows DNA era. Specifically, true language independence is now a reality, because every language that is implemented on the CLR must conform to a common language specification (better known as the CLS). The CLS dictates what is acceptable and how source code is compiled to Microsoft Intermediate Language (MSIL, or just IL). In addition, the CLS specifies that all code must be described by the implementing languages, which is achieved by using metadata to describe every class.

Language interoperation is achieved because the CLR is "language agnostic," which allows code written in any compliant language to be reused by any other compliant development environment. So the problems of writing code in VB that cannot be used by C++ applications, and vice versa, are no longer an issue.

A COM component in the Windows DNA era was the only way a VB application could benefit from code written in C++, by way of loose relationship between VB and C++. But if you wrote non–COM C++ classes, such as a collection of methods to implement some Internet service, there was no way to reuse the classes in VB. The same problem occurred in reverse: functionality written in VB was not directly accessible to any C++ developer.

The plumbing is now in place under the floor of the CLR. With the support of the CLR, creating components is far easier and less problematic than struggling in COM. By conforming to the CLS and the CTS, you are free to develop interfaces and components in any language, and your components can be consumed by another compliant language.

As you will see in Chapter 2, all .NET compilers emit intermediate language. Every compiler emits the same IL code so that, at the IL level, every language is essentially identical. Now add the metadata to the mix and the CLR gets to know where everything is. The issue of tying applications to the correct versions thus disappears when classes and objects become part of the all-knowing and all-consuming runtime.

This means that we no longer need to register components and applications with the registry, so the idea of XCOPY deployment or side-by-side deployment now becomes possible. See Chapter 2 for more discussion on this type of deployment.

Is .NET Another Java?

This question begs to be asked in any introductory book on .NET, and it deserves its place in this book because more than a few VB developers have raised the question: "Since we have to learn new stuff for VB.NET, why not just move to Java?" There are a few similarities.

First, the .NET CLR is similar to the JVM, which runs in the Java runtime environment for Java applications, applets, JavaBeans, and so on.

Second, Java also publishes an extensive collection of base classes (one that has been growing since 1995). It is also a managed language. It produces bytecode, which is run on the JVM, and the code is checked and garbage collected. But Java code can also be compiled to run on the JVM because the runtime also deploys a just-in-time (JIT) compiler to compile Java code. .NET code is also JIT compiled, as discussed in Chapter 2.

Third, the Java and .NET object models are similar. Both are based on a single-inheritance object hierarchy. All classes, base or custom, are derived from a single root class called **Object**.

And fourth, managed environments manage memory for you; this is done by a runtime system called the *garbage collector* (GC). The GC is responsible for all object finalization and resource reclaiming. Both Java and .NET are garbage-collected environments.

Managed GC systems make life easier for software developers because they spare them the burden of reference counting and having to ensure that the memory is properly released when objects are disposed of. Anyone who has built a large application or service in unmanaged code knows how much time this can take. And God help you if your application springs a memory leak. Trying to locate the "hole" can take up many frustrating days of picking through code.

Finalization in both environments is nondeterministic, with some services that make it possible to maintain tighter control over the firing of finalization events. Both the .NET and Java environments are thus unsuitable for development of critical applications that require absolute control over systems resources—specifically processors, memory, and hardware—or that need to maintain absolute control over the time it takes to process an algorithm.

NOTE

Nondeterministic finalization *means that you cannot control exactly when an object is disposed of.*

These four points are pretty much where the similarity of the two environments begins and ends. .NET goes the extra mile because it is truly language agnostic, while Java is not. The .NET Framework is currently supported by more than 20 languages. Whatever you do in VB.NET today can be consumed by any other .NET-compliant language, such as C#, Perl, Cobol, and so on. You have a ready market for consumers of your .NET classes and components by developers in any one of the supported languages. Not so with Java.

NOTE

As a VB 6 and earlier developer you probably cared very little about the intricate workings of the VB runtime. It's possible to have the same attitude toward the CLR. When the CLR ships with every OS, it will become to many developers as transparent as the classic VB runtime DLLs.

We cannot say that Java is "Write Once, Run Everywhere" (a trademarked marketing statement of JavaBeans), and that the .NET Framework is only a Windows thing. The promise that Java is a "write once" language is highly debatable, but we won't go into that here. In addition, if you examine the .NET Framework SDK and the .NET Compact Framework you will quickly see that the CLR is a portable technology.

NOTE

As admirable as Java is, writing good graphical Windows applications with it prior to the release of the Windows Foundation Classes (WFC) was clumsy and crude.

Microsoft has already published a subset of the CLR called the Common Language Infrastructure (CLI), whose sole aim is to "export" .NET to the likes of FreeBSD. It is unlikely that applications running on BSD will be able to load Windows forms, however, because Microsoft will not port the Windows look and feel (just because it's free does not make it an ideal platform). However, it *is* likely that future classes for the CLI will provide graphical resources for those platforms as well, such as X Windows or Motif.

Why .NET Depends of Visual Basic

This new .NET model is expected to become the standard for developing software (at least on the Windows platform) for the next decade. Despite the anticipation surrounding C#, which was built from the ground up as a .NET language, only one language is truly set to light the .NET world on fire. That language is Visual Basic. Why?

According to Microsoft, there are more than 8 million Visual Basic programmers in the world. True or not, and even if 4 million is closer to an accurate number, VB programmers are still by far the largest group of programmers in the world.

Visual Basic has been rebuilt from the ground up and, yes, to take advantage of the new object-oriented syntax and new style of programming VB developers face, there is a learning curve. But the essential syntax and idioms of the language are still in place, allowing you to become proficient in Visual Basic.NET very quickly.

A language and a technology are bound to be successful if a large number of people support them. That Visual Basic.NET is going to catch on far quicker than Java is a certainty. Remember, by the time Java was officially released in 1995, few people could claim they were Java programmers.

The remainder of this chapter looks back at the legacy of classic VB, and sets the scene for the new era of Visual Basic programming.

The Legacy of Visual Basic

When Windows was introduced toward the end of the 1980s, it held great promise as a GUI-decked operating system. But it needed applications, and it needed them fast.

BASIC and languages like Borland C/C++, Turbo C, Microsoft C, and Turbo Pascal dominated the character-based arena. But programming Windows was more like rocket science in the first years. We needed to hire master's-level "engineers" to build dialog boxes and interact with the highly complex graphical device interface (GDI) and the hardware layers. Trapping a mouse click was more like trying to isolate a brain cell than to connect a simple string of 1s and 0s.

It was difficult to be creative, because most of our time was spent sending and trapping messages and painstakingly drawing controls. Memory management contributed a great deal to the failure of many Windows application projects, as did the enormous amount of code we had to write. Nevertheless, products like Visual Basic and Borland's ObjectVision began to ease the pain—ever so slightly.

Born in 1991 as the visual programming environment from Microsoft, Visual Basic is today's most widely used programming language. However, Visual Basic's roots go back several decades to the 1960s, the beginning for many software development languages. It began in 1964 at Dartmouth College, where the *Beginner's All Purpose Symbolic Instruction Code* (BASIC) was developed by John G. Kemeny and Thomas E. Kurtz.

BASIC was designed to be a simple language to learn, and also one that would be easy to translate. Kemeny and Kurtz wished it to be a stepping-stone to more powerful languages of the time, such as FORTRAN and ALGOL. Microsoft had other ideas. As long as an easy-to-learn language could be used to create applications for Windows, the future of programming for Windows was set in the stone: Visual Basic.

Don't Mind Us: We're Making Moolah

While the rest of the world was aggressively adopting object-oriented technology and focusing on the shift from procedural languages, Visual Basic was focusing on building applications. Since its advent, the programming model was centered on the *form*. VB lets you create a form, drop visual controls on it, and then program the events that would or could result from a user interacting with the form and its controls. You could, and still can, create a form-based application in VB that does absolutely nothing in less time than it takes to spell out VB.

To this day, with all the power that VB.NET now offers, VB programmers still grope for a form when they start up Visual Studio.NET. There was simply no other way to program in the earlier versions of VB, and old habits tend to stick around. (The aim in this series of books is to encourage the VB programmer to focus on the class or object at the center of his or her bits-filled world, instead of the form. In this regard we have spent a little time talking about the philosophy of object-oriented software development in Chapter 4, because so many VB programmers—and many other programmers—are still mystified by it.)

NOTE

This does not mean VB developers don't know anything about OO. In fact they have been on their knees begging for true inheritance and other OO features for years.

Componentware Arrives with OLE and COM

Ironically, VB's specific weaknesses as an object-oriented language and development environment significantly fueled the component and control business. Using the early OLE 16-bit technology (VBX, for VB custom control), then finally OLE custom control (OCX, which was built on COM) and ActiveX, many programmers and independent software vendors (ISVs) began to write both visual and nonvisual components that could be dropped into VB applications.

OCX components accelerated the move to componentware or component factories and helped reduce complexity in programming for the Windows platform. VB developers were able to develop extensive applications rapidly by consuming self-contained, yet amazingly interoperable components for just about any business application. If, for example, a VB program required a data-bound grid, several full-featured products that were much better than the freebies Microsoft was shipping could be purchased over the Internet and "bound" to the application. Still, a major drawback to OCX and COM components was the need to register the components in the Windows registry.

OCX and COM components did a great job separating interface and implementation. What gets bound in the application is the interface and the visual aspects of the component. The implementation—the guts of the component—sits in the DLL.

Delphi also sprouted an active component industry. But its solution was much more elegant, much like .NET today. Components were built with the Object Pascal–based Visual Component Library (VCL) and not based on COM at all. While there was no need to register components, Delphi's solution tended to perpetuate the *monolithic* application habit, a habit we were trying to shake.

Deployment was a cinch for the Delphi applications compared to the early VB applications, which made the programmer wade through DLL deployment hell just to get to the splash screen. Deployment and delivery of components that need to be specifically registered with the operating system was one of the key reasons OCX technology never quite took off in the world of thin clients and Web-based applications. Java has tried to satisfy the demand with JavaBeans.

However, the mass of VB developers was a much bigger and more lucrative market than the Delphi component market or the JavaBean market. Surprisingly, Borland finally supported OLE 2.0 and OCX controls by wrapping them in Object Pascal. The components still had to be registered, however.

Death of a C++ Programmer

Without a doubt, C++ (and of course Delphi, Java, and others) had been a far superior language to Visual Basic. Structured exception handling (SEH), free threading, and true inheritance are just a few areas in which Visual Basic could not compete.

The key to staying in business for many companies and ISVs is getting product to market as quickly as possible. Because it's so quick and easy to use, Visual Basic, hands down, made that possible. So when project managers had deadlines to meet and tight budgets to control, VB was usually the language of choice for developing the prototypes, GUIs, and frontend applications.

Project managers often found that VB programmers delivered robust applications. Even when a C++ programmer would be hired supposedly to code a superfast algorithm, the team often ended up using the VB version anyway because it was fast enough and was completed in half the time. So many C++ programmers hung up their C/C++ tools and became either full-time beach bums or full-time Visual Basic programmers.

NOTE

With the release of Visual Basic versions 5 and 6, many large, mission-critical products were being written in VB.

The Legacy of ASP

Despite the critical success of Java, which had more than a million programmers in its ranks by 2001, it never quite managed to steal away the lucrative Internet programming market from the VB community. Microsoft, however, after struggling to make dynamic and data-aware Web pages work with the burdensome Internet Server API (ISAPI), finally turned to Active Server Pages (ASP).

Programming the ASP model was no picnic, but the demand for dynamically loading HTML, imbued with data, on millions of Web sites, intranets, e-commerce applications, and various Internet-based services was driven to unexpected levels by the end of 1999. And many VB programmers got fat on the market's demand, not minding that their code looked less than beautiful.

When Microsoft introduced the Visual Basic Scripting Edition (VBScript) to the ASP market to make it much easier to develop ASP, it knew it had an established programmer following that was already familiar with the syntax and grammar of the language. The introduction of VBScript to ASP development gave many VB developers a market to chase, which directly competed with Java and Java Server Pages (JSP). But the problem with VBScript and ASP technology was, and is, that using them to code large ASP projects can be nightmarish. ASP code is hard to manage and maintain, and it's not very scalable. Plus, it is about as object-oriented as methane gas. But ASP.NET changes everything. It does away with VBScript's spaghetti code—because it supports .NET classes and the server engine is an IIS hosted version of the CLR—and allows you to code directly against it with VB.NET.

NOTE

The Internet and Information Services (IIS) and VBScript 5.0 supports classes, but these classes were anything but object oriented.

While you can also code against ASP.NET with C#, Cobol, and any of the .NET languages, the ASP market is likely to be dominated by VB programmers for some time, because the VB community owns the knowledge base and the installed base for Web development. This translates to a serious lack of expertise for programmers of Delphi, C++, Cobol, and other languages.

And the VB Machine Rolls On

In November 2000, at a special summit for Microsoft authors, the VB.NET development team told us that the VB of the 1990s has been completely transformed. They said, "To move VB into the next century and for it to prevail and develop the new generations of applications and Web services, we had to rebuild the language from the ground up. It was not a matter of just adding new features, or retrofitting the language; we essentially had to start all over in many areas."

Perhaps, more than any other feature of the .NET Framework that brought VB as we know it to an end, is its radical adoption of object orientation for software development.

And then Along Came a Cpider?

At the same time Microsoft announced VB.NET, it also announced C# (pronounced "C Sharp"). The C# language—architectured again by Anders Hejlsberg—and VB.NET have become uneasy bedfellows in the .NET homestead.

NOTE

Anders Hejlsberg is the chief architect for C#, and also one of the key proponents behind .NET. He is working on Microsoft's effort to achieve standardization for C# and the .NET Common Language Runtime (or at least a subset of it).

C# is an important language for Microsoft. A C/C++ derivative language, it competes directly with Java in several areas, especially Internet applications, Web services, and components. The existence of C#, however, puzzles many developers and project managers. And it begs the question "Why bother any longer with VB, when C# is here?"

"The question should not be why there is a VB.NET… the question should rather be why is there a C#?" This sarcastic quote, lifted off a VB newsgroup, asks why Microsoft has made such a big investment in C# when most of its developer base are VB programmers. There are many reasons they've done this—one of the most obvious has to do with the Sun v. Microsoft court case.

Microsoft was not going to just walk away from Java with its tail between its legs. Here was a proven technology and language that the company had been involved with for several years. In many respects, while it lost the court case, it actually gained more than Sun did.

There are also millions of programmers who have never learned VB, and C# is a much easier language to learn, especially for Java programmers who might "see the light" and Cobol, Pascal, Eiffel, and other language followers. This latter fact is especially true of C/C++ programmers, many of whom would find it *infidig* to learn VB.NET.

VB programmers currently have the upper hand as an established development force. There are probably 1000 VB programmers to every one C# programmer—as of June 2001. It is one thing to recruit an army of millions, but it is another to train them to fight. VB programmers currently have a distinct advantage in that the language they know can suddenly turn them all into superheroes if they get up to speed on its new features as quickly as possible. Think about it. A C# programmer cannot say that he or she has more than a decade of experience with the language. And we don't believe a dozen years of C++ experience is going to go far on a .NET project.

NOTE

See Chapter 7 about job opportunities for Visual Basic programmers.

On the other hand, there are also *many* new things to learn. Several of them are foreign to the overwhelming majority of VB programmers, but not to C#, Delphi, or Java programmers. It is probable that VB.NET will not only prosper, but it will live up to Gates's Tech-Ed 2001 proclamation that it will become the most popular—*and* the most powerful—software development language of all time. And you don't need bifocals to see that.

Entering VB Nirvana

The remainder of this book deals with Visual Basic.NET essentials, and, although it is a mile-high view of Visual Basic.NET and the .NET Framework, reading it can get you quickly on the road to programming Visual Basic.NET stuff like a wizard. A number of areas are going to take you a little more time to grasp because they will be so new to you. So let's get you a little warmed up first with a brief introduction to the most important new stuff. It will not be long before you discover that with little effort you can enter VB nirvana.

The following is a list of the important features accessible to the Visual Basic.NET language:

- ▶ True object orientation
- ▶ Structured exception handling
- ▶ Delegates
- ▶ Interfaces
- ▶ Multithreading
- ▶ Managed execution
- ▶ ADO.NET
- ▶ ASP.NET

True Object Orientation

Like an eight-year-old nagging his father for a new bicycle, VB programmers have for years been asking for true object orientation, especially inheritance. Finally, Visual Basic is object-oriented down to the last screw.

For starters, the new inheritance capabilities of VB now allow you the ultimate flexibility in designing "lovely" applications, components, and services. The tried-and-tested patterns that have been adopted by the object-oriented world for many years now can be easily adopted in VB.

NOTE

I am testing to see whether "lovely application" is a better choice of words than "killer application."

The object-oriented nature of the .NET Framework, where everything is an object, and the support of the CLR provide extremely powerful polymorphism and encapsulation features. Chapters 4 and 5 examine the OO functionality in some depth. Attributes and access modifiers let you hide and share members, functionality, and data as you need to for whatever service, application, component, or implementation you might be doing.

NOTE

By saying "everything is an object," I mean everything, *even the primitive data types (see Chapter 4).*

The following features, while not new to languages like C++, Java, or Delphi, are new features that VB programmers will have to get used to as quickly as possible.

Overloading

VB.NET allows *overloading* of properties and methods. Overloading allows you to define members using the same name in a class, but using different datatypes and different implementations of the member. By overloading your methods using the **Overloads** keyword, you will be able to define as many implementations of a method as you think you need using the same method name, but different parameter lists.

This gives the appearance of a single method, while offering alternative implementations and alternative input and return data. For example, you might have a method called **SendError** that in one implementation sends one string and requires that the consumer passes one string argument, and in another implementation the method would send two strings and would thus require the consumer to dispatch two arguments to the method. This is demonstrated in the following code:

```
Overloads Sub SendError(ByVal s1 As String)
'Add code here
End Sub

Overloads Sub SendError(ByVal s1 As String, ByVal s2 As String)
'Add code here
End Sub
```

Visual Studio automatically enumerates overloaded methods, allowing consumers to iterate easily through the list of methods. The **WriteLine** method in the **Console** class is a good example of this feature at work. When you make a call to **WriteLine** you get a choice of 18 methods from which to choose.

Overriding

Often you will want to inherit from a class but will find that not all of the methods and implementation are useful to you. VB.NET allows *overriding,* which—using the **Overrides** keyword—lets you derive a method from a class and then reimplement the method in the inheriting class. You can only override a method that has been marked as overridable.

The ability to override methods is required to implement pure abstract classes or abstract methods inherited from a base class. The abstract class and method, like the interface, is a specific design pattern used in object-oriented software development. Any method you override will have the same signature as the method definition in the base class; however, the implementation is what gets replaced, or provided.

A good example of overriding can be taken from some of the methods that are inherited from the root **Object** class. For example, the **Equals** method in its default implementation does not compare two objects, data for data, but compares only the reference variables. You are thus allowed to override the method and change the implementation to obtain an actual comparison of the object data. The following code demonstrates overriding the root **Equals** method.

```
Public Overloads Overrides Function Equals(ByVal Obj As Object) As Boolean
'Add new implementation here and then return True or False
End Function
```

Constructors and Destructors

VB.NET objects require *constructors* and *destructors.* Constructors are methods that control the creation and initialization of the object. You can even overload constructors as demonstrated in this code:

```
Overloads Public Sub New()
  Me.Text("Starting")
End Sub
```

Destructors are methods that are used to free system resources when objects are placed out of scope or when their use is explicitly terminated.

While you can call for the destruction of an object, exactly when that happens is indeterminate. The CLR is responsible for freeing memory through the garbage collection process, a feature of managed execution. So destruction is not as deterministic as you may be used to in the unmanaged world. Nevertheless, destructors and finalizers are useful for explicitly tearing down objects, such as ensuring that data is persisted, that settings are restored to defaults, and the like.

See Chapter 4 for more discussion on constructors and destructors.

Structured Exception Handling

While VB still supports the **On Error** and **GoTo** constructs for error handling, structured exception handling (SEH) that has been supported in languages like C++, Java, and Delphi for years is now fully supported in VB. SEH is a process in which objects can be "thrown" to catch and deal with errors in a protected segment of a method.

The CLS implements an enhanced version of the SEH **Try ... Catch ... Finally** syntax. To write exception-protected code you place the potential exception causing statement between the **Try** and the **Catch** blocks as follows:

```
Public Sub ArrayTest()
Dim d(10) As Integer
  Try
   d(0) = 1
   d(100) = 10
  Catch e As IndexOutOfRangeException
    'deal with it here
  Finally
  'finally fix it
  End Try
End Sub
```

The optional **Finally** segment (which will always be run) can be used to reset values or provide some finalization to the entire exception handler.

Programming with SEH is a big design shift for VB programmers and will fundamentally change the way you construct and maintain your applications. There is a lot more to exception handling than demonstrated here. You will need to learn how to work with the base exception classes and how to code your own exception classes, which can be used by any other .NET language.

The **On Error** syntax should be used for backward compatibility and migrating classic VB code to .NET.

Structured exception handling is explored in more depth in Chapter 5.

Delegates

Another feature of object-oriented languages that has been around for a while is *delegates* or *delegation*. Delegation is the practice of creating objects that call the methods of other objects on your behalf, and it is a formal definition of how this is achieved at runtime. How you delegate the calls is a matter of design, and tested patterns have put delegation to use effectively when objects need to assume the roles of other objects for various reasons.

The delegate event model provides a framework that integrates event handling in components and services, allowing us to pass the method calls of independent objects as arguments. In this regard, a delegate is often described as a type-safe function pointer.

Interfaces

Interfaces play a critical role in modern object-oriented languages. An interface is built in a class file using the **Interface** keyword and describes the properties and methods for implementation in descendant classes. You will be able to create interfaces for your own projects and the projects of others. Consumers of your interfaces will be able to implement the interfaces into their programming environments, no matter what CLS-compliant language they use.

You can also fully implement interface definitions in your own classes using the **Implements** keyword. And many of the base classes in fact provide interface inheritance for you to implement in your classes. See Chapters 4 and 5 for more information on interfaces.

Multithreading

The CLR fully supports *free threading* or *multithreading*, which lets you write applications and services that can perform multiple tasks concurrently and independently. Like the true object-oriented abilities now available to VB programmers, free threading is a long overdue addition to the VB developer's skill set.

While a full discussion of threading is beyond the scope of this book, if you look at the methods of the thread classes, you will see all the methods you need for starting, stopping, sleeping, synchronizing, and pooling threads are provided.

Classic VB did not offer any such user-controlled thread access. In some project types you could set the threading from "single" to "apartment" or set a thread pool rather than using a thread-per-object approach. However, creating a true multithreaded application—for example, one that processed a long list sort in the background while the user kept working in the foreground—could only be achieved with clumsy timers, complicated APIs, and a lot of unsupported black magic.

Managed Execution

VB.NET is now a fully implemented *managed* language. This means that by being both CLR and CLS compliant, you give up a lot of execution control to the framework, particularly the CLR. While it might take some getting used to for features like nondeterministic finalization, gathering classes and interfaces into assemblies, and so on, the new benefits far outweigh not handing your fate over to the runtime.

Chapter 2 explores the CLR and the managed execution process in more detail.

ADO.NET

ADO.NET is the new database technology that Microsoft has created for the .NET Framework. While it is a successor to ADO (Active Data Objects), ADO.NET does not really replace ADO. And you instantiate and work with ADO.NET objects just as you do with ADO objects. It's really what goes on in the actual objects and how they are implemented that has completely changed.

The ADO library is a collection of COM components principally encapsulating the functionality of OLE DB. It has been the key provider to Microsoft's database technology for a number of years now. ADO encapsulates the functionality to easily access the OLE DB provider, which at the lower level sports a very difficult API to program against. ADO is a very connection-centric object model.

ADO.NET sports an inherently disconnected architecture and principally encapsulates access to a native SQL Server data provider (discussed in Chapter 5) that is extremely fast. You connect directly to the data source, send down a query, and retrieve the data to populate a client-side **DataSet** object. Then you disconnect, returning only when you need new data or data needs to be updated. The dataset can hold a number of virtual tables that can mirror the referential schema on the datasource, which provides much more data manipulation utility than a pure ADO **RecordSet** object can.

ADO.NET is not based on COM at all but rather on XML. As such, this means that ADO.NET objects can freely pass through firewalls as serialized and streamed

XML data, and can be passed between applications and across process boundaries far more easily than COM. COM is binary standard and not easy to pass around widely distributed applications and processes that may even reside on remote computers (especially if a firewall filtering out binary data separates the processes).

ASP.NET

In 1997 Microsoft introduced the world to Active Server Pages. Version 1.0 came bundled as part of Internet Information Server 3.0 (IIS). No longer would developers have to rely on the Common Gateway Interface (CGI) and the clumsy Internet Server API (ISAPI) for their Web site creation. Microsoft brought rapid Web development to its developers—at least that was their intention. Like all products in their infancy there was room to grow—and in the case of ASP, the room was the size of an airplane hanger.

ASP allowed programmers to create dynamic Web pages without the difficulty associated with CGI/ISAPI. A developer could create an HTML page and include VBScript or JScript (or JavaScript) that would be processed on the server when a client requested a page. This allowed developers to rapidly create dynamic sites that were both database and user driven.

Problems arose though when it came time to manage the code. Intermingled within the HTML was script that was used by the ASP processor. This made code next to impossible to read, and when it came time to modify the code you might as well bring a sleeping bag to work and forget weekends because it was going to be a while.

Over the past few years with the release of Visual InterDev 6.0 and ASP 3.0 (IIS 5.0), things improved dramatically for developers. The development environment was friendlier, color-coded script made it easier to read, and InterDev's support for IntelliSense made it easier to write script. Even with product enhancements and the knowledge of ASP growing, Web development still required time, skill, and patience.

Microsoft has taken everyone's suggestions and criticisms and has taken the time to create a best of breed ASP. Microsoft called it ASP.NET and has included it in the .NET framework. It is no longer just a preprocessor for Web pages as it was previously in IIS. ASP.NET is an entirely new approach to Web development.

One of the first things that you will notice when you start to use Visual Studio.NET is that there is no more Visual InterDev. Microsoft wanted Web development to be just like any other type of software development, and they did this by incorporating InterDev's best features into the Visual Studio Integrated Development Environment (IDE). With this you now have a single unified solution upon which to do all of your development. This is a great benefit because now you no longer need to learn the ins and outs of more than one development environment.

Along with Windows applications, services, and controls, the Visual Studio environment allows you to create Web applications, Web services, and Web components. Here are some of the benefits of moving to ASP.NET:

▶ The unified programming environment lets you use one IDE (Visual Studio.NET) for everything.

▶ ASP.NET pages are compiled, which allows pages to render faster and developers to use a true object-oriented programming language to code and not just a scripting language such as with VBScript and JavaScript. This allows the use of inheritance, security, garbage collection, structured exception handling, and any other feature available in the .NET Framework.

▶ No more "spaghetti code" intermingled in the HTML. The visual HTML display is separated from the code with the "code-behind" feature, which allows you to place a reference in your ASP page to a separate file that contains all of the code for that page. This enables simplified code upgrades and greater readability.

▶ ASP.NET hosts the Web controls and Web services so other applications can be written to use or access them over the Internet.

▶ State management has been improved in ASP.NET. It is now much easier to maintain session or application state across Web server farms. Pages that post back to themselves can easily maintain their values using the features like **ViewState** and **PostBack**.

▶ ASP.NET also provides the framework for Web services, using Simple Object Access Protocol (SOAP) method calls and XML data, which replaces the multitiered glue that COM provided for Web and distributed applications. See Chapter 5 for ASP.NET and Web services in action.

Observations

COM never fully implemented any of the principles we discussed earlier in this chapter. Yes, Internet interoperation and integration has been achieved (although DCOM did not quite work out as planned), but little of our six principals discussed earlier was put in place under COM. Language independence is a reality with .NET, and so is versioning, XCOPY, and side-by-side deployment. And with the new object-oriented framework comes less cost of ownership and more return on investment, and we can get to market in far less time than before. Still, we should not bash COM too much, because without it we would not have .NET.

 NOTE

XCOPY is simple file copy routine that is typically run from the DOS command line.

That .NET, CLR, CLS, and the new features in what was is essentially Visual Basic 7 are radical changes for VB developers is probably the software development understatement of the year. Be that as it may, I have had a lot of opportunity to work with programmers who have specialized in VB for a number of years. And VB.NET in their hands is going to light up the software development world like never before.

VB programmers are wizards at performing miracles with little to work with, and patronizing and irritating cockamamie drivel from developers, authors, and other so-called experts warning of complexities that might be over the heads of VB programmers is not only irritating but downright ridiculous. Yes, there's lots of new stuff to learn, but .NET for the most part is easy and fun. Microsoft has put the fun back into programming by taking on all the hard work we once had to do ourselves.

It is clear that not only VB developers, but C++ and C# developers, and the gurus from more than a score of other CLS-compliant languages, are going to find interesting times developing for .NET. The .NET Framework is going to change the way we develop software for the Windows platform, and in the future (if our prayers are answered), on all manner of platforms—mobile, free, or otherwise.

Introduction to the Common Language Runtime

IN THIS CHAPTER:

Common Language Runtime Basics

Understanding Assemblies and Their Contents

The Common Language Specification

Managed Execution

Security and Deployment

The Common Language Runtime (CLR) is the managed execution environment for running .NET code. Managed execution is not a new thing, and many lessons about this subject can be learned from our Java friends in the valley. CLR technology is as revolutionary as it is simple. Coding to the CLR is a boon for developers, especially for Visual Basic programmers, because for the most part coding against the CLR is transparent. Developers find it far easier to write code for the CLR than not to use it, because only the most critical algorithms, a tiny percentage of life-and-death code, are not suitable for the CLR.

As we said in Chapter 1, the current model of programming for the Windows platform requires that you spend a lot of time tinkering with the plumbing of both the operating system and COM (the Component Object Model). You know how tedious working with COM can be—keeping track of the prolific GUID "magic numbers," the type libraries, registry entries, and tricky installation procedures. But in writing managed code, most of these kinds of burdens are taken away.

You can write managed code without concerning yourself with the CLR and how it operates. Of course, if your code is to be installed on machines that are not configured with the .NET runtime, you have to install its binaries before you can run anything on the target machine. But this is also a trivial matter, because the CLR is installed to the operating system (OS) without any need for you to crawl behind or under panels. And the future .NET server and client operating systems in the making at Microsoft will have the CLR already in place for you.

You do need to concern yourself with a few aspects of how the CLR works and how you distribute your code, but this is limited to producing your executables and the components that you will need to drop onto the target. We decided to keep this chapter short enough to give you a "heads-up" on the CLR, without detracting from the tasty development issues you are probably anxious to sink your teeth into in the other chapters.

The CLR Is More, by Far

The CLR is more than just an execution engine for managed code. If you are a Java or Delphi programmer and you visualize the CLR by comparing it to a virtual machine or engine, that's fine. But the CLR is a lot more than a virtual machine, or even a runtime environment, as you will quickly discover.

A Hosted Execution Environment

The CLR is a *hosted execution* environment, which means that before a CLR can be run on a target platform, that platform's specific CLR host must be installed or supported on the target machine. Microsoft has already released several hosts, including Windows 2000, Windows XP, Internet Information Services (IIS), and SQL Server 2000. Other newly created hosts are targeting mobile or compact platforms. Windows XP and the .NET servers *natively* support the CLR—that is, the code to support the CLR is already (kind of) part of the operating system. (We say "kind of" because it's actually debatable—and the decidedly anti-Microsoft lobby threatens to make this a legally contended issue—whether the CLR is *part* of the operating system, or an *added feature*.)

> **NOTE**
>
> *A subset of the CLR known as the* Common Language Infrastructure *is being proposed for international standardization. Microsoft intends to target non–Windows/Intel (Wintel) platforms with the CLI, so it is not unreasonable to predict, with a measure of skepticism, that a form of the runtime, which will probably target Web services and the like, will be included with FreeBSD and Linux.*

You can think of the CLR as a proxy service that sits between your application and the operating system. Figure 2-1 illustrates the CLR, sitting atop its host, which is a thin veneer of binary support for non-CLR-aware operating systems, and interacting with the operating system.

The CLR proxies requests from your applications to the various layers of the OS, such as the network stack, the graphics devices, file system operations, and so forth.

Services and Forms
Data and XML
Base Classes
CLR
HOST
OS

Figure 2-1   *The CLR atop its operating system host*

An alternative view of the OS-CLR stack is represented in Figure 2-2, which shows the CLR as the third ring from the operating system, which is at the center. Applications thus execute on the outer ring, and requests for services from the OS are passed down to the inner ring and then routed back in again to the "outer circle."

An Execution Manager

Managed execution is not something George W. invented for the state of Texas—it refers to several processes at work in the CLR, and not just one. If we look at the .NET Framework as a stack of processes, as illustrated in Figure 2-3, you can see what transpires between you writing code and the CLR executing it:

1. Code is generated by the developer.
2. Code is "compiled" to Microsoft Intermediate Language (MSIL, also known as managed code, and IL for short).
3. Code is described with metadata and assembled into an assembly.
4. Code is checked, prior to execution, and marked as "kosher" (or not).
5. Code is just-in-time (JIT) compiled if it *is* kosher.
6. Code is executed.
7. Code execution is managed.
8. Code is terminated, and resources are freed.

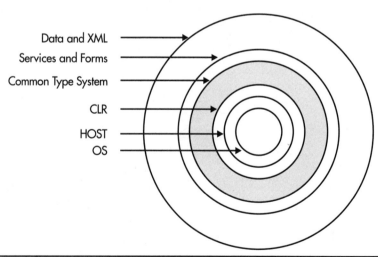

Figure 2-2   *The various layers of the CLR (a bird's-eye view)*

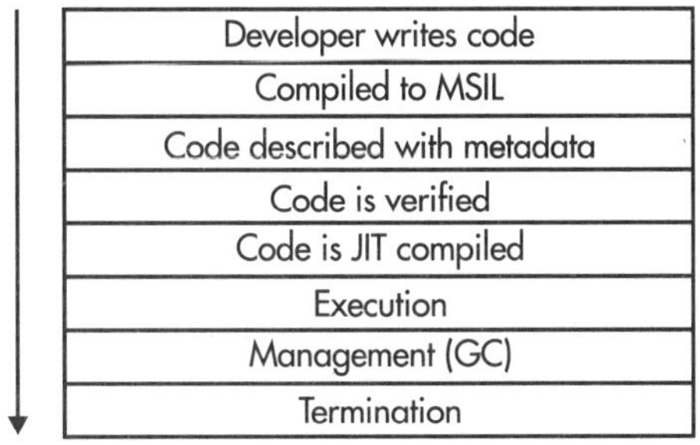

Developer writes code
Compiled to MSIL
Code described with metadata
Code is verified
Code is JIT compiled
Execution
Management (GC)
Termination

Figure 2-3 *The CLR's execution stack*

Examine Figure 2-3, and it should be clear that the developer is most concerned with the upper levels of this execution stack. What takes place at the lower levels is handled automatically by the CLR. (Although you can do a few tricks at the lower levels, a detailed discussion is beyond the scope of this book.)

What occurs up and down the CLR execution stack is all part of managed execution. After the developer generates the code, it is executed in the development platform, where it can be examined in the debugging process that can step through managed execution before packing it off to another CLR.

The package of code is compiled to IL and placed into self-contained files. These self-contained files are similar to packages in Delphi and Java (which you know about if you program in these development environments); they are managed according to a namespace hierarchy that was adopted from C++. The self-contained files, called *assemblies*, are central, and critical, to everything you develop for .NET, so we will devote some time to understanding what they are, what they do, and how they work.

Assembly Basics

As you have no doubt discovered, everything in .NET is an *object*. While that's useful information for you, the developer, to know, the CLR does not know an object from an elbow unless you describe the elbow (or the object) first. Something needs to tell the CLR how to provide the various type implementations that applications and services need to work with, and, in fact, how to execute an application.

A little digging around in the legacy, unmanaged world of Windows sets the scene. In the old days of computing, the Windows executable—monolithic binaries that read code in .INI files—loaded up various contexts, data, states and modes, and so on. Life was programming hell is those days (remember Windows 286?).

Then came the invention of dynamically linking files, and those mega-sized binaries shrunk, as various unwanted family members were kicked out of the binary house.

Microsoft published a pair of standards called the Microsoft Portable Executable (PE) format and the Microsoft Common Object File Format (COFF). These standards were created for the benefit of the OS, so that it would know how to load and execute the files. The standards had to be adopted by compiler makers or their customers would not have been pleased.

The files carried a certain amount of metadata in the form of PE/COFF headers. The OS scanned several sections for data, text, images, resources, and other information needed to render and execute in a manner that the developer expected. But when the application or dynamic-link library (DLL) needed to alert the environment of its needs and wants, this was done (after dumping .INI files) via the services of the registry.

Today, we still have portable executable and DLLs, but the step of compiling source code and populating the PE/COFF files with binary or machine code has been postponed. Instead, an intermediate language in .NET replaces the binary code to achieve a number of objectives of the .NET Framework, one of which is *language interoperability*, which we will talk about later in the chapter.

The IL code in the PE/COFF file is not machine code that the native operating system now understands, and it will not be able to execute the application that you spit out of VB.NET, C#, or other .NET languages. You can think of the IL code as the universal translator on *Star Trek* that allows Klingons, Ferengi, Cardassians, and humans to understand each other. The CLR knows what to do with this new quasi-compiled, intermediate language.

The CLR scans the .NET PE file for metadata that can help it interpret the IL code in the PE/COFF file. The metadata section is a new section that Microsoft has added to the standard PE/COFF combination. The metadata not only helps the CLR figure out what to do with the file, but the file itself publishes metadata to describe itself to the rest of the .NET "dominion." The .NET adaptation of the PE/COFF file also contains a native image section, as it did in the old era.

Now have a look at Figure 2-4, which illustrates how the contents of the PE/COFF file are assembled. The last issue Microsoft needed to address is what to call this new assemblage of data in the PE/COFF file. The word *package* was already taken by Borland and Sun (for use by Delphi and Java respectively), and *assembly* had a nice ring to it. The rest is history.

It's going to take Windows programmers some time to stop calling the files that come out of the compilers *executables*, because these files are not really executable anymore (at least not outside the CLR). No matter whether you have built a collection of classes compiled as a DLL or an application with an .EXE extension, in CLR the file is known as an *assembly*.

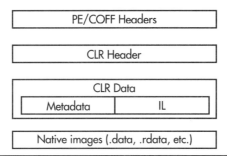

Figure 2-4   *The PE/COFF file (assembly)*

Before we go further into developing with VB.NET, you need to know two things about assemblies:

▶   Understand what goes into the assembly—although you don't need to know how to read or generate the assembly itself, unless you are keen to develop a compiler for .NET.

▶   More important, understand how assemblies are used, distributed, and deployed as your application, or class library.

For a quick peek at IL code in an assembly, open an application or a class library into the IL disassembler application (ILDASM.EXE) that ships with the .NET Framework Software Development Kit (SDK). This is demonstrated in Figure 2-5. You can dump the assembly contents into a file and get a better look at the manifest, metadata, and entry points of the file. The assembly opened in Figure 2-5 is exposed as follows:

```
.method public static void  Main() cil managed
{
  .entrypoint
  .custom instance void [mscorlib]System.STAThreadAttribute::.ctor() =
    ( 01 00 00 00 )
// Code size       141 (0x8d)
.maxstack  3
.locals init ([0] int32 cClearanceLevel,
         [1] string cPassWord,
         [2] string cUserID,
         [3] bool ItsAGo,
```

This break is not IL coded in this manner; it's broken here due to page-width constraints.

```
                [4] class [Crew]Crew.WarpIngineer We1)
   IL_0000:  nop
   IL_0001:  newobj     instance void [Crew]Crew.WarpIngineer::.ctor()
   IL_0006:  stloc.s    We1
   IL_0008:  ldstr      "Please enter a user ID"
   IL_000d:  call       void [mscorlib]System.Console::WriteLine(string)
   IL_0012:  nop
//abridged
} // end of method Module1::Main
```

While we have not listed the entire contents of the file, you can download the code for this demonstration (the example in Chapters 4 and 5) from the Osborne Web site at **www.osborne.com**.

The .NET Class Library or Base Class Library (BCL) files are also distributed as assemblies. Knowing how the BCL assemblies and your customer assemblies are named, grouped, listed, and referenced is important for getting code off the development environment and into the world of .NET.

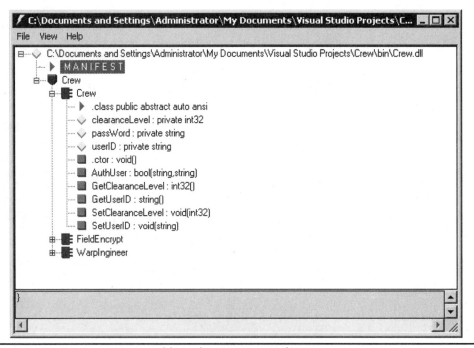

Figure 2-5 *Exposing an assembly in the ILDASM application*

Assemblies Exposed

Now that you know what goes into an assembly, it is not too difficult to appreciate that an assembly is essentially *the* unit of deployment, versioning, execution, reuse, security, and interoperation of the .NET Framework. Specifically, the role of the assembly is as follows:

▶ An assembly is a *unit of deployment.* When an application starts, its assembly and any assemblies it initially needs to reference must be visible to it. Other assemblies that need to be reached come into the picture as needed. They are also not immediately JIT compiled the first time the application loads; rather, they are compiled for the first time when they are needed. The degree of latency that becomes noticeable obviously depends on the assembly.

▶ An assembly is a *unit of security.* It forms a security boundary between what can be executed and the conditions of execution. Permissions are both requested and granted on the execution of assemblies. Assemblies also publish trust information. They can be signed as public entities, and their signatures can be verified under public key infrastructure.

▶ An assembly is a *type boundary.* Types published in the assembly identify themselves by the identity in which they reside. No two assemblies can be identical, which means that while two types could be identical, they would be separated by the assemblies in which they reside.

▶ An assembly is a *unit of versioning.* Everything in an assembly is versioned under the assembly's uniqueness, and it is thus the smallest unit of versioning in .NET. Even two identical types in the same assembly are unique because they are enumerated in that assembly and they can each be uniquely resolved. Assembly versioning is what makes *side-by-side* execution a possibility. In side-by-side execution, two identical applications, dependent on different assemblies, can be executed concurrently without corrupting each other's data.

▶ An assembly forms the boundary of a *reference scope.* An assembly's metadata, its manifest, specifies the level of exposure a type and its resources have outside the assembly.

▶ An assembly, most importantly, is a *unit of execution.* An assembly can be executed. The manifest provides the metadata for the CLR to determine how to execute the assembly's executable code. It also exposes the single entry point for the CLR to load the executable, which must be one of the following members: **DLLMain**, **WinMain**, or **Main**.

▶   The assembly can be *dynamic* or *static*. Dynamic assemblies can be downloaded or executed directly into memory, and they can also be persisted and then reloaded into memory. Static assemblies can comprise classes and resources (like images and icons), and are PE files that are stored on disk. Static assemblies are the more common of the two types.

NOTE

If you are confused about the difference between a PE file and an assembly, you are not alone. An assembly is a PE file because it includes PE/COFF header information the CLR can use to load the executable or dynamically link the file.

The Elements of the Assembly

Each assembly has four essential sections: assembly metadata, type metadata, MSIL (your code), and resources (images, etc.). The manifest is the critical requirement because it contains the assembly metadata. The assembly can also contain a second set of metadata, which describes the types stored in the assembly (this metadata is not present if no types are resident in the assembly). If you *do* have types in the assembly, you will obviously find MSIL code in the assembly. Finally, the assembly can also hold resource files (even past issues of *Fortune* magazine), and thus an assembly is meaningless without either type code or resource files.

The assembly contents may also span multiple files. This is known as a *multi-file assembly*. For example, as Figure 2-6 demonstrates, you can place assembly metadata in one file and type metadata and MSIL in another file. You can even place resources in a third file. As long as the manifest logically links the files as a unit, they can be subdivided in this fashion.

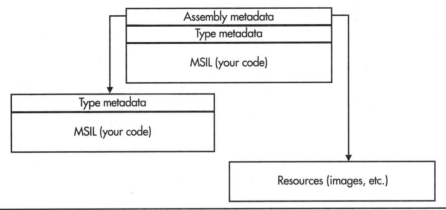

Figure 2-6   *The assembly can be partitioned across multiple files.*

Assemblies are created transparently by the development environment you work in. Advanced assembly management, such as creating multi-file assemblies (or modules), is beyond the scope of this book. However, we will not be outdone in our quest to get you up and running pronto (otherwise you would not be getting a head start), so we have included a section at the end of this chapter on JIT deployment of your code.

Generating MSIL

You do not have to generate managed code *consciously*. Building and compiling from Visual Studio.NET or using the VB.NET command-line–enabled compiler (as demonstrated in Chapter 3) does this for you. And while you don't need to do explicit linking, it is reasonable, and required, that you distribute IL code to target environments and link and build "on location."

IL code is CPU and platform independent. The CLR and its host care about the platform specifics; so as far as you are concerned, the entire world is .NET enabled. (I am already at work building a host and CLR to run in a matchbox that will manage my entire home entertainment system, security system, sprinkler system, and so on. I am calling it the Common Author Runtime, or CAR, because it will allow me to write more .NET books. Osborne is sponsoring the CAR!)

Writing managed code lets you concentrate on what you do best: designing and developing applications that are going to change humanity for the better. And with managed code, you don't need to know too much about the CLR, unless you plan to write one yourself or you've been hired to write one for a toaster or lawnmower manufacturer. (Forget about trying to write one for another operating system, because someone is probably already at work supporting your favorite, or most hated, kernel.)

Every compiler that generates code to target the CLR generates the same IL code. So if you are writing in C# or VB.NET or COBOL, whatever the compiler spits out is the same IL code that another language's compiler would spit out. The standard that makes this possible is the Common Language Specification (CLS).

Actually, I just threw you a marketing pitch, because every language has something unique that might not be fully understood by another language a developer is using. For example, properties are a .NET feature, but not every language treats them the same way. C#, for example, has a teeny-weeny difference of opinion about what it thinks of properties versus how VB sees them. But these peculiarities are not important in getting you the Common Language Specification head start you are after and some of them might change by the released version and future service packs.

The Common Language Specification

You might think of the CLS as a knitting machine. Every manufacturer has its own ideas about the features it wants to include in the knitting machine. Some have fancier pedals than others, and some allow you to program in a pattern loaded from a computer, and so on. But at the end of the day, every machine spits out the same garment (don't let your favorite knitter read that).

The compiler vendor is also free to bend a few rules and do some tricks that the CLR can support—or that can be targeted to the unmanaged execution environment. For example, the first version of VB.NET (or would that be the seventh version?) does not support the ability to overload operators. However, the C# development team decided that they would add operator overloading. Does that mean that C# is now a more powerful language? No; it just means that the C# people had more time on their hands, because they built C# from the ground up to target the CLR(Microsoft was certainly talking about its "new" OOP language long before the advent of the CLR); and the VB egg had to be refried all over again.

NOTE

This is not really true. Both Java and VB.NET can do operator overloading and they do. The + operator is overloaded in both languages. But any custom operator overloading is prevented to some degree by the makers of each language.

Fact is, the CLS lists operator overloading as a feature the CLR can support but does not really approve, along with such features as shift operators and unsigned variables. But if you go nuts on features that are not specifically CLS compliant, or that are not supported by the broad base of languages, you risk losing some programmers of other languages who won't be able to use your code.

Table 2-1 provides an abridged list of software development features that must meet CLS compliance rules. (See *Visual Basic.NET: The Complete Reference,* Osborne/McGraw-Hill, 2002, for more commentary.)

Language Interoperability

Language interoperability, one of the Holy Grails of software development, means that your code is in one language but everyone else can use it. Imagine that you could create components that could be used by any language or development tool. Aside from the obvious benefits, though, programming life might get boring (and Sun and Microsoft might be the best of friends).

Despite what comes to mind when thinking about language interoperability, filtering source code down to compliant IL produces a degree of language interoperability

Feature	What must be CLS compliant
General	Visibility and exposure; types that are exposed must be compliant, but global static fields and methods are not
Naming	Characters, casing, keywords, uniqueness, and signatures
Types	Primitives (boxed types are not compliant), visibility, interface methods, closure, and constructor invocation (typed references are not compliant)
Type members	Overloading, uniqueness, and conversion
Methods	Accessibility and calling conventions
Properties	Accessor metadata, accessor accessibility, modification, naming, and parameters (see the "Methods" section in Chapter 3)
Events	Event methods and metadata, accessor accessibility, modification, naming, and parameters
Pointers	Pointers are not compliant
Interfaces	Signatures and modification
Reference types (objects)	Construction and invocation
Class types	Inheritance (all classes must inherit) from at least one compliant class
Arrays	Elements, dimensions, and bounds
Enumerations	Underlying types, the FlagsAttribute, and field members
Exceptions	Must derive from the base **System.Exception** class
Customer attributes	Value encoding
Metadata	Compliance marking

Table 2-1   *Abridged Version of the CLS*

that many of us can live with. In this day and age, absolute language interop is still far off, because the dozen or so languages that are supporting the CLR are—at the source level—very different. VB has done things for VB developers in its own peculiar way for more than a decade now. So writing VB.NET source to achieve one end may actually produce some strange nuances when reduced to IL and then opened up in the C# compiler.

The C++ days of writing components for "paint-by-number" projects in VB are over. And for many VB programmers, .NET brings about a role reversal. VB.NET programmers can now create components and class libraries that can be targeted to other CLS-compliant platforms. You would still need to test a VB class reference in a C# application, however, because a particular bit of code might mean one thing to the VB programmer and something else to the C# programmer (actually there's a lot more that they *don't* agree on).

But the immediate benefits are apparent:

▶ Classes that were produced in one language can be inherited by classes used in other languages.

▶ Objects instantiated from the classes of one language can be passed to the methods of objects whose classes were created in other languages.

▶ Exception handling, tracing, and profiling is language agnostic. In other words, you can debug across languages, and even across processes. Exceptions can be raised in an object from one language and understood by an object created in another language. You can start debugging in Florida and end up stepping through SQL code in Tokyo!

Language interop helps maximize code reuse, which is one of the founding principles of all object-oriented languages. And this interoperability is achieved largely thanks to the metadata that describes the information in assemblies.

Metadata

Suppose you have built an assembly that has a .DLL extension or an executable with an .EXE extension. But the code cannot be executed just yet, because the CLR must first JIT compile it to machine code. IL directs how all the objects in your code are laid out; what gets loaded; how it is stored; which methods get called; and a whole slew of data on operations, control-flow, exception handling, and so on.

NOTE

Many "papers" discount .NET as something akin to a p-code interpreted environment. The JIT compiles to code that is native to the CPU architecture and the CLR has access to its host's resources. In fact, there is no interpreter available at this time.

When you "compile" your code at design time, the compiler also infuses the file that is storing the IL code with metadata. This metadata describes the classes used, signatures of methods, and the referencing required at runtime (which is what gives you such powerful stuff as reflection and delegation). It also describes the assembly by exposing the following data:

▶ The identity of the assembly (name, version, public key, culture context, and so on)

▶ Dependencies, or what other assemblies this assembly depends on

▶ Security permissions, which are set by an administrator

▶ Visibility of the type

▶ The parent of the type, or what it inherits from

▶ Type membership (methods, fields, properties, events, and so on)

▶ Attributes, which are additional elements used on types and their members

All this data is expressed in the metadata and essentially allows the assembly contents to be self-describing. Think of it as being like trying to make your way through passport control at Kennedy airport. You turn up with your passport, which keeps "metadata" about you. If you look like the person in the book, your hair is combed, you have the correct security clearance, you are not on "America's Most Wanted," and you don't sweat like a guilty smuggler, you might just be allowed to enter.

Self-describing code makes all the hassles of registration, type libraries, and Interface Definition Language (IDL), as discussed in Chapter 1, a thing of the past. Adding "and then some" would be an understatement because the metadata achieves so much more.

Self-describing files do not need to be identified or registered with the operating system. By packaging metadata within the file itself, the identification is a self-propagating reality on the part of the assembly. You can also trust a self-describing assembly more implicitly than you can a file that publicizes itself in the registry, because registry entries date rapidly. Registry entries and their implementation counterparts also can become easily separated.

Language interoperability is now a reality, because at the IL level all code is the *same* code. If you build your files and distribute them to consumers as assemblies, as long as they are in IL format the target development system will be able to use the assembly transparently. This, of course, means that if you intend your classes to be totally language agnostic, they need to conform to the CLS and not include elements not supported by all CLS languages. Because so many CLS languages are here now, and because many more CLS languages are on their way, you might want to keep a copy of the CLS next to you whenever you design classes and write code.

Down to Executable Code

Just because you have all your metadata and instructions in place does not mean that your code is passed directly to the JIT compiler. First, the IL code must undergo a thorough inspection. We call this making sure the code is "kosher." The code is given a verification test that is carried out according to the wishes of the network administrator, who might have specified that all .NET code on the machine must be executed according to a certain security policy. The IL code is also checked to make sure nothing malicious has been included.

The code is also checked to determine whether it is type safe, that the supporting compiler has done a good job of making sure the code does not try and access memory locations it is restricted from accessing, and that references reference what they are supposed to reference. Objects have to meet stringent safety checks to ensure that objects are properly isolated from one another. In short, if the verification process discovers that the IL code is not what it claims to be, it is deported (and you might never be trusted again).

Naturally, it might bother you that IL is not really as secure from prying eyes as machine code, and that reverse engineering MSIL is obviously a lot easier than reverse engineering classic compiled executables. And you are right to be bothered (especially because, as you will see in the first example in Chapter 4, the password value is fully exposed in IL). But, as the Java community has learned with its bytecode, decompiling intermediate code is not really worth the effort. To go the extra mile, however, Microsoft and some third-party vendors are working on

"JIT'er" Bugs Beware

The .NET JIT compiler is a platform-specific, processor-specific technology. This means that the code you write is not necessarily write once, run everywhere. Microsoft is not marketing .NET as a platform-neutral technology; let's face it, the Holy Grail of software development is just that, a Holy Grail.

From the get-go, you need to know for what platform you intend to target your code, and as of this writing, that platform is a shade of Windows running on Intel processors. If it comes to pass that someone announces a CLR and JIT compiler for BSD or something X'ish, at least you'll know that your fancy Windows look and feel does not stand a dew drop's chance in daylight of presenting itself on that X-rated platform.

obfuscating technology that will make IL code harder to decompile. If you plan to email your class libraries or to allow them to be downloaded by your customers, they must be signed and then encrypted for travel.

Managed Execution

The .NET JIT compiler has been engineered to conserve both memory and resources while performing its duties. It is able, through the code inspection process, to figure out what of your code needs to be compiled right away and what can be postponed until it is needed. This is the essence of a JIT compiler.

Applications and services thus may appear to be slow on startup the first time, because subsequent execution obviates the need to pass the code through the "JIT'er" again. You can also force compilation or pre-compile code if necessary. But for the most part, or at least until you have a substantial .NET project underway, you will not need to worry about getting your spanner into the JIT'er.

During execution, the CLR manages the execution processes that allocate resources and services to the executable code. Such services include memory management, security services, cross-language interop, debugging support, and deployment and versioning.

Managed execution also entails a lot more than reading IL, verification, JIT, and so on. It also describes what the CLR does once it has loaded and executed an application. Three sophisticated operations of the CLR worth noting are *side-by-side execution,* isolating applications and services into *application domains,* and *garbage collection.*

Side-by-Side Execution

The autonomous, independent, self-describing, unique, versioned nature of an assembly allows you to execute multiple versions of an assembly simultaneously. This is a phenomenon known as side-by-side execution. This is not something that has never been done before. It is, however, something that could never be done easily, and it could not be done with just any application.

Side-by-side execution has brought about the end of DLL hell, because you no longer have to maintain backward compatibility of libraries and components when new applications and assemblies are installed on a machine. Instead, applications that depend on yesterday's version of Smee's component (the same one mentioned in Chapter 1) will not break because a new application was installed with today's version of Smee's component. And when you need to junk the various versions of Smee's component when they are no longer being used, you can hit DELETE.

Side-by-side execution is possible because an executable assembly expresses a dependence on a particular assembly (the old Smee component). So as long as the old component is still around, any application that needs it still works. However, versioning on .NET is a little more intelligent than simple version numbers and assemblies that can be gone in a SHIFT-DELETE. Version policy can specifically force an application to upgrade to the new version of Smee's component.

NOTE

Just because you can run applications and assemblies side-by-side on the same computer, and even in the same process, it doesn't mean that conflicts won't crop up. You need good application design and proven patterns of software development to ensure that code applications are safe and reentrant.

Application Domains

Well-written applications with properly encapsulated data usually provide a certain level of isolation from other applications in legacy processing environments. In some cases, however, when two applications are closely related, risk accessing the same resources, or spawn threads, they can collide.

In the past, we have had to engineer such applications to run in separate isolated processes, often requiring layers of proxy code to manage cross-application data exchange and task synchronization. This is usually resource intensive and still risks clashing and corruption. Two or more high-end mail servers or Web services are good examples of the kinds of applications that need to be properly isolated from each other. Scalability is severely hampered by the hoops you need to jump through to achieve the best isolation.

The CLR provides a much higher degree of application isolation through the code verification process, type checking, and so on. But the CLR can further protect the violation of application process space through the creation and deployment of applications in application domains.

An application domain is created in the runtime host and sets up a safe execution environment around a CLR within which a target application will run. A domain is created before the CLR is bootstrapped to accommodate application execution. Multiple application domains can actually be spawned in the same process, which dramatically increases processing bandwidth and thus scalability. The SQL Server runtime host would be a suitable target to run server-side functionality in application domains.

Application domains are also extremely lightweight, so you could engineer a service that spawns multiple application domains in a single browser process, and you could do this in a way that prevents controls operating in the browser from trespassing into each other's backyards.

Using application domains, the faults and failures of applications are also isolated from other applications. So it is feasible to keep an application running in one domain and maintain a standby application in an isolated instant, where it would be ready to take over processing—like a form of software fault-tolerance. Applications cannot be executed in the domains until the assemblies have been loaded into the domains. The application developer programs specific support for the application domains—however, the specifics of this programming technique are beyond the scope of this book. See *Visual Basic.NET: The Complete Reference* (Osborne/McGraw-Hill, 2002).

Garbage Collection

A boon for developers coding to .NET is the automatic memory management that it provides. This has been achieved using a sophisticated memory-management algorithm called a garbage collector (GC).

If you have programmed for Java, you are already familiar with garbage collection, because Java also manages memory for you. The GC, and how it is controlled, is fully investigated in *Visual Basic.NET: The Complete Reference*. If this is the first time you have programmed in a garbage-collected environment, read on. Life is going to change for you.

Let's set the scene with an analogy. If you are a single person, you know what a drag it is to schlep the garbage out in the morning. If you are not single, you may also know what a drag it is to be asked to schlep the garbage out in the morning. And if you have kids, you know what it is like to argue with them and still have to take the garbage out yourself.

See yourself in that picture? Programming and managing memory without a GC can be a drag. Now imagine that every morning, the garbage bag simply dissolves and you no longer have to worry about it. This is what the GC does for you. It *eliminates* the chores of managing memory in programming.

In Chapter 4, we discuss the object reference model and how the object you control is connected to a reference variable you can manipulate. When you no longer need the object and nix the reference variable, when you assign the reference variable to another object, or when something just happens to cut the reference variable from the object, the object gets lost (it has *gone out of scope*). This means that you no longer have a way of referencing the object to reuse it.

In VB 6 and earlier days, objects that go out of scope, get lost, or simply are not needed anymore have to be explicitly disposed of (remember **Terminate events** [VB], **Destroy or Free** [Delphi], or **AddRef/Release** [C++]). The problem in manual memory management is that when you have a lot of objects, you sometimes forget to dispose of them, you lose track of how many were created, and so on. So some of these objects never get cleaned up and you slowly start to "leak out memory." The .NET GC does not let this happen, because these "lost" objects are removed and the memory they occupied is freed.

This, of course, could mean that you can write a heck of a lot of code without having to worry about memory management. However, we need to say "yes, but" and add a big disclaimer: You *can* write a lot of code and never have to worry about freeing objects. And you will see that in the examples provided in this book. But the concept of not having to worry about memory management ever again is simply untrue—untrue for the .NET languages and untrue for Java.

To demonstrate, let's say you create an application that is opening up sockets all over the Internet and about 10 threads are each running in its own little "slice" on the system, activating objects and basically being very, very busy. The algorithms in the application that work the threads need to create objects, work with them, and then dump them (for whatever reason, they cannot be reused by the thread). In this case, chances are that you are going to run out of memory just as quickly as you would in the unmanaged world, because the GC cannot clean up after your threads as quickly as you need.

You might think that you could just call **Finalize** after each object is done with. But, sorry folks, GC algorithms do not work that way. You see, the finalization of objects in the GC world of managed execution is *nondeterministic,* which means that you cannot predict exactly when an object will be cleaned out. Objects aren't removed chronologically, so that those that died earlier than others may end up getting removed out of order. GCs do not just stop and rush over to do your bidding. Like kids, they don't come running immediately when the garbage bag is near bursting.

There is something else you need to think about. Garbage collection can itself be a bottleneck. The boon of not having to set objects free has this trade-off: The GC is under the control of the CLR, and when the collector stops to take out the garbage, your threads have to mark time. This means that not only do you have garbage stinking up the place, but your threads get put on hold while the GC's dumpster pulls up at your back door. So now you no longer have memory leaks to worry about, but you might have "time leaks" instead.

Before you tear up this book and decide to go into shrimp farming, know this: The CLR allows you some management over the GC. A collection of GC classes and methods are at your disposal. This does not mean that you can force collection or make the cleanup *deterministic*, but it does mean that you can design your applications and algorithms in such a way that you have some degree of control over resource cleanup.

Here is something else to consider. Just because managed code is garbage collected does not mean you can ignore application design and common sense. If you are coding applications that lose or nix objects, the GC is not going to work for you. In fact, you *should* return this book to the store (don't tear it up, though) and go into shrimp farming. Your patterns and design should be using the objects you create until the application or service shuts down. And objects that have to be removed should be kept to a minimum.

Despite our warnings, the GC is actually very fast. The time you might lose to collection is measured in milliseconds in the life of the average application on a fast machine. In addition, the GC can be deployed on multiprocessor machines, allowing its threads to be allocated to one processor while yours run on the other. And because the GC is such an important part of the CLR, you can bet that Microsoft will often send it back to the workshop for tune-ups, oil changes, tire-rotation, and so on.

The .NET Security Model

A number of mechanisms are in place to secure resources and assemblies from unauthorized users, hostile code, and viruses. Here are the three basic security levels:

- ▶ **ASP.NET Web Application Security** This mechanism provides the means for controlling access to a Web or Internet site through authentication. Credentials are compared against the NT file system or against an XML file that contains lists of authorized users, authorized roles, and HTTP verbs.

- ▶ **Code Access Security** This mechanism uses permissions to control assembly access to resources and operations. By setting permissions, you can protect the system from malicious code while at the same time allowing bona fide code to run safely. This form of *evidence-based security* is managed by administrators.

- ▶ **Role-based Security** This mechanism provides access to assemblies based on what it, as the impersonator of the user, is allowed to do. This is determined by user identity, role membership (like the roles you have in SQL Server 2000), or both.

As a .NET developer, you need to consider security on a number of levels. You need to determine how your code will run in the target environment, how it will resist attack, and how you can handle security exceptions that are raised when your code is blocked.

NOTE

We don't condone writing assemblies for malicious or hostile use, but nevertheless there are developers out there with less than amicable intent who will be reviewing the .NET security model to figure out how they can get assemblies onto the .NET runtime.

You can protect your assemblies from invasion through the technique of *strong naming* or *digital signing*. If your assemblies are going to find their way into the public domain, it is recommended that you both sign and strongly name them.

NOTE

A strong name is a unique name that is generated from the contents of an assembly, such as version numbers, simple names, digital signatures, culture information, and so on.

You should fully investigate both strong naming techniques and digital signing of the assembly—which is achieved through public key encryption technology (PKI)—because most chief technical officers (CTOs) are going to demand it, and because it is for your own protection.

Just-in-Time (for Tea) Deployment

Application or service deployment no longer requires intricate installation procedures, like registry infestation and creating and setting keys and values. However, you can distribute applications to target runtimes in several ways. As a head start, however, you can simply place your compiled assemblies (.DLL and .EXE files, and any multi-file assembly members) into a private folder. Double-click the target's icon and Bob's your uncle.

The following list shows the available deployment scenarios:

▶   Explicitly install into the global assembly cache (GAC).

▶   XCOPY a collection of files, or just drag and drop them, into a folder or the GAC.

- ▶ Use the Windows Installer (version 2.0).

- ▶ Download (into the ASP.NET runtime).

- ▶ Use just-in-time (also known as on-the-fly) deployment.

Each computer that carries the CLR is endowed with a GAC. This "repository" for assemblies is a machinewide code cache that stores assemblies that have been designated for sharing by more than one application on the machine.

NOTE

The GAC is usually created in the root of your operating system folders. For example, on Windows 2000 this might be C:\Winnt\assembly.

The purpose of the GAC is to expose the assemblies placed in it—to applications and services that depend on them. When the CLR needs the assembly required by the application, it will find it in the GAC.

NOTE

COM interop code does not have to be installed in the GAC. See Chapter 6 for further interop information.

If assemblies do not need to be shared among applications, you should rather store them with their "friends" in private locations. Administrators can then protect the folders if need be, and some of the assemblies can be placed entirely off-limits to anything but the assemblies that depend on them.

You can use the Windows Installer, or any other .NET-compliant commercial installer, to deploy into the GAC or private folders. The .NET SDK also provides a utility called the Global Assembly Cache tool (GACUTIL.EXE), which you can use for putting stuff in the cache.

NOTE

Assemblies placed in the GAC must have strong names. See the section, "The .NET Security Model," earlier in this chapter.

Assemblies deployed for ASP.NET applications can be XCOPY'ed or FTP'ed. When you allow Windows forms or Web service assemblies to be downloaded that can be packed as either DLL files or compressed .CAB files, you can simply hook up the source via FTP or HTTP and allow the client to download the file through a simple link.

Applications installed with the services of the Windows Installer, which generates .MSI packages, benefit by integrating .NET installation with the Add/Remove Programs option in the Control Panel. You can allow installation, removal, and repair in this way.

Observations

The idea that a Common Language Runtime, managed execution, and a garbage collector are now available for Windows applications might at first sound like daunting concepts. Sure, programming to the CLR is a major paradigm shift for many Windows programmers; however, the classic VB runtime provided a similar degree of transparency for VB developers. Many classic VB applications do not require the same level of memory management that C++ or Delphi applications do. And you do not have to free an object explicitly, because the old VB runtime would, supposedly, take care of this for you—although at times this made you feel a little lazy and led to occasional memory leaks.

It really doesn't take long to understand the nuances of the CLR and its various components. In fact, most of the developers on your team writing code targeting the CLR need never really worry about the CLR at all. Instead, you can elect one or two people to be CLR "diligent."

CLR specifics—especially the GC, application domains, and security—need to be hashed out in the design and modeling stage. Provide specific support for exception handling (by delegating the duty of adding security exceptions to your custom exception classes), and not only will projects come in ahead of schedule, but you can take Fridays off to go sailing or horseback riding!

CHAPTER 3

VB.NET Building Blocks

IN THIS CHAPTER:

Getting Started

Operators

Execution Control

Iteration

Arrays and Collections

Working with Strings

Methods

S tarting with this chapter we are going to build support for the initial login and authorization facility for a space exploration program. If enough of you VB programmers buy this book, we might be able to afford a warp drive and build the spaceship by the next version of Visual Basic! Building this software together will teach us a lot about programming .NET in general, and VB.NET in particular. It will not take long for you to learn what you can (and cannot) do with this marvelous language. This chapter, however, investigates Visual Basic.NET building blocks, and we will get to the real meat of the login facility in Chapters 4 and 5, which will demonstrate OOP with Visual Basic.NET and will show off some of the neat stuff you can do with the latest version of VB.

If you are an expert programmer and have had some insight into how to write basic software using VB.NET you can skim over the beginning of this chapter. However, I suggest you sit back with a hard lemonade because you never know what you might uncover.

Even if you're not planning your own intergalactic travel program, you should get a good look and feel for VB.NET. Perhaps you need to move your VB applications over to .NET. Or you're ready to move your ASP-driven Web site to ASP.NET to take advantage of the new ASP programming model and the power of the new ASP.NET host—or the new ADO.NET and XML stuff, which might transform an idea brewing in your head into the next killer application or service.

You need to start somewhere, and this chapter provides the basics of the VB.NET language. The language is huge, so many of the subjects introduced in this chapter are implemented (excuse the pun) in their own chapters in a much bigger reference. But you wanted a head start, and a head start is what you will get. So don your code helmet and fasten that seat belt.

Let the Mission Begin

One of the objectives of this book, and others that follow, is to introduce a fundamental shift from the traditional Visual Basic programming model you're probably accustomed to. Programming in VB.NET is a fundamental change from the forms-based model VB programmers have been using for the past decade and longer. Now that VB is at last perfectly object-oriented (OO), you programmers need to adopt a new mindset for OO programming in VB.NET that will feel comfortable and that will allow you to get up to speed as quickly as possible. I know many of you are Java, Delphi, or C++

(dare I say that) programmers looking to add VB.NET to your arsenal, so object-oriented software development is more in line with your experience.

As discussed in the first chapter, VB became the world's most successful language and development environment because it was by far the only programming language and development tool that could make you productive within minutes of starting it up.

Programming in classic VB is as easy as 1, 2, 3:

1. Open the IDE and choose New Project, Standard EXE.

2. Drop a button on the form and double-click the button.

3. Write code in the button's sub-procedure.

As soon as you double-clicked the button, VB added the button click hander code for you and then you could go in and add the code needed to make the button do something. For those of you not fortunate enough to have experienced classic VB, here's a look at the code behind the sub-procedure form construction (all five words):

```
Private Sub Command1_Click()
End Sub
```

For Delphi or Java programmers, programming like this was quite a shock. VB had a lot of stuff going on under the hood, and the hood was welded shut by Microsoft. For OO programmers like me, it took some getting used to.

As for VB.NET, you've probably already opened Visual Studio.NET and generated a trial application. When you take a peek at the code behind the form, what do you see? About 200 words of stuff that most VB programmers have never seen before. Welcome to the world of object-oriented software development. At last, the hood has been opened —not that it matters, though, because the entire engine has been rebuilt and, at the outset, if you don't know true OO programming, you don't know what to look for.

NOTE

I am not trying to be cute or belittle classic VB. The intention is to get you productive as quickly as possible (not in a few weeks, after spending $4000 on an "official curriculum" course). This is where you start in classic VB, and you can build some pretty powerful stuff. Classic VB has a reputation of being easily taught to anyone. However, that ease of use comes with a price when a programmer needs to write complex and difficult algorithms. VB.NET might not be as popular as classic VB, but then to solve real-world problems you need the right tool to do the job.

In VB.NET, the first bit of code that you need to notice is the bit that declares the form:

```
Public Class Form1
    Inherits System.Windows.Forms.Form
```

This code tells you immediately that you are dealing with a pure OO language, because the form is immediately declared as a *class,* and the class inherits from **System.Windows.Forms.Form**. Every class in an OO language must inherit from a *base class*. In this example, the form inherits from the base class **Form**.

By now, you probably realize that there is a lot to coding in VB.NET. In fact, there is little difference, conceptually, from writing code in VB.NET, C#.NET, or for that matter Java and Delphi. If you are unfamiliar with the idioms you see in VB.NET, you may get stuck while trying to understand both syntax and OO issues.

This chapter will not get into the specifics of OO programming in VB (see Chapter 4 for a short introduction, however), because you'd be better off simply cranking out some code that works as soon as possible. We are also going to dispense with the overused "Hello World" cliché and do something constructive here: we are going to enter the world of OO at warp speed.

Goodbye World, Hello VB.NET

Close that form and close down Visual Studio.NET, completely. Open Notepad. *Seriously,* Notepad is better for quick and dirty (and some big and dirty) code building. We don't need a billion-dollar integrated development environment (IDE) to crank out a seven-line application. So follow along for the ride:

1. In Notepad, type the following code:

    ```
    Imports System
    Module GoodbyeWorld
      Sub Main()
        Console.WriteLine("Goodbye World")
        Console.ReadLIne()
      End Sub
    End Module
    ```

2. Save the file in your source code folder. You can save it as goodbye.txt (after all, it is a simple text file), or you can save it as goodbye.vb (this is a good idea so you can get used to the new *.vb* extension for class files).

3. Find the VB.NET command-line compiler. This is the same compiler that Visual Studio invokes, but you can invoke it from the command line (and

it's amazingly powerful and fast). The compiler, VBC.EXE, is stored in the .NET Framework SDK folder (if you have not installed the SDK, do so now).

You can issue a slew of directives to the compiler and get totally confused. Still, if you need to change a few variables or knock out a bug in a program, compiling from the command line is very useful. After the SDK and the Common Language Runtime (CLR) is on your machine, you can copy VBC to any folder and run it from anywhere. You can also place it into a path so that it can be invoked from any folder.

4. Compile goodbye.vb from VBC as follows:

```
\vbc goodbye.vb.
```

5. The executable assembly is immediately built and plops the file goodbye.exe (an assembly) into the folder. You can execute the application by double-clicking it. Or you can compile and execute the application with a combination of directives directly from a DOS batch file.

NOTE

To discover a collection of directives that can be thrown at the compiler, type **vbc | more** *at the command line. The directives are also listed in the SDK documentation. There are too many of them to list here.*

You can compile and execute on the fly from the command line using VB.NET. What else do you see happening here? The application is a *console* application. How does it know to display itself as a console application? First you have to tell it to find the console classes in the system namespace (assemblies and namespaces are discussed in Chapter 2). This can be done in one of two ways: at the top of the file, before any class or module declaration, you can type the **Imports** keyword; or you can point the compiler to the functionality, as demonstrated in boldface text here:

```
Module GoodbyeWorld
  Sub Main()
    System.Console.WriteLine("Goodbye World")
System.Console.ReadLIne()
  End Sub
End Module
```

Calling the method **Console.WriteLine** creates a console window and lets you process various console commands, such as reading input and displaying output. It's very useful to hang a "window" on a service or some application that needs little interaction on the part of your user. While we could create a "formless" application in earlier editions of VB, we could not create a console application or a system service without a third-party wrapper component.

NOTE

If you skipped Chapter 2 or just need a refresher, here's the definition of namespace and assemblies: A namespace is a collection of classes that are partitioned according to a naming system. That system is designed in a dot-notation hierarchy, similar to the domain name system (DNS) or Active Directory namespace. Assemblies are mainly dynamic-link library (DLL) files that store the classes and the metadata needed by the Common Language Runtime to support them.

That's the simplest VB.NET application you will ever get to write. Every VB.NET application like this must contain a **Main** method to run. If you omit the method, the VB compiler will go bust with an error that it can't find **Main**. The **Main** method is also where life begins *and* ends for your applications. You can pass command-line arguments to **Main** and you can also get a return code from **Main**, which is an application "exit" code that is sent out to the operating system, where it can be queried on the Windows ERRORLEVEL stack. In other words you can return a 0 indicating that the application performed normally, or something else (like –1) if it did not.

If you return an Exit Code, then **Main** must be overloaded as a shared function (because it returns a value) and not a simple subprocedure, as demonstrated in the following code (with command-line arguments included):

```
Overloads Public Shared Function Sub Main(ByVal CmdArgs() As [String]) As Integer
   If (appState = 1) Then
     Return 0
   End If
     Return - 1
End Function
```

Return is a new way of returning a value from a function; however, the old VB method of returning function values still works. For more discussion on methods and return values see "Methods" later in this chapter.

Of course, you could do this from Visual Studio.NET, but why would you want to? Visual Studio is not the only way to write and compile an application. Notepad would also make an excellent IDE if it had *IntelliSense*, a debugger, the ability to manage an application as a project or solution, a movie browser utility, pizza ordering screens, and credit card processing ability. In addition, you can create an application in VB that no longer needs the forms baggage. (The old way to get a service going in VB entailed a third-party add-on that turned the application into a service, sort of. Or you had to keep a form continuously running on the desktop, which would have to be manually executed, or placed into some startup folder.) Now a simple integration with the console classes is sufficient.

A console application is convenient for demonstrating the VB.NET language and building blocks, and that's what we are going to do in some places in this chapter. You can also use the **System.Diagnostics** namespace that lets you write output to the Output Debug windows in VS. It works like the VB 6 **Debug Print** and Java's **System.Out** feature.

Before moving on, though, you should notice that I am using a *module* in the above console code. A module is a class in VB.NET that has been kept around for backward compatibility. But 99.9 percent of the time, you'll be working with classes, console apps, or otherwise.

Option Compare, Explicit, and Strict

VB.NET currently provides three "Option" directives that can be placed before any code in your class, which governs syntactical and idiomatic behavior in your code during both design time and runtime. These directives are explained here:

- ▶ **Option Compare** This statement is optional and sets the default comparison method when a string of data is compared. If you set **Option Binary**, then the method used is binary. **Option Compare Text** specifies text comparison.

- ▶ **Option Explicit** This statement forces the explicit declaration of all variables in your class. While the statement is optional you can set it as follows: **Option Explicit On | Off**.

- ▶ **Option Strict** This is a new option statement that prevents conversion that would result in any data loss. See the section on conversion next. The option is on by default so for the most part you can leave it out. Using both **Option Explicit** and **Option Strict** is redundant since **Option Strict** implies **Option Explicit**.

Data Type Conversion

When you try and change data from one type to another, your code is put through a process called *conversion*. In software lingo we say that the conversion may be either a *widening process*, which means that there is no chance for data loss (like putting the contents of a small cola bottle into a big bottle), or a *narrowing process*, which risks data loss (like putting the contents of a big bottle into a smaller bottle). The new **Option Strict** directive (see the previous section) prevents data loss by preventing a narrowing conversion.

VB.NET allows both implicit and explicit conversion and supports conversion or cast operators that will be familiar to VB 6 developers. An implicit conversion does not require the use of a conversion or cast operator. For example, if you convert an Integer to a Long, the conversion process is implicit, as this code suggests:

```
Dim smallBottle As Integer = 100
Dim bigBottle As Long = smallBottle
Debug.WriteLine(smallBottle & " and " & bigBottle)
```

Some variables, however, require special cast operators, depending on the data and the circumstances. If you try to perform the conversion implicitly you will receive a compile error (unless of course you set **Option Strict** to the **Off** position). Conversion of types always requires the use of a cast operator (**CType**) and you will see such explicit conversion in action in Chapter 5.

VB.NET Operators

There are two primary groupings of operators supported by the Common Language Runtime: Unary operators, Binary operators, and a small collection of operators that are used with objects. Unary operators take one operand and use prefix notation, such as **+x**. Binary operators take two operands, one to the left of the operator and one to the right (for example, **A + B**).

In this section, we'll discuss both of the primary groupings of operators; but first let's talk about True.

The Value of True Is −1

For reasons that are not clearly known, Microsoft long ago decided that the value of True in Visual Basic 6 and earlier was equal to −1. The Common Language Runtime, however, does not see it that way. True is 1 and False is 0 along with every other modern language in existence, and if you pass True to, say, C#, you'll see that True is passed through as 1.

During Beta 1 of VB.NET, Microsoft changed the value of True so that it was the same as all the other CLS compliant languages (1); however, by Beta 2 it was changed back to –1. You can, however, avoid a lot of confusion by just writing code with the keyword **True**.

Operator Precedence

In VB.NET when expressions contain more than one operator the precedence of the operator, not the order of appearance, controls the order in which the expressions are evaluated. Binary operators such as **X + Y** are left associative, which means that the operations on the expressions are performed left to right.

However, precedence and associativity can be controlled using parentheses. For example, in the following code if we simply change the order of one of the operators, we get an entirely different result. The first attempt

```
Dim Value As Double
  Value = 7 * 2 / 5 ^ 2 + 9 - 50
Debug.Writeline(Value)
```

writes -90.9845679012346 as the output window. But the following example

```
Dim Value As Double
  Value = ((7 * 2) / 5) ^ 2 + 9 - 50
Debug.Writeline(Value)
```

writes -33.16 to the output window. Why is this happening? First, parentheses are included in the expression, which changes a lot because precedence and associativity can be controlled using parentheses in expressions. The parenthetical expressions are always evaluated first—in other words the parentheses override the precedence of the operators.

The following table lists the precedence of operators when evaluating expressions:

Class of Operator	Precedence of the operators in the class
Primary	(x), x.y, foo(x), foo[x], x++, x--
Exponentiation	^
Unary	+, -
Multiplicative	*, /
Integer division	\

Class of Operator	Precedence of the operators in the class
Modulus	Mod
Additive	+, -
Concatenation	&
Relational	=, <>, <, >, <=, >=, Like, Is, TypeOf...Is
Conditional NOT	Not
Conditional AND	And, AndAlso
Conditional OR	Or, OrElse
Conditional XOR	Xor

Here is a short list of additional rules to remember:

▶ Math operators evaluate first, followed by comparison operators, followed by logical operators.

▶ The concatenation operator (&) precedes all of the comparison operators, but it follows the mathematical operators.

▶ The comparison operators have equal precedence.

Unary Operators

There are three unary operators supported by the CLR: **+**, **-**, and **Not** (**Unary Plus**, **Unary Minus**, and **Unary Logical Not**, respectively). They are defined as follows:

▶ **Unary Plus** is simply the value of the operand.

▶ **Unary Minus** is the value of the operand subtracted from zero.

▶ **Unary Logical Not** for **Boolean** is the logical negation of the operand; for Byte, Short, Integer, and Long (and all enumerated types) the result is the bitwise complement of the operand.

Assignment Operators

What would a computer language be without its assignment operators, which are used to assign value to variables. The assignment operators come in two forms, simple and compound assignment.

The following table lists the simple and the compound assignment operators and the actions they perform:

Operator	Description	Action/Usage
=	Equal assignment	*Value = Expression*
+=	Addition/Concatenation assignment	*Variable += Expression*
–=	Subtraction assignment	*Variable -= Expression*
*=	Multiplication assignment	*Variable *= Expression*
/= and \=	Division assignment	*FloatingPointVariable /= Expression* *IntegerVariable \= Expression*
^=	Exponentiation assignment	*Variable ^= Expression*
&=	Concatenation assignment	*Variable &= Expression*

NOTE

When you declare variables, you can use a shortcut to make your code more concise and readable by assigning the value of the variable in the same line as its declaration. Check this out: Dim X As Integer = 5 is the same as Dim X As Integer, X = 5.

Have a look at how the compound operators work with an example of the addition/concatenation operator (+=). This code

```
Dim fName As String = "Donald"
Dim lName As String = " Duck"
fName += lName
Debug.WriteLine(fName)
```

writes "Donald Duck" to the output window.

When using the assignment equals compound operator remember that if the expression is numeric, the operation will be addition. However, if the expression is a string, the operation will be concatenation.

Relational Operators

The relational operators are used to evaluate an expression on the right side of the equal sign and return **True** or **False** (Boolean) depending on the comparison. The following table lists the comparison operators and the actions they perform:

Operator	Description	Action/Usage
Is	Compares objects	*Result = objectX **Is** objectY*

Operator	Description	Action/Usage
Like	Compares string patterns	*Result = String **Like** Pattern*
TypeOf...Is	Tests for the type of object	*If (TypeOf Object Is) Then*
<	Less Than	*Expr1 < Expr2*
<=	Less Than or Equal To	*Expr1 <= Expr2*
>	Greater Than	*Expr1 > Expr2*
>=	Greater Than or Equal To	*Expr1 >= Expr2*
<>	Not Equal To	*Expr1 <> Expr2*
=	Equal To	*Expr1 = Expr2*

NOTE

*Using this operator can be tricky because it does not always perform a comparison at the object level, but rather at the reference variable level (see Chapter 4). In other words, if two reference variables refer to the same object, you will receive **True** from the comparison. Use the **Equals** method that is always inherited from the root **Object.** You may override and provide your own implementation of code that compares two objects.*

The following table lists the pattern-matching syntax for character, numeric, and wildcard character matching using the **Like** operator:

Character	Meaning
?	The wildcard for matching any single character
*	The wildcard for matching zero or more characters
#	The wildcard for matching any single digit (0-9)
[...]	The character list surrounded by the square brackets can match any character in the list you provide—example [VB.NET]
[!...]	The character list surrounded by brackets but prefixed by an exclamation point (bang) can match any single character not in the list
X – X	The characters separated by a hyphen can specify a range of Unicode characters

The following example demonstrates the **Like** operator and pattern matching in action:

```
Dim X As String
X = "boody"
If (X Like "b??dy") Then
  Debug.WriteLine("True")
End If
```

Concatenation Operator

The concatenation operator, represented by the ampersand (**&**), combines string variables with string expressions. The usage is

*Value = expression **&** expression*

Here is an example:

```
Dim X As Integer = 1
Dim Y As Integer = 23
intBoth = X & Y
'Returns 123
```

Bitwise Operators

The following table lists the **logical** (**Boolean**) operators and the **Bitwise** operators and the actions they perform:

Operator	Action/Usage
And	**Byte**, **Short**, **Integer**, **Long**, Enumerated types: The result bit is 1 if both bits are 1; otherwise 0.
Or	**Byte**, **Short**, **Integer**, **Long**, Enumerated types: The result bit is 1 if either is 1; otherwise 0.
Xor	**Byte**, **Short**, **Integer**, **Long**, Enumerated types: The result bit is 1 if either bit (not both) is 1; otherwise 0. For example: 1 **Xor** 0 = 1 and 1 **Xor** 1 = 0.
Not	**Boolean:** *result = Not expression*. If expression is **True** then result is **False**. If Bit in Expression = 0 then bit in result = 1. If Bit in Expression = 1 then bit in result = 0.
AndAlso	If *Expression **AndAlso** Expression = True* then result is True; otherwise **And** is performed as above.
OrElse	If *Expression **OrElse** Expression = True* then result is True; otherwise **And** is performed as above.

Short-circuiting

The **AndAlso** and **OrElse** are new short-circuit operators introduced to VB.NET. If you use the **And** operator, VB.NET will evaluate the entire expression even if the first part of it was false. The default on the CLR is to "short-circuit " the comparison if the first operand is false. The best way to understand this is to have a look at some code.

```
Private Sub LogicTest()
 Dim x As Integer = 1
 Dim y As Integer = 1 'First Test:

  If A(x) Or B(y) Then
    Debug.WriteLine("x= " & CStr(x) & ", y = " & CStr(y))
  End If   If A(x) Or B(y) Then
  'X=2, Y=2 'Second Test:

  If A(x) OrElse b(y) Then
    Debug.WriteLine("x= " & CStr(x) & ", y = " & CStr(y))   'X=2, Y=1
  End If
End Sub

Function A(ByRef v1 As Integer) As Boolean
  v1 = v1 + 1
  Return True
End Function

Function B(ByRef v1 As Integer) As Boolean
  v1 = v1 + 1
  Return True
End Function
End Sub
```

Arithmetic Operators

The following table lists the VB.NET arithmetic operators:

Operator	Description	Action/Usage
+	Addition	*Value = Expression + Expression*
-	Subtraction	*Value = Expression – Expression*
*	Multiplication	*Value = Expression * Expression*
/ and \	Division	*Value = Expression / \ Expression*

Operator	Description	Action/Usage
Mod	Modulus (division returns only the remainder; % in Java, C#, C++, etc).	*Value = Expression **Mod** Expression*
^	Exponentiation	*Value = Expression ^ Expression*

Execution Control Statements

This section covers the execution control and iteration statements supported by VB.NET. The **On Error** statement is referenced here as well, but for a much larger treatise of error handling and the new structured exception handling (SEH) support, see the section on exception handling in Chapter 5.

The following table lists the collection of statements that allow you to control execution in a program. These are also known as *conditional* or *switch* statements, because branching and decision-making occurs on a condition—the state of an object or a value.

Desired Action	Statements
Branching	GoTo, On Error
Decision-making and switches	If...Then...Else, Select Case, Switch

Branching

Branch statements are used to redirect the flow of execution through a code segment. They are often referred to as "jump" statements, a term that our C# brothers and sisters prefer.

GoTo

GoTo transfers execution from the current statement to a label elsewhere in the code block. In the syntax for **GoTo** shown here, the *Label* parameter represents the label your code will jump to:

GoTo *Label*

While you can achieve any functional objective without **GoTo,** you might require its use in a number of situations, especially when porting applications from earlier versions of VB. In error handling, for example, you might consider preserving **GoTo** statements until you are in a position to replace them with exception code.

The .NET Framework supports **GoTo** and its use in VB.NET is as follows:

▶ **GoTo** can be used to branch to regions of code only within the code block in which it is used.

▶ **GoTo** can be used in **Try...Catch...Finally** blocks, but a **GoTo** in the **Try** block cannot direct execution to a label in the **Catch** or **Finally** block of the same **Try** block. (**Try** blocks are covered in Chapter 5.)

▶ A **GoTo** statement anywhere in the **Try** block cannot direct execution to any label outside the **Try** block in which it appears.

The following code illustrates usage of **GoTo** in redirection:

```
Dim Num As Integer
Dim Str As String
 Start:    Str = Console.ReadLine()
           Num = CInt(Str)

           GoTo Line0    'Check num and branch to its corresponding label.
 Line0:    If Num = 1 Then Goto Line1 Else Goto Line2
 Line1:    Console.WriteLine("This is Line 1 and you typed 1")
            GoTo Line3
 Line2:    Console.WriteLine("This is Line 2 and you typed 2")
            GoTo Line3
 Line3:    If Num > 2 Then Console.WriteLine() Else GoTo Start
```

On Error

The **On Error** statement causes a branch or redirection in program execution. The following list of **On Error** statements are supported by VB.NET:

```
On Error GoTo label
On Error Resume Next
On Error GoTo 0
On Error GoTo -1
```

The **On Error GoTo** *label* statement causes program execution to jump to an error handler at the label specified in the *label* argument. **On Error Resume Next** causes the execution to jump to the statement that immediately follows the statement where your error occurs. The **On Error GoTo 0** or **On Error GoTo –1** statement disables any active error handler, resetting it to **Nothing**.

Decision-making and Switches

The three core decision-making and switching statements used to control the flow of code execution are **If...Then...Else**, **Select Case**, and **Switch**.

If...Then...Else

This construct evaluates a Boolean expression. When a condition tests **True**, the statement after **Then** is executed; otherwise the execution is transferred to the **Else** section in the single-line construct, or to the **ElseIf** section in the block construction. The **Else** and **ElseIf** statements are optional and are executed only if their related statement blocks return **True**.

This statement illustrates single-line syntax:

> If *condition* Then [Then *statements*] Else [Else *statements*]

When the conditions are placed on one line, the statement can be used as follows:

```
If a = b Then Console.WriteLine("True") Else
Console.WriteLine("False")
```

In the single-line syntax, you can also execute multiple statements if the **If** condition is **True**, as demonstrated with the following code:

```
If a = b Then Console.WriteLine("True") : _
 b = CInt(Console.ReadLine()) : Console.WriteLine("Done")
```

The **If...Then...Else** statement can also be used as follows:

```
If Condition Then
 (IF Statements)
ElseIf Condition-n Then
 (ElseIf Statements)
Else (Else Statements)
End If
```

Nothing appears after the **Then** statement in this syntax, which is the clue that the program needs to execute the **If** block according to the block's syntax. The entire **If** block must be terminated with the **End If** statement. Take a look at an example:

```
If NationalDialtone Then
    RoutePattern = 1
ElseIf LocalDialtone Then
    RoutePattern = 2
Else
    RoutePattern = DefaultRoutePattern
End If
```

The **Else** and **Else If** statements are optional, and you can nest multiple **If** statements in the original block, like so:

```
If A = 1 Then
  If A > 0 Then
    Debug.WriteLine("Yes it is")
  End If
End If
```

Using the Choose Function and the TypeOf Operator

You can also use the **Choose** function and the **TypeOf** operator with the **If...Then ...Else** construct. **Choose** provides a means of retrieving a value on which to base redirection of execution or flow-control logic based on a condition. The function simply returns a type or a value based on a list of arguments that are provided as choices. The first element in the list is **index 1**, the second element is **index 2**, and so on. The **Choose** function looks like this,

Choose(index, *choice-1*[, *choice-2*, ... [, *choice-n*]])

and it works as demonstrated here, where it has been enclosed in a function that passes the index value used to retrieve an object:

```
Function PullLever(ByVal Index AS Integer) As Object
    PullLever = Choose(Index, "Cherry", "Bar", "Bell", "Jackpot")
End Function

If PullLever(SpinNum).ToString = "Jackpot" Then
  PayToHopper(Jackpot)
End If
```

The four objects on the slot machine's pay-line are indexed 1 through 4. The argument **Index** is an integer that is initialized to *4* in the example. When calling the function, the result of calling **Choose** and passing *4* as the index value for **Index** results in the fourth item—**Jackpot**—selected from the list.

If you pass *0* or a number greater than the total elements in the list, the **Choose** function will throw an exception. Inside the **If** construct, the **TypeOf** operator can be used to make a decision based on a test to determine whether an object is or is not what you think it is. The following code does just that:

```
If TypeOf textComponent Is TextBox
 Me.strControl.WordWrap() = False
End if
```

Select Case

The VB.NET **Select Case** conditional or switch construct executes one or more statements based on the value of an expression. The syntax is as follows:

```
Select Case expression_to_test
Case Value1
  Statements-for-value1
Case Value2
  Statements-for-value2
Case Else
 Case-Else-Statements
End Select
```

If the target of the evaluation compares to the case value, the statement of that case value is executed. Here is an example:

```
Select Case Status
Case 1
  CallString = "0" 'transfer to company operator
Case 2
  CallString = "*5" 'transfer to local operator
Case 3
  CallString = "*6" 'transfer to international operator
Case Else
  CallString = "*9"
End Select
```

If **Status** is equal to *3*, **CallString** is initialized as "*6". A **Case Else** "safety net" can be used to provide a default initialization in the event the case value is not in the **Select** statement.

Iteration Statements

VB.NET loop statements let you execute one or more lines of code repetitively while a condition is **True**, or until it becomes **True**. The following loop statements are supported by VB.NET:

- ► **Do...Loop**
- ► **For...Next**
- ► **For Each...Next**
- ► **While...**

Do...Loop

The **Do...Loop** construct repeats the execution of a block of statements for as long as a condition *is* **True**, or until it *becomes* **True**. The two variations use the keyword **While** or **Until** to test a condition for **True**. If you need to test a condition *while* it is **True**, use the **While** keyword; to test the condition *until* it becomes **True**, use the **Until** keyword. The syntax for both tests is as follows:

```
Do [{While | Until} condition ]
   statements
Exit Do
   statements
Loop
```

Another variation supported by VB.NET is as follows:

```
Do
   statements
Exit Do
   statements
Loop [{While | Until} condition ]
```

Newcomers often ask this question, "When should you use **While** and when should you use **Until**?" The right answer is, "Use the one that makes your code more readable."

The following is a simple example of the **Do...Loop**:

```
Do  Number = Number + 1
 Console.Write("*")
Loop Until Number = 50
```

You can also place the condition on the **Do** line, which will guarantee at least one interation. And we can nest to some extent as follows:

```
Dim Incr As Integer = 0
Dim Cond As Boolean = False
   Do
     Do While Incr < 500
       Incr += 1
         Console.WriteLine("Now at: " + CStr(Incr))
          If Incr = 500 Then
           Cond = True
           Console.WriteLine("Now at: " + CStr(Incr) + " and Finished")
           Exit Do
          End If
     Loop
   Loop Until Cond = True
```

NOTE

*One of the tech reviewers, Amir Liberman, went berserk testing how many levels of **Do...Loop** constructs he could nest before VB.NET took notice (to see "if" there were any limitations). He gave up trying at 21 and said that if you have a reason to nest like that then your logic upstairs has gone for a loop.*

For...Next

The **For...Next** statement lets you iterate through an array or collection. The following example illustrates this loop:

```
sArray = s2.Split(seps)
  For I = 0 To Ubound(sArray)
   Console.WriteLine(sArray(I))
  Next I
Console.WriteLine(s2.Join("*", sArray))
```

For Each...Next

The **For Each...Next** statement works similar to **For...Next**; however, it is used extensively to execute statements while looping through the elements of arrays and collections. See "Arrays" and "Collections" later in this chapter.

While

The older **While** statement executes a block of statements *while* a certain condition is **True**. **While** works in the same way that it did for earlier versions of VB; however, this loop now needs to be terminated with **End While** and not **Wend**. The syntax for **While** is as follows:

While *condition*
  statements
End While

The *condition* parameter can evaluate to **True** or **False**. If the value is null, it is considered **False**. When the condition evaluates to **False**, the loop will end; as long as the condition continues to evaluate **True**, the code in the *statements* section will be executed. The following example is another way of executing the **Do...Loop** example provided earlier (**While** is harder to read when taken to several nested levels):

```
Dim Incr As Integer = 0
Dim Cond As Boolean = True
  While Cond = True
    Incr += 1
    Debug.WriteLine("Now at: " + CStr(Incr))
    If Incr = 500 Then
       Cond = False
       Debug.WriteLine("Now at: " + CStr(Incr) + " and finished")
    Exit While
    End If
  End While
```

The **Exit While** statement is redundant in this loop but included for illustration. The loop will end at the next iteration of the outer loop because the Boolean value **Cond** will evaluate to **False** when the counter **Incr** value reaches 500.

NOTE

*You can no longer use **Wend** to end a **While** loop as you could in VB 6.*

The .NET Framework provides rich support for sorting and searching of data structures and the management of collections. A number of built-in functions provide simple sorting and binary searching; however, the **Array** class (**System.Array**) and the **Collections** class (**System.Collections**) provide a variety of methods for tackling fundamental data processing using objects and OO techniques. These .NET objects are allocated space on the heap, as opposed to the native datatypes you worked with as a legacy VB programmer.

Arrays

Arrays in the .NET Framework are objects derived from the parent class **System.Array**. Not all variables referenced by the array type are referenced in the same way. String objects, for example, are *referenced by references* to separate string objects (in other words, the array's string elements are just "pointers" to other reference types). Numeric data, on the other hand, is stored directly in the array.

NOTE

The differences between VB 6 arrays and .NET arrays are discussed in Chapter 6.

You refer to the element of the array as the *element type.* The element type is created when you create the array and destroyed when the array is destroyed. Naturally, the only type that cannot be the element of the array is array itself.

Arrays are classified according to a ranking system. The rank determines the number of elements that are associated with an index. An array of one dimension is referred to as a *single-dimension array*, and its rank is *1.* An array rank higher than *1* signifies a *multi-dimension array*.

Arrays are stored in the garbage-collected heap of the .NET runtime environment.

Declaring and Initializing Arrays

When you create an array, you need to assign a *length* to its dimensions. The length of the array is the number of elements that you need to store. .NET array elements are referenced through *zero-based indexing*, which means the first element of the array is given index value *0*. To specify the length of the array, you defer to the range of indices counting 0. In other words, an array of 10 elements is 0 through 9 in length.

The simple step to declaring an array in VB.NET is demonstrated as follows:

```
Dim Days(20) As Integer
```

NOTE

The VB 6.0 syntax of specifying lower-bound to upper-bound elements, such as **Dim Days(1 to 20) as Integer**, *is not supported in VB.NET.*

Alternatively, you can also declare the array with the **New** keyword and provide curly braces for optional initial values in the array. The syntax for both of the following examples is acceptable to the .NET runtime:

```
Dim Days1() As Integer = New Integer(5) {} 'or
Dim Days2() As Integer = {1, 2, 3, 4, 5}
```

Typical method usage on an array is as follows:

```
Days2.Length 'gets you the length of the array
Days2(3) 'gets you the fourth element of the array
```

Working with Arrays

VB.NET arrays are simple to work with—although they do have their nuances, as you will see shortly. The initial value of an array is null. In other words, in the Days1 arrays shown earlier, each element of the five-element array is null. This is true no matter the datatype—in an array of strings, until the strings are assigned values they also default to null. Referencing the null value is not impossible, as the following code shows:

```
Dim Incr As Integer
Dim Cond As Boolean = True
Dim ListIndex(10) As Integer
Dim List(10) As String
Incr = ListIndex(0)
  While Cond = True
    Debug.WriteLine("Element " + CStr(Incr) + " = " +
    CStr(ListIndex(Incr)))
      If Incr = 9 Then
```

```
      Cond = False
        Exit While
      End If
        Incr += 1
  End While
```

This chunk of code reports the value of each element in the array. Since nothing in the code is assigning values to the elements, the routine correctly displays null values for integer elements as zeros. The output is as follows:

```
Element 0 = 0
Element 1 = 0
Element 2 = 0
Element 3 = 0
. . .
Element 9 = 0
```

Let's now assign values to the elements and check the results:

```
Dim Incr As Integer
Dim Cond As Boolean = True
Dim ListIndex(10) As Integer
Dim List(10) As String
Incr = ListIndex(0)
  While Cond = True
      ListIndex(Incr) = Incr
      List(Incr) = CStr(ListIndex(Incr))
        Debug.WriteLine("Element " + CStr(Incr) + " = " + List(Incr))
          If Incr = 9 Then
            Cond = False
            Exit While
          End If
            Incr += 1
  End While
```

The output now shows values:

```
Element 0 = 0
Element 1 = 1
Element 2 = 2
Element 3 = 3
. . .
Element 9 = 9
```

Notice that we have set the Boolean test (**Cond**) to *9* to end the **While** loop. This demonstrates that the array is zero-based (0 to 9). If we change the Boolean test to *10*, the method would throw an out-of-range exception (**IndexOutOfRangeException**) when it tries to access the nonexistent eleventh element.

The UBound and LBound Functions

To find the upper bound, or *size,* of an array, or the lower bound we use the **UBound** and **LBound** statements respectively. The syntax is as follows:

UBound(*arrayname*[, *dimension*])

LBound(*arrayname*[, *dimension*])

The *arrayname* parameter is the required name of the array, while the *dimension* is an optional parameter of the long datatype, representing the dimension of the array from which you wish to retrieve the upper bound. Use 1 for the first dimension, 2 for the second dimension, and so on. In the following example, we use **UBound** to get the array's upper bound before starting the **For...Next** statement:

```
For intX = 0 To UBound(x)
  Debug.WriteLine(CStr(x(intx)))
Next
```

By using **UBound** in this manner, you will never get an exception that says you passed the boundary limit of an array, so your code will be less troublesome.

NOTE

If you do not specify a dimension for a multi-dimensional array when calling the **UBound** *function it will return the size of the first dimension.*

Working with the Array's Upper Boundary

VB.NET does not allow you to specify the **LBound** to **UBound** of the array **Dim Days(1 to 20) as Integer** as was common with earlier versions of VB. But the .NET Framework arrays still support explicit redeclaration of the arrays using a **ReDim** statement, and thus they grant you the ability to keep expanding the array as needed. The cool aspect of this new behavior, which is still supported, is that you can preserve the data of the original array. Essentially, the array can keep growing *ad infinitum,* as you will see shortly. The **ReDim** syntax is as follows:

```
ReDim [Preserve] varname(size) [AS type][= initexpr]
[,varname(subscripts)[AS type][= initexpr]]
```

The syntax takes the following arguments:

▶ **Preserve**   An optional keyword that you use if you want to keep (preserve) existing array data when expanding the upper limit of the array dimension

▶ **Varname**   Required name of the variable name of the array

▶ **Size**   Required size of the new array dimension

▶ **Type**   Optional variable datatype

The array must be initialized before the upper bound can be changed. In other words, you must first declare the array, and then subsequent calls to resize the array can be achieved with the **ReDim** statement.

NOTE

*Be careful when using the **ReDim** statement. If you use the **ReDim** statement to make the array smaller, the elements in the upper bounds of the array that you eliminate will obviously be gone forever.*

*The architects of VB.NET have gone a long way to ensure the type safety of the framework, and any type of data that the array contains cannot be changed willy-nilly. For example, if the array is declared as **String**, you cannot change the datatype of the array to **Integer**.*

In the following example, we have taken the code demonstrated previously and increased the array size by 1:

```
Dim Incr As Integer
Dim Cond As Boolean = True
Dim ListIndex(10) As Integer
Dim List(10) As String
Incr = ListIndex(0)
While Cond = True
 ListIndex(Incr) = Incr
 List(Incr) = CStr(ListIndex(Incr))
 Debug.WriteLine("Element " & CStr(Incr) & " = " & List(Incr))
 If Incr = 9 Then
  Debug.WriteLine("Old boundary ended here")
```

```
  Incr += 1
  ReDim Preserve ListIndex(Incr)
  ReDim Preserve List(Incr)
  ListIndex(Incr) = Incr
  List(Incr) = CStr(ListIndex(Incr))
  Debug.WriteLine("New: " & CStr(UBound(ListIndex)) & " = "
    & CStr(UBound(List)))
   Cond = False
   Exit While
 End If
  Incr += 1
  End While
End Sub
```

The new output to the console is as follows:

```
Element 0 = 0
Element 1 = 1
Element 2 = 2
Element 3 = 3
. . .
Element 9 = 9
Old boundary ended here
New: 10 = 10
```

Some rules to follow when playing with a "spandex" array:

▶ You cannot change the number of dimensions in the array.

▶ **ReDim** does not allow you to change an array from one datatype to another.

▶ When working with multi-dimensional arrays **ReDim** lets you extend only the **Ubound** of the last dimension (see the next section).

▶ If you shrink the array, you will no doubt lose the data stored in the eliminated indices.

The Erase Statement

The **Erase** statement releases the instance of an array, essentially "erasing" the array values. You can equate **Erase** with the VB 6 **set object = nothing** statement. If you wish to clear more than one array, you can pass a comma-delimited list of array names to the **Erase** statement. This is how your syntax should look:

Erase *arraylist*

Now consider the following example:

```
Dim x() As String
ReDim x(1)
  X(0) = "Dog"
  X(1) = "Cat"
Erase X 'Now the array is cleared . . . and truncated
```

The IsArray Function

The **IsArray** function returns a Boolean indicating whether a variable is an array. The syntax to use the function is as follows:

IsArray(*variablename*)

Consider the following example:

```
Dim strBooks(10) as String
Dim intCount as Integer
Debug.WriteLine IsArray(strBooks)        ' returns true
Debug.WriteLine IsArray(intCount)        ' returns false
```

Collections

A collection is similar to an array in that it is an object that maintains a collection of types that can be referenced and managed as a unit. The most important difference between the **Collection** class and the **Array** class is that the members of a collection object can be of any type, while the elements of an array must be of the same type. Collections are created as follows:

```
Dim MailHeader As New Collection
```

The collection object is a basic and easy-to-use structure that comes equipped with three methods you use to manage the elements of the collection. The methods are **Add**, **Remove**, and **Item**. The following example creates a collection of string objects; it is used as follows:

```
MailHeader.Add(Me.ToBox.Text)
MailHeader.Add(Me.FromBox.Text)
MailHeader.Add(Me.SubjectBox.Text)
```

And you can reference the object's information at a specific position in the collection using the **ToString** method, as follows:

```
Me.FromBox.Text = MailHeader.Item(2).ToString
```

Besides sort and search algorithms, the collection is useful as a structure to store and reference objects in visual components that manage strings or graphical elements, such as icons and bitmaps. **ListBoxes** and **ComboBoxes** are good examples of collections of strings that can be referenced as a unit. The **System.Collections** namespace provides industrial-strength data structure manipulation capability, as discussed next.

NOTE

While arrays and collections are similar in function, arrays with their type restriction provide a performance benefit over collections. Arrays are thus more suited to sorting and searching operations than a simple collection object. Collections, on the other hand, provide more flexibility in the management of elements and allow the creation of custom types.

The Collections Namespace

The .NET Framework provides advanced support for data structure management in the form of the **System.Collections** namespace and its posse of data-management classes. The namespace provides classes that create objects for sorting, storing, and searching such as **ArrayList**, **HashTable**, **Queue**, **Stack**, and so on. The **System.Collections** namespace also offers up several interfaces that define functionality and can be used to enumerate, populate, and author collections. Table 3-1 lists all the classes and interfaces that are offered by the **System.Collections** namespace.

Classes/Methods	Purpose
ArrayList	An array object that gets dynamically increased as needed
BitArray	An array object of bits; use Boolean expression to determine whether the bit is on or off
CaseInsensitiveComparer	Compares two objects; ignoring case
CaseInsenstiveHashCodeProvider	Provides a hash code for an object; ignores case
Comparer	Used for case-sensitive comparison of objects
DictionaryBase	Used for a collection of closely associated keys and values (like a hash table)
HashTable	A collection of keys and values organized as hash codes

Table 3-1   *Classes and Interfaces Offered by the **System.Collections** Namespace*

Classes/Methods	Purpose
Queue	A collection of objects organized on a first-in, first-out basis
ReadOnlyCollectionBase	A collection of read-only objects
SortedList	A sorted list of keys and values that can be accessed by keys and indices
Stack	A last-in, first-out (push-pop) data structure
Interface	**Purpose**
Icollection	Defines the size, enumerators, and synchronization methods for collections
Icomparer	Exposes the **Comparer** method
Idictionary	Represents a dictionary of keys and values
IdictionaryEnumerator	Enumerates the dictionary
Ienumerable	Exposes the **Enumerator** method
Ienumerator	The **Enumerator** method
IhashcodeProvider	Exposes the hash code provider
Ilist	Represents a list of objects referenced by indices

Table 3-1   *Classes and Interfaces Offered by the **System.Collections** Namespace
(continued)*

The **System.Collections** namespace also provides a single structure called the **DictionaryEntry**, which represents the key-value pair that makes up dictionary entries.

NOTE

*The **System.Collections.Specialized** namespace provides an additional level of functionality for data structures and data management. Of particular interest is the **StringCollection** class, which is used for advanced management of a collection of strings.*

Strings

This section deals with VB.NET's important string processing and manipulating ability —functionality provided by the **System.String** base class. In just about all applications you write you will have a reason to work with a string of characters in some form or another. In addition to the new methods of the **String** object, the legacy VB-style string-manipulation functions listed in Table 3-2 are available to .NET applications.

Action	Function
Compare two strings	**StrComp**
Convert strings	**StrConv**
Convert from uppercase to lowercase	**Format**, **Lcase**, **Ucase**
Repeat characters	**Space** and the **String** function
Determine the length of a string	**Len**
Format a string	**Format**
Manipulating strings	**InStr, Left, Ltrim, Mid, Right, Rtrim, Trim**
Comparison rules	**Compare**
ANSI and ASCII values	**Asc, Chr**
Replace one string with another	**Replace**
Return a string array based on a filter	**Filter**
Return a string array based on the delimiter	**Split**

Table 3-2   *VB-Style String-Manipulation Functions*

Working with Strings

The following code instantiates the **String** object and initializes its string field.

```
Dim Str As String = "I love VB.NET"
```

You can also convert the **String** object to objects of other types, such as **Char** and **Byte**.

The Methods of System.String

Table 3-3 lists the important string and character manipulation methods available in the **String** class.

Clone

Like most of the .NET types, **String** packs a **Clone** method that enables you to declare a new object and then clone another object to it bit for bit. You can then

Action	Method
Clone the object	**Clone()**
Compare two strings	**Compare(), CompareOrdinal()**
Compare this object to another object	**CompareTo()**
Join one string to another	**Concat()**
Copy one string object to another	**Copy()**
Copy characters into an array	**CopyTo()**
Evaluate the beginning and ends of strings	**StartsWith(), EndsWith()**
Test the equality of one object to another	**Equals()**
Format numeric output	**Format()**
Obtain the index location of a character in a string	**IndexOf(), LastIndexOf()**
Insert sub-strings into a string	**Insert()**
Obtain a reference	**Intern(), IsInterned**
Joining and splitting	**Join(), Split()**
Padding	**PadLeft(), PadRight()**
Remove characters	**Remove()**
Replacing characters	**Replace()**
Extrude a sub-string from a string	**SubString()**
Trim from both ends of strings	**Trim(), TrimEnd(), TrimStart()**

Table 3-3   *String and Character Manipulation Methods in the* **String** *Class*

work with the new object in place of the cloned one. The following code demonstrates the cloning of a **String** object:

```
Dim sTxt, sTxtDis As String
Dim zClone As Object
sTxt = "I big yours"
zClone = sTxt.Clone()
sTxtDis = zClone.ToString()
Console.WriteLine("Result: " + sTxtDis)
```

Compare

The **String.Compare** method provides a facility for comparing two strings to each other. This static method returns an integer that indicates the equality of the two strings. The syntax is as follows:

String.Compare(*StrA*, *StrB*)

Consider the following code:

```
Dim sText, sNewText, sTextDisplay As String
Dim n As Integer
sNewText = "hello planet"
sTextDisplay = "hello planet"
n = sText.Compare(sNewText, sTextDisplay)
Console.WriteLine("Result: " + CStr(n))
```

The strings are found to be equal and the output to the console is

```
Result: 0
```

The following table lists return codes provided by the **Compare** method:

Integer Returned	Action
Negative	StrA < StrB
0	StrA = StrB
Positive	StrA > StrB

A similar method in the **String** object is **CompareOrdinal.** However, this method compares the **String** object while disregarding language or culture. For example, the following line returns the same three result integers as the **Compare** method:

```
n = sText.CompareOrdinal(sNewText, sTextDisplay)
```

CompareTo

The **CompareTo** method is similar to the already discussed compare methods; but instead of taking two string objects as parameters, this method compares the string parameter to the owner of the method. Consider the following code:

```
Dim sText1, sText2 As String
Dim n As Integer
```

```
sText1 = "hello human"
sText2 = "hello human"
n = sText1.CompareTo(sText2)
Console.WriteLine("Result: " + CStr(n))
```

The strings compare as equal, and the output to the console is **Result: 0**.

Concat

The **Concat** method concatenates two or more strings and returns a new string that contains the characters from the concatenated strings. The minimal syntax is as follows:

> s1.concat(s2)

This joins s1 and s2 to form a new output string. However, the method can take up to three strings and has application in array types (see the "Arrays" section earlier in this chapter).

```
Dim s1, s2, s3 As String
s1 = "Houston, "
s2 = "we have a problem."
Debug.WriteLine(s3.Concat(s1, s2))
```

The output to the console is the string representation of s3, which is the concatenation of s1 and s2. Note that the original strings s1 and s2 are not modified in any way. The result to the console is as follows:

```
Houston, we have a problem.
```

The s3 variable's original string does not change. It is just used to invoke the **Concat** function.

Copy

The **Copy** method provides a simple means of copying one string object to another. The original string is left untouched. The **Copy** syntax is demonstrated in the following example:

```
Dim s1, s2 As String
s1 = "Houston, we have a problem."
Debug.WriteLine(s2.Copy(s1))
```

And if you cannot guess what gets written to the output window, we really do have a problem!

CopyTo

The **CopyTo** method is a little more complex than the **Copy** method. The method takes a character at the source position in a string and then copies the character to a destination position in a character array. The base syntax is as follows:

Str1.CopyTo(Int1, myArray, Int2, Int3)

The character at Int1 is the starting point or source index in the source string. The parameter **myArray** is a destination array you provide. Int2 is the starting index or destination index in the array and Int3 or count is the number of characters to copy from the source string.

```
Dim I As Integer
Dim s1 As String = "Houston, we have a problem."
Dim myArray(5) As Char
   s1.CopyTo(0, myArray, 0, 4)
   s1.CopyTo(10, myArray, 4, 1)
For I = 0 To 4
   Console.WriteLine(myArray(I))
Next I
```

In this code example, an array (**myArray**) of type **Char** holds five characters. Then four characters (count) are copied into **myArray**, starting at index 0 and ending at index 3. Next, using string **s1**, character *e* is copied in position 10 in the string to the index position 5 in the array. The characters copied into the array are *H*, *o*, *u*, *s*, and *e*.

Finally, to write the array contents to the console, a **For...Next** loop is used, which loops four times to output the characters and display the following:

```
H
o
u
s
e
```

EndsWith and StartsWith

The **EndsWith** and **StartsWith** methods are useful for simple Boolean checks on strings—in particular, what you designate as the end strings or the starter strings. The syntax is as follows:

Str.EndsWith()
Str.StartsWith()

Here is an example:

```
Dim s1 As String = "Houston, we have a problem."
  If s1.EndsWith("problem") Then
    Debug.WriteLine("not true")
  End If
```

In this example, the output to the console can never happen because the period has been omitted from the **EndsWith** test and the statement is thus false.

Equals

The **Equals** method provides a means of determining, through the return of true or false, whether a certain string of characters is equal in value to another string. Thus, if we think the **str1** value is "X," the **Equals** method allows us to determine whether it is indeed "X." This method is convenient for testing values of strings to control flow in a method. The syntax is as follows:

str1.Equals(str2)

Now consider the following code (note that case is important):

```
Dim s1 As String = "Houston, we have a problem."
 If s1.equals("Houston, we have a problem.") Then
  Console.WriteLine("true")
 End If
```

You can also use the equal operator (=) to obtain the same results. We need to change only one line, as follows:

```
If s1 = "Houston, we have a problem." Then
```

Format

The .NET Framework contains a numeric string formatting method that wraps the standard numeric formatting functions found in modern languages and class libraries, including legacy Visual Basic. The numeric types are formatted through the **Format** method applicable to the datatype being rendered. The basic syntax is as follows:

Str.Format()

The **String** class also provides for custom formatting for more flexibility, which is illustrated in the next few sections. The standard format string comprises a character that represents the format, such as currency or decimal, followed by digits that represent the precision. The following table lists the standard formats supported by the **Format** method:

Specifier	Returns
C,c	Currency
D,d	Decimal
E,e	Exponential or scientific
F,f	Fixed-point
G,g	General
N,n	Number
X,x	Hexadecimal

Currency   Use the currency format string to convert a numeric value to a currency value. The currency value can contain a locale-specific currency amount. The format information is determined by the current locale but you can override this by passing in the **NumberFormatInfo** object as an argument. The default in the United States is, of course, U.S. dollars—for example:

```
Console.WriteLine("{0:c}", 125.88)
Console.WriteLine("{0:c}", -125.88)
```

NOTE

The **Console.WriteLine** method automatically calls **String.Format** as demonstrated in these examples.

The output to the console is the following:

```
$125.88
($125.88)
```

Decimal Use the currency format string to convert a decimal value to an integer value. For example,

```
Console.WriteLine("{0:D}", 12588)
```

writes *12588* to the console, but

```
Console.WriteLine("{0:D10}", 12588)
```

writes *0000012588* to the console, representing 10 digits (5 as passed by the parameter and 5 zeros for left "padding").

Exponential This is the scientific (exponential) notation that formats the value passed to the string in this form:

$$m.dddE+xxx$$

As indicated, the decimal point is always preceded by one digit. The number of decimal places is specified by the precision *specifier* (six places is the default). You can use the format specifier to determine the case of the letter *e* in the output, as illustrated in the following example:

```
Console.WriteLine("{0:E}", 125.8)
Console.WriteLine("{0:E10}", 125.88)
Console.WriteLine("{0:e5}", 125.88))
```

This example writes the following to the console:

```
1.258000E+002
1.2580000000E+002
1.25880e+002
```

Fixed-Point Use fixed-point formatting to convert the value to a string and then specify the number of places after the decimal point with the user of the precision specifier. For example, the following code

```
Console.WriteLine("{0:F}", 125.88)
Console.WriteLine("{0:F10}", 125.88)
Console.WriteLine("{0:F0}", 125.88)
```

provides this output:

```
125.88
125.8800000000
126
```

General   Use the general format to convert the string to a number of either fixed-point format or scientific format. This format is often used in calculator software to write to a more compact format. For example, the following code

```
Console.WriteLine("{0:G}", 12345.67)
Console.WriteLine("{0:G4}", 12345.67)
Console.WriteLine("{0:G6}", 12345.67)
```

provides this output to the console:

```
12345.67
1.2345E4
12345.7
```

Number   The number format allows you to convert a large number that has a decimal point to a number that can be better read with commas. The default is two decimal places; in the second example shown next, three decimal places were specified. The following code

```
Console.WriteLine("{0:N}", 12345.67)
Console.WriteLine("{0:N3}", 12345.670)
```

displays the following on the console:

```
12,345.67
12,345.678
```

Hexadecimal   If you need to convert a string value to a hexadecimal format, use the X specifier. The uppercase *X* gives you uppercase letters (and vice versa using lowercase *x*). The minimum number of digits to display is set by the precision specifier. If the number is smaller than the precision specifier, it will be "padded" to the digits specified. The following code provides examples (note the case differentiation):

```
Console.WriteLine("{0:x}", 123)
Console.WriteLine("{0:X3}", 123)
```

And the output is as follows:

```
7b
07B
```

Custom Formatting   If you need specific control on the output, the ability to create custom formats can be useful. When you use the custom format option, special characters are used as a template to shape the output. Characters that are not recognized are copied to the output.

Using a Digit or Zero for a Placeholder   The following code formats the output to the designated number of digits using a 0 as the placeholder. If there are more placeholders than digits passed in the argument, the output is left-padded with the placeholder 0's. For example, this code,

```
Console.WriteLine("{0:111}", 1234)
Console.WriteLine("{0:00}", 12)
Console.WriteLine("{0:0000}", 123)
Console.WriteLine("{0:0000}", 1234)
```

provides the following output:

```
111
12
0123
1234
```

In this output, the first line generates three *1*'s, because this placeholder is not recognized by the method and is thus simply copied to the output and the number as the argument is ignored. The second line shows output limited to two digits. The third line shows output limited to four digits, but because we provide only a three-digit string as the argument, the number is left-padded with a *0*. The fourth line shows four numbers formatted to a string of four digits.

Using a Digit or Pound for a Placeholder   The pound (or hash) character can be used as the digit or space placeholder. This placeholder works just like the 0 except that a space or blank is inserted into the output as no digit is used in the specified position. For example, this code

```
Console.WriteLine("{0:####}", 123)
Console.WriteLine("{0:####}", 1234)
Console.WriteLine("{0:##}", 123456)
```

displays the following output to the console:

```
123
1234
123456
```

Custom Positioning of the Decimal Point   You can determine the position of the decimal point in a string of numerals by specifying the position of the period (.) character in the format string. You can also customize the character used as a decimal point in the **NumberFormatInfo** class. Here is an example:

```
Console.WriteLine("{0:####.000}", 123456.7)
Console.WriteLine("{0:##.000}", 12345.67)
Console.WriteLine("{0:#.000}", 1.234567)
```

The following code displays the following strings on the console:

```
123456.700
12345.670
1.235
```

Using the Group Separator   The comma (,) group separator is used to format large numbers to make them easier to read. You typically add the comma three places after the decimal point to specify a number such as 1,000.00 or higher. The character used as the specifier can also be customized in the **NumberFormatInfo** class. The following example illustrates placement of the group separator:

```
Console.WriteLine("{0:##,###}", 123456.7)
Console.WriteLine("{0:##,###,000.000}", 1234567.1234567)
Console.WriteLine("{0:#,#.000}", 1234567.1234567)
```

The output to console is as follows:

```
123,457
1,234,567.123
1,234,567.123
```

Using Percent Notation   You can use the percent (%) specifier to denote that a number be displayed as a percentage. The number will be multiplied by 100 before formatting. Take the following example,

```
Console.WriteLine("{0:##,000%}", 123.45)
Console.WriteLine("{0:00%}", 0.123)
```

and you get the following percentages displayed in the console:

```
12,345%
12%
```

IndexOf and LastIndexOf

The **IndexOf** and **LastIndexOf** methods provide a facility for locating a character or a set of characters in a string. In a word processing application, for example, you can provide users the ability to search for and replace strings. Consider the following code snippet:

```
Dim s1 As String
s1 = "The small brown fox"
Console.WriteLine(s1.IndexOf("x"))
```

It is rather easy to work out in your head the output to the console. It is the integer *18*, of course—being the last character in the above string. If the character is not present in the string, an error value of –1 is returned.

The method **LastIndexOf** provides a slightly different facility. It reports the last occurrence of a particular character in the string. In the above example, there is only one occurrence of "x", so the return value is again 18. But if we searched for "o", for example, we would get 17 as the return value because there are two occurrences of "o" in the string, and we are looking for the last one.

Insert

The **Insert** method inserts a string into another string in a location specified in the method. Here's the syntax:

> String.Insert()

Consider the following code:

```
Dim s1 As String
s1 = "The small brown fox "
Console.WriteLine(s1.Insert(20, "jumped over the wall"))
```

The string argument "jumped over the wall" is inserted at integer 20 in the string s1 to display to the console the following:

```
The small brown fox jumped over the wall
```

Intern and IsInterned

String objects can get quite large, and the task of comparing them can become slow in computing terms. The **Intern** method provides a facility for obtaining a reference to a string that speeds up comparison operations by an order of magnitude. The **Intern** method is also useful for creating strings on the fly and then providing an immediate facility for using the string in a number of operations.

When you invoke the **Intern** method of different string objects that have the same content as the original string object, you will obtain a reference to the first object. For every object instantiated that is the same as the original object, you will obtain multiple references to the same object by interning each new string object. Interned strings can be compared with the equal operator (=) instead of calling the more resource-intensive **Intern** method, which literally has to compare each character in the corresponding string.

NOTE

See the section, "The .NET Object Reference Model," in Chapter 4.

The following code demonstrates the interning of string objects:

```
Dim s1, s2, s3, s4 As String
s1 = "The small brown fox"
s2 = "The small brown fox"
s3.Intern(s1)
s4.Intern(s2)
  If s3 = s4 Then
    Console.WriteLine("Jeez that was quick")
  End If
```

The string object also contains the method **IsInterned**, which when called provides a reference to the string if it has already been interned. Otherwise, it returns null and you can proceed to call **Intern** or handle the null return value as an exception. Look at the following code. The string 'Test' will appear in the pool once and some string space will be preserved! If you create a string on the fly, it will not be in the intern pool. Calling **Intern** will return the string from the pool and if not found it will place it in it first. **IsInterned** differs by not placing a string in the pool; rather, it will return Null/Nothing for strings that are not in the pool!

```
Dim a1 As String = "Test"
Dim a2 As String = "Test" 'The string is in the Pool
Dim s1 As String = "Test1"

Debug.WriteLine("<" & s1.IsInterned(s1) & ">")  'Will print '<Test1>'
Dim s2 As String = New _
```

```
   System.Text.StringBuilder().Append("Tes").Append _
  ("t2").ToString() 'Test2 is not in the pool
   Debug.WriteLine("<" & s1.IsInterned(s2) & ">") 'Will print <>
   Debug.WriteLine("<" & s1.Intern(s2) & ">") 'Places Test2 in the Pool
'and will print <Test2>
   Debug.WriteLine("<" & s1.IsInterned(s2) & ">") 'Will print <Test2>
```

Join and Split

The **Join** and **Split** methods are used with arrays. The **Join** method copies the string elements occupying an array of type **String** and connects them with separators or characters to assemble a string. The **Split** method can be used to chop up a string at the characters in the string you designate as separators. The pieces of strings can then be slotted into a string array.

The following code first designates a separator character. In this example, we designate the blank character (" ") as the separator (s1). The code shows that s1 is passed as a **Split** into an array of type **Char.** We then use the element of the array as the specifier for chopping up the string s2 (s2 is split at the blanks in the lines). At this point in the execution, **sArray** holds a string (each word in the sentence) in each element or index position in the array.

```
Dim I As Integer
Dim s1, s2 As String
Dim seps(1) As Char
Dim sArray(6) As String
s1 = " "
s2 = "The cow jumped over the moon"
s1.CopyTo(0, seps, 0, 1)
sArray = s2.Split(seps)
For I = 0 To 5
   Debug.WriteLine(sArray(I))
Next I
Debug.WriteLine(s2.Join("*", sArray))
```

> ### NOTE
> *Regardless of the declared size, VB will resize the array to fit all elements.*

The first console output is derived from a loop that copies each word from the array and displays it to the console. The second console output joins copies of all the elements of the first array into a sentence, using the asterisk character (*) as the separator. The console's output for the first call to **WriteLine** is as follows:

```
The
cow
jumped
```

```
over
the
moon
```

The next output for the second call to **WriteLine** is as follows:

```
The*cow*jumped*over*the*moon
```

PadLeft and PadRight

The padding methods either left or right align a string in its field and then pad the other end of the string with spaces or a specified character to fill the specified length of the field. The following code works for both left and right padding of strings:

```
Dim s1 As String = "Holy cow"
Dim dot As Char = Convert.ToChar(".")
Console.WriteLine(s1.PadLeft(20, dot)) 'or
Console.WriteLine(s1.PadRight(20, dot))
```

The output to the console is as follows:

```
Holy cow............
............Holy cow
```

NOTE

*Observe the **Convert.ToChar** method used in the padding code to change a character literal to a char value. Changing a character literal to assignment of type **char** is not supported in Beta 2 of VB.NET.*

Remove

Remove lets you remove a designated number of characters from a particular start index in a string. The following code demonstrates this as follows:

```
Dim s1 As String = "Holly cow"
Dim s2 As String = s1.Remove(3, 1)
Console.WriteLine(s2)
```

Replace

Replace lets you replace a character in a string with a new character. Consider the following code:

```
Dim s As String = "Holy cow"
Dim c As Char = Convert.ToChar("w")
Dim c2 As Char = Convert.ToChar("d")
```

```
    s = s.Replace(c, c2)
Console.WriteLine(s)
```

The console output is as follows:

```
Holy cod
```

SubString

The **SubString** method lets you split a string into two strings at the index location in the string and then return the substring, including the character at the index location. In the example provided next, we want to return just the substring and not the blank or space character, which is the location for obtaining the substring. The following code adds 1 to the location of the blank or space between the two words. We used the **IndexOf** method to find the blank space:

```
Dim s As String = "Holy cow"
Dim i As Integer = s.LastIndexOf(" ")
s = s.Substring(i + 1)
Console.WriteLine(s)
```

This returns just the word "cow" to the console.

ToCharArray

The **ToCharArray** method lets you copy a string to a character array. You can easily reference the character array as follows:

```
Dim s As String = "Holy cow"
Console.WriteLine(s.ToCharArray(0, 2))
```

The console output is as follows:

```
ho
```

ToLower and ToUpper

Often you might need to convert characters to either lowercase or uppercase. The methods **ToLower** and **ToUpper** allow you to toggle text as lowercase or uppercase. For example, the code

```
Dim s As String = "holy cow"
s = s.ToUpper()
Console.WriteLine(s)
```

writes HOLY COW to the console. **ToLower** converts uppercase to lowercase. Incidentally, the method does not take an argument.

Trim, TrimEnd, and Start

The **Trim** functions let you trim white spaces from the beginning and end of strings. **Trim** lets you trim the start and end of strings with one call.

NOTE

*Everything is an object in the .NET Framework—that is, everything except the primitive or basic types. The **String** class's methods thus do not directly alter or manipulate its value. Instead, the object is automatically cloned and the new version is manipulated. When working with multiple string objects that form the source of new strings, using the standard string methods can be cumbersome. Working with multiple string objects can also be resource intensive. The .NET Framework provides the **StringBuilder** class that makes working with strings a lot easier. Further exploration of this fast class is, however, beyond the scope of this little book.*

Methods

A *method* is a module of functionality within a class or an object. As you know, your programs can comprise multiple methods, organized in the objects, and accordingly combined to provide an algorithm or implementation that contributes to an algorithm. Inherited methods can be overridden and your class can contain multiple methods with the same name, which is known as overloading in OO parlance (see Chapters 1 and 4 for examples of both overriding and overloading).

The generally accepted OO style for organizing methods in classes is to categorize them into two groups: *accessor methods* and *modification methods*.

▶ **Accessor methods**   Often called "get methods," accessor methods are used to access information from an object and do not manipulate the object or change its data in any way. An example of an accessor method in your class is one that would allow you to compute values and extract data without actually changing the state or data of the object. While properties are supported in .NET, I believe accessor methods provide a different utility to properties (see the following discussion). Accessor methods are also often used to perform calculations and compute data.

▶ **Modification methods**   Often called "set methods," modification methods let you manipulate an object and change its data. For example, in an **injector** class, you can write a modification method that changes the state of the warp drive, from on to off and vice versa.

Some discount the idea of grouping like this and believe that accessor methods should be replaced by .NET properties, or that accessor methods are too Java-ish. But there are a number of reasons not to discount the notion and style of classifying methods in this way:

▶ Classes become easier to manage and document when you group your code into methods that change data and methods that just compute and return data.

▶ A property generally exposes access, while an accessor method can be used to hide data and computation completely within a class, making if off limits to everything but the members of its class.

▶ The property architecture is not ideal for an accessor method that needs to perform computation for sophisticated algorithms, like working with data structures, advanced sorts, lists manipulation, and so on.

While accessor methods can be used as properties (which might initially appeal to Java converts because Java has no notion of properties), this job is better served by the property architecture—which is actually the combination of two methods, one that can modify a data field and one that reads a data field. Properties are fully investigated in Chapter 4.

Both accessor and modification methods can access the object's data (the instance variables and constants). The accessor methods access data and they can even be activated or called by other members of the class. The modification methods also use the data provided by the instance fields to perform computations and carry out the processing required by the client or consumer.

NOTE

See Chapters 4 and 5 for examples of both accessor and modification methods.

You should name methods in such a way that consumers of the class can tell at a glance whether the method is an accessor method or a modification method. For example, accessor method names are usually prefixed with *Get,* as in **GetUserID** or **GetObjecRef.** Modification methods, on the other hand, are given names that describe what they modify, change, or compute. For example, the modification method that changes data might be called **SetUserID**.

Sub-procedures and Functions

VB.NET defines two method types: one for procedures that do not return values, called *sub-procedures* or *sub-routines*, and another for procedures that do return values, called *functions*. The VB.NET syntax to declare them is as follows:

```
Sub routines = [Attributes][Modifier] Sub [Name][(params)]
Functions = [Attributes][Modifier] Function [Name][(params)]
[As [Attributes] TypeName]
```

We will touch on the various options for both method types in the chapters to follow.

Observations

Well, no sign of the warp drive yet, but we have gained a lot of ground in this chapter. You should now have the necessary building blocks and the essential understanding of how VB.NET works at the fundamental problem solving or algorithm level.

I introduced you to one of the key base class namespaces **System.String**, which is even being extended as we speak. I chose just one class out of many to give you an idea of what's possible with VB.NET and its base class libraries. The next two chapters will provide some insight into how classes like this are implemented, how the functionality is reused, and how to create and extend your own classes.

Object-Oriented Software Development Using VB.NET

IN THIS CHAPTER:

The .NET Object Reference Model

The .NET Value Type Reference Model

Inheritance

Interfaces

Polymorphism

Encapsulation

Designing and Modeling Object-Oriented Applications

Creating Base Classes

Extending Classes

Creating Applications with Custom Classes

An object-oriented (OO) system is not necessarily something that exists solely in the world of computers. In fact, the early object-oriented software languages (it all began with *Simula* back in the late 1960s) were designed to build software objects that represented the object-orientation found in nature.

If you think about the human body, for example, it contains zillions of objects (cells) that work in unison for the common good of the individual, and thus, in mysterious ways, for the good of mankind. The human body is so complex that it is impossible to reproduce it, object for object, or cell for cell; such is the wonder of life. Sometimes the objects begin to do things that work against our anatomical and neurological system, which threatens our existence. Cancer is an example.

Object-based programming allows us to play god on our computers. For example, by creating a little agent on a Web site, you can create a little "life form" that can "grow" into a substantially useful tool. Such a "being," an agent, built by associating many "talking" and "listening" objects, contains methods and data, and it can be instructed to do things independently of the software applications it hangs around. Like humans, the agent exists in its own little processing space, waiting to interact with its environment.

Such an object-oriented application contains the methods that allow it to compute and then interact with a user that needs help locating information on, for example, a Web site—or anything else, even another application or computer. To build such an agent, we would first provide it with methods and data to give the agent character. Data can provide the agent with information about its current state, its location on the screen, whether it is unhidden, and so on.

It seems easy so far to create an object, tell it things it needs to know (data), and create the methods that allow the object to function. But once the object is created, how do you communicate with it? How does the object know how to show itself, or hide for 60 seconds, or speak, or figure out if you can make it to your next paycheck? For that matter, how do we humans know when to eat, why we think, why we do what we do, and why we never seem to make it to our next paycheck? Sometimes our own messaging systems go nuts. Ever scratched your ear and felt your fingernails scratching at the end of your little toe instead? Mankind has even pondered for thousands of years why we even exist. We don't have an answer yet—but that's a thread for Deepak Chopra.

The creators of Visual Basic have tried to get seats on the OO train for years, but version after version, the train left the station without them because of other pressing needs (all those demanding customers and all that *cha-ching* at the cash registers sounding in our ears). But Visual Basic.NET changes everything, and the *cha-ching* rings louder.

Not only do VB programmers now have a true OO language with VB.NET, but they have been given seats in first class, along with C# and all languages that are compliant with the common language specification. Wait a minute, even Java is on this train! Only not in this coach.

NOTE

You will no doubt read or hear about how only Java and C# count in the world of OOP, or nonsense like "VB.NET is just a hack of a procedural language." These statements are such cockamamie nonsense that quoting the sources would only serve to legitimize their worth. VB.NET, it could be argued, is even more OOP than Java, as you will see in the next two chapters. In Dirty Harry's famous words, our response to the VB.NET bashers is: "Do you feel lucky?" Rather than just talk about OO software development and how VB.NET conforms, we will use the next two chapters to also show you OO software development using VB.NET.

Types

The Common Type System (CTS) supports two fundamental types: *value types* and *reference types.* All of the primitive datatypes (such as **Integer**, **Char**, **Double**), enumerations, and structures are value types; modules, interfaces, arrays, and delegates are reference types.

What makes the .NET languages in general and VB.NET in particular different (or special, depending on how you look at it) is that *all* types are derived from a common root type, **Object (System.Object)**. **Object** is the *numero uno* of the .NET type system in that he (or she) is neither a reference type nor a value type, but a first cause of all the data types, custom or base. **Object** provides the base members and implementation common to any datatype.

NOTE

*Java's primitive types are simple types, like the types provided by non-OO languages, such as C and Pascal (but their values can be wrapped). VB.NET and C# (the CLS primitives) types derive from the root **Object**, by way of the **ValueType** object. Declare **Dim One As Integer = 1**, and then type **Debug.WriteLine(One.ToString)** and you will see the result: "1". And the statement **Dim X As System.Double** is exactly the same as the statement **Dim X As Double**. Java opted out of making its primitive types objects because its makers felt that it degraded performance. The .NET architects felt otherwise, even though .NET primitives are stack rather than heap allocated.*

The .NET Value Type Reference Model

Value types are stored directly on the stack and are always referenced directly. A variable or constant of a value type always contains the literal value of that type, but it cannot be null. The following table lists the available .NET value types.

Value Type	Description
Primitive	Declarable literal values, as variables and constants
Enumeration	Represents a set of values of a primitive
Structure	Represents data structures with members (data and functions)

Primitives and *enumerations* are simple to work with and, for the most part, few of us will care about how they are made and how they get onto the stack. We can work with primitives in the same way that we worked with primitives in VB 6 (although new primitives were introduced in "VB 7").

Structures, also known as *structs* in the world of C/C++ and C#, are a different story. Structures are like classes or objects because they can contain methods and data, but they can work like built-in types because they are value types and thus they can also go directly to the stack and do not require heap storage. Why is that so special?

The *object reference model*, which we will look at next, carries the burden, or overhead, of reference variables. Structures can thus work like objects and provide encapsulation, which is useful for creating custom datatypes that behave like primitives. But without the burden of referenced objects, structures are not resource intensive and are very fast.

NOTE

Further investigation into how value types, and structures in particular, work would take us into the subject of "boxing," which is beyond the scope of this book.

The .NET Object Reference Model

The .NET Framework treats everything as an object. Reference types are not stored on the stack, but rather the runtime heap, and as you will see in this section, they can be referenced only with a reference variable to the location in memory where the actual type is stored.

To succeed as a VB.NET developer, and especially as a developer of OO software, you need an unshakable understanding of how classes and objects are referenced in .NET and how they work. This referencing scheme is known as the *object reference model* of an OO language and is explained here.

NOTE

The class is the unit of functionality and data in OO software development. While a class is often thought of as a blueprint for an object, it is also a datatype. The classes you create are also known as custom classes *or* custom datatypes.

Early OO software development languages created an instance of a class when a variable of the class type was declared. The *variable* and the *object* in memory were one and the same. Modern OO languages instead create a *reference*, which is a type of pointer that points to a location in memory where the actual object—its data—will be stored after it is created. Languages such as Eiffel, Delphi, and Java also use the object-reference model.

When you declare an object—in other words, when you declare its *reference variable*—you do not immediately create that object in memory. You only *reserve* a *place* in memory for the object reference. Object references in VB.NET are created using the following syntax:

```
Dim Result
```

NOTE

The directive **Option Strict On** *will not allow you to declare a variable without the* **As** *clause to link it to the type.*

This instance variable might be more clear if illustrated. See Figure 4-1.

This code creates an object reference variable called **Result**. At the moment of creation, **Result** is just an object reference variable, and no object of any type has been created. In other words, **Result** refers to nothing and is essentially unusable. To create the reference variable and associate it with an object, you would use the following line of code:

```
Dim Result As Object
```

The instance variable is created and immediately points to the object, as illustrated in Figure 4-2. However, **Result** still points to nothing more than a copy of **Object**.

You have now *created* (or as they say in some OOP circles, *activated*) an object of the type you specify following the **As** keyword. Reference variables allow you to refer to the object and its members in your code. From this point on, the type is connected to the reference like a dog on a leash. Lose the leash and you lose the dog.

Figure 4-1   *An instance variable, not yet pointing to any object*

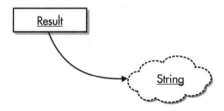

Figure 4-2   *The instance variable points to the memory location where the created object is stored.*

But how does the object get created? We can use the keyword **New** to create the object if this class is destined for instantiation. **New** is a constructor that is inherited by every class, all the way down from the root **Object**. When you call **New**, it creates the actual instance of the class as an object, initializes its data fields, and places it in the memory location to which the reference variable is pointing. (All classes that are to be instantiated must support the **New** method.)

You can set properties in the object, if it exposes properties, like this:

```
Result1.ResultCode = 0
```

Or you can call its public methods like this:

```
Result2.ComputeResult(50, 69)
```

We'll get back to how you create the classes for your objects, and their members, in the "Creating Classes" section later in this chapter. For now, let's return to the object reference model.

The object's reference variable is a versatile feature. In unmanaged OO languages like Delphi (see Chapter 6) or C++, you would have used it to destroy or free an object from memory (for example **Result.Free** or **Result.Destroy**). In managed languages like VB.NET and C#, you don't have to worry about destroying and freeing the object (but you can call methods like **Finalize**—but more about that later).

In managed OO programming, you can alert the garbage collector (GC) to clean up objects you are no longer using in a number of ways. One way is to make the reference point to thin air, as shown here:

```
Result1 = Nothing
```

The effect of this statement is illustrated in Figure 4-3. This code has effectively removed the pointer to the object, like cutting a lifeline. Eventually, the GC will come and sweep the object off the heap—after that, the object is toast.

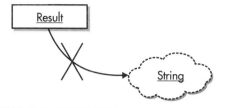

Figure 4-3 *Cutting the object off from its "lifeline"*

Another way to point the reference away from the original object that was created for it is to assign the variable to another object. To do this, of course, you need to create another object, which, of course, would entail another reference variable along for the ride. The following code achieves this:

```
Dim Result1 As Object
Dim Result2 As Object
```

You have now declared two references, called **Result1** and **Result2**. **Result1** and **Result2** now both refer to **Object**. The two object references and any associated objects are illustrated in Figure 4-4.

What do you think will happen if you add the following line of code?

```
Result1 = Result2
```

You're correct if you said that after this assignment, **Result1** and **Result2** would refer to the same object. The assignment is illustrated in Figure 4-5.

NOTE

You can also clone an object (make a copy) without having to declare an additional reference variable.

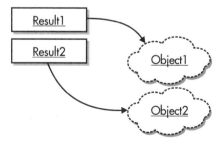

Figure 4-4 *Result1 and Result2 refer to the root Object.*

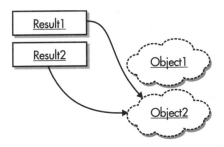

Figure 4-5 *Result1* and *Result2* refer to the same object; the same location in memory.

Inheritance, Encapsulation, and Polymorphism in VB.NET

Object-oriented software development is like a three-legged stool. If one of its three essential legs—*inheritance, encapsulation,* and *polymorphism*—is not present (even in a most basic form) the stool falls over. So has it been with earlier versions of Visual Basic.

Inheritance

Inheritance is not a difficult concept to understand. Consider Muhammad Ali's daughter Laila Ali, who is aiming to "float like a butterfly and sting like a bee" in the ring like her dad. In April 2001 she told reporters that she is driven to box by a force she doesn't understand. And what drove gifted musician James Raymond, who was given up for adoption at birth, to bang away at the ivories and ebonies? In 1995, nearly three decades after Woodstock, he discovered he was the son of rock n' roll great David Crosby of Crosby, Stills & Nash fame. Any of us can look at our children to see inheritance—and if we are programmers, we can understand how and why this is so important to software development.

Inheritance in software development lets you derive classes from other classes that have data and implementation that we can reuse. Why should we waste time and add complexity to an already highly complex vocation by creating new classes with new data and implementation when other classes already exist to convey what we need? In VB.NET, you can derive from existing classes and then some. You can also extend the base class in the new class. You can then allow the new class to also be derived from, and another class to further extend, the class you started with.

NOTE

A base class is called many things: super class, parent class, or root class; and a subclass also goes by many names, such as child class, derived class, extended class, and inheriting class. All are correct.

"Is a Kind of" Objects

The pure form of inheritance that is offered by the .NET common language specification is new science for Visual Basic programmers. Inheritance caters to everything you do with VB.NET, and unless you fully understand what it does, how it works, and how to use it, you might as well go and look for something else to do for a living.

NOTE

You will no doubt stumble across programmers who will tell you that "inheritance is overrated." That's not a good start to understanding inheritance and how you use it because such a statement detracts from the importance of inheritance. Inheritance is just one aspect of object-oriented technology and separating responsibilities in programming teams is just one area where it is useful. Not to mention that dozens of proven inheritance patterns have been deployed in millions of applications.

Inheritance caters *inter alia* to reuse, consistency and standardization, error reduction, documentation, maintenance, design, and ultimately time to market and a quality product. It achieves this by collecting classes in *families*, in which classes can inherit definitions and implementations from one another.

While deciding whether to inherit a class in your new child class, ask yourself whether the class you are going to create is similar enough to another class that they should be logically related. If a new class can use a substantial number of methods and data from another class, and it's not just a matter of inheriting one class to beef up another, it makes sense to inherit one from the other if the potential parent allows it.

Get one thing straight: You cannot program in VB.NET without inheriting from at least one class: **Object**. **Object** is the basic root class in VB.NET. Because you always implicitly inherit from **Object,** there is really no such thing as a *noninheriting* class.

A new class, **C1**, always extends **Object**. As such, **C1** is considered a subclass or subtype (or child) of **Object**. If you now create a second new class, **C2**, and inherit from **C1** (or, to say it differently, **C2** *extends* **C1**), class **C2** is a subtype of **C1**, which is a subtype of **Object**. This is illustrated in Figure 4-6.

This chapter provides an example of a class that represents a crewmember on a spaceship. We could start our crewmember class hierarchy with a class called **Crew**.

As *a kind of* crewmember, a derived **Engineer** class can inherit the base methods and data needed to interact with the crewmember database and obtain services common to all crewmembers. The new class is now free to extend the **Crew** class as it needs.

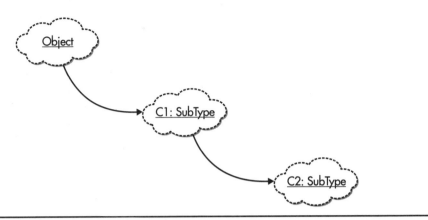

Figure 4-6   *The class inheritance hierarchy*

In the next chapter, the **Engineer** class will extend **Crew** by adding new methods pertinent to the extended class.

Further down the hierarchy, a **WarpEngineer** class may implement its own clock-in/clock-out time processor, based on three-day shifts. Warp engineers have very stressful jobs (one slip and they can get sucked into mini-black holes), and they are thus required to work for three days at a time and then rest for four days. This short shift is not a requirement for all crewmembers, so it makes no sense to implement such functionality in the base class **Crew**. The **WarpEngineer** object thus needs its own implementation for keeping track of dangerous shifts and pay.

However, we don't have to create a new class or methods to accommodate **WarpEngineer**; we can inherit the base class's method definitions, and then simply *override* the method's implementation in the *derived* class.

A cook, on the other hand, logs very different hours than a Warp engineer; a **Cook** subclass would also extend **Crew**, but it would implement only the functionality useful to the **Cook** class. This represents a hierarchy of relationships on our spaceship, which is illustrated in Figure 4-7. (If you look closer at .NET's base Form types, such as Windows forms, you will see that they also inherit from a base form class, because all forms share common features.)

Code reuse is one of the key philosophies behind Java (and all OO languages, for that matter), and this is why Java classes have multiplied as fast as bunny rabbits. The .NET Framework is pursuing the same philosophy, and as you get into coding in .NET, you will connect with millions of other .NET programmers around the globe who are willing to share their classes with you (either out of the goodness of their heart or to make lots of money). (I am also going to give you lots of .NET source code and components for free, as long as you buy my books!)

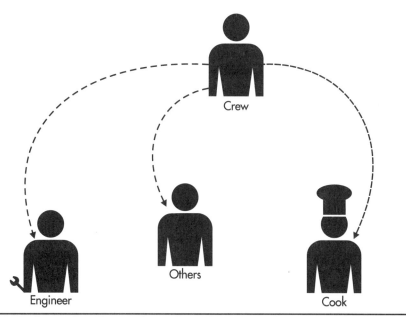

Figure 4-7   *The hierarchy of **is** a relationships of our spaceship's Crew classes*

Multiple Inheritance

The inheritance subject now brings us to a highly controversial and hotly debated subject, *Multiple inheritance*. Multiple inheritance allows a design and implementation phenomenon known as a *"mixin."* A mixin means that you can inherit more than one nonabstract method from a number of different classes and thus create a new class that now contains inherited functionality from all the mixed-in classes. Figure 4-8 illustrates the mixin multiple inheritance model.

Multiple inheritance in software, some believe, is too problematic for the rank-and-file software nerds. Both Sun and Microsoft (and not to forget Borland *et al.*) claim that multiple inheritance causes too many problems in OOP to be useful. This is valid to some extent because while inheriting from multiple parents may on the face of it sound straightforward, it turns out to be rather complex in many cases.

The purest form of multiple inheritance lets a subclass inherit implementation from different parents at the same time, and many developers believe that the added flexibility and power is worth the extra care required during implementation. One of the most common problems encountered with multiple inheritance deals with identical method names in different classes. The problem: Which method do you implement? How do you tell them apart? How can they both be supported if they achieve different results? And with the new world order of the Internet and the World Wide Web, developers

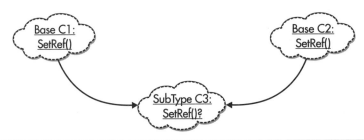

Figure 4-8   *Mixing-in implementation in multiple inheritance sounds easy, but the "matching" causes a lot of problems.*

now have access to millions of new classes being authored across the planet, which means there is no easy way of resolving conflicts.

C++ changed to multiple inheritance after the language was introduced. Eiffel, on the other hand, was built from the ground up using multiple inheritance. Languages like Java and Delphi have opted for single inheritance only, and this is the case with the .NET languages. (In fact, if you try and add a second **Inherits** statement to a VB class, the compiler will politely tell you to get lost.)

NOTE

The single inheritance model in .NET has not stopped the aggressive adoption of it by such languages as Eiffel and C++.

But single inheritance does not necessarily mean you can have only one super or parent class. The .NET language inheritance can be implemented only through a single-object hierarchy, while a language like C++ has multiple-object hierarchies. In .NET, the root **Object**'s members always manifest in every new class. So a child class not only derives from your new custom base class, but also from **Object**. You can by all means derive from your custom class, and thus you could create a new child class that contains elements of *three* super classes. This is acceptable (if not overdone), as long as only one logical hierarchy exists. The hierarchy of classes begetting classes is illustrated in Figure 4-6.

Inheritance does not make sense when a class's characteristic changes from an *is-a-kind-of* object to *is-a-role-played-by* object. That means that when a class sometimes needs to behave more like another class (other than the one it derives from), inheritance is not the answer. There are many such *role-played-by* circumstances in our applications, and delegation patterns come to the rescue. We will discuss *delegates* and *interfaces* briefly; this book does not provide the forum for an in-depth review.

Inheritance and Interfaces

Interfaces are fundamental to the .NET Framework. Microsoft's implementation for the Common Type System (CTS) is no different than interfaces in C, C++, Java, or any other language (although there are many differences in opinion on how interfaces extend the type system). An interface is simply a class that defines the methods—the essential metadata required to implement the members in a class that "contracts" with the interface. An interface is not very different from a completely abstract class because you are not allowed to provide any implementation in the interface; the implementation must be provided entirely by the *implementor*—the developer exposing the interface in a new class.

While reviewing .NET languages, you will often hear that the languages support multiple inheritance through interfaces. I fail to see how this is true, and both Sun and Microsoft shout this out aloud from their respective minarets. While declaring that interfaces are inherited is technically correct, and such language is used in the lingo of all object-oriented languages, the statement declaring "interface" inheritance as a "substitute for multiple inheritance" is really confusing. The two concepts are entirely different and serve very different purposes.

First, *you cannot inherit implementation from interfaces.* You can only expose an interface in your class and then provide the implementation of the interface's members, according to the interface members' definition.

Use of the word "inherit" to mean the same thing as "expose" is unfortunate. Interface inheritance by no means makes up for forgoing the perceived benefits of multiple inheritance. However, having said that, you can *implement* from multiple interfaces. You just have to be careful to resolve duplicate definitions from multiple interfaces, which is one of the main reasons the architects left true multiple inheritance out of the .NET picture in the first place. Interface construction and implementation is a very important subject but unfortunately beyond the scope of this book.

Encapsulation

Classes should always ensure that data is hidden. Hiding data from the consumers of classes (the applications that use them) ensures that these members are not accessed, which could leave the object in an unstable state. The less that consumers know about the data within a class, or how it is manipulated, the better. There are several reasons for this.

NOTE

Data hiding is one of the founding principles of object-oriented software development.

First, data hiding promotes a *loose coupling* between the class and the consumer, which means that the consumer is less dependent on the class. In other words, a loose coupling insures that if the consumer decides to choose another interface, the de-coupling from the first interface will not break the application. The CTS is an excellent forum for this level of coupling. You might use a class written in C# today, and find a better one written in VB.NET tomorrow. It's like, in the real world, if you hear that the SUV you have been driving to *schlep* the kids to school has a habit of shredding its tires and doing a break-dance on the interstate, you can simply dump it and use another one.

Second, data hiding (or at least hiding the fields) allows the class's creator to change the accessor and modifier methods—or how the data is manipulated—without breaking the code at the client. The creator is thus free to continue to improve the class without breaking the contract with the consumer.

Back to the SUV example: consumers are not required to know how the internals of the vehicle operate, nor do they need to know what lies under the hood. The contract you have with the manufacturer promises that you can expect the thing to work when you turn the key in the ignition. The manufacturer is thus free to recall the product a dozen times, and the consumer is free to buy another product (or at least get it fixed), if all that you get when you turn the key is a click.

Third, data hiding promotes security. If a field holding valuable data is exposed (it happens) and the data becomes publicly available... well, this scenario is just too horrible to continue.

TIP

Fields, variables, and constants should generally be private; methods should generally be public. Fields can be public when you are 100-percent sure (which almost never happens) that their definition will not change or that changing them directly will not put the application at risk.

Fourth, data hiding helps reduce errors by ensuring that data in a field is changed or modified only through a method or property that properly checks data being passed to it and that it properly handles the exceptions that arise (it is good practice to provide pre- and postcondition checks in all your methods; and it makes it easier to follow). Consider the following code:

```
'the provider's field
Public myDate As Date

'the user's string
myDate = "2/31/02"
```

Clearly, if the date string in this code snippet is used, the object will behave in predictable ways. But if the field access modifier were declared **Private**, in other words *sealed*, the consumer would not be able to send such a string. With all due respect to programmers, you and me included, we have an uncanny knack for breaking things. If you give us two seconds to get inside a class, we'll break it beyond repair or accidentally expose its vital data to the world. Given that the Internet is everywhere, this is not something we should risk. Data hiding clearly separates the class creators from the class breakers.

Finally, encapsulation ensures that objects are fully *reentrant*—in other words, encapsulation ensures that objects of a type can be safely instantiated numerous times with the knowledge that the data of one of the objects is not going to interfere with the data of another object. While the nature of object-orientation can ensure reentrance and isolation, the issue becomes more critical when more than one thread is at work in the application.

NOTE

In my opinion, public fields are really global variables, and as such they are dangerous. If you declare a public field in an object and then create a second instant of the object, there is a chance that changing the data in one object will change the data in the second object as well.

One final note on encapsulation. Hackers love to hack. If a class exposes a member, a programmer will likely call it or directly implement it in his or her software. Once exposed, always exposed. If you try and go back and hide data or a member of a class that has been distributed, your life will be trash as long as you have an email address or a phone number.

NOTE

The idea of hiding data and implementation goes back further than the advent of OO. A library, which heralds to the early days of C and before, hides the implementation of its functions and data. The functionality is exposed through a contract between the consumer and the creator. The consumer does not need to know the specifics of the implementation, and the creator is bound to fulfill a contract that ensures that the functionality serves the consumer.

Polymorphism

The root of the word *polymorphism* come from Latin, meaning "many forms." How polymorphism pertains to OO software development can be difficult to explain, because the concept manifests in many areas, so we turn again to Mother Nature and ask her for examples. Many life forms can change shapes or take on different forms depending on the signals they get from their environment. Sea anemones, for example, shrink practically to nothing when they became threatened. The lungfish can place itself into a state of suspended animation (encased in mucus) when the lake it lives in dries up, and it can remain inanimate between rainy seasons, encased in rock-hard dry mud, waiting for new rains that will give it a reason to swim again. We humans head for the fast food drive-through when our stress levels begin to rise.

Polymorphism in software development is similar to the polymorphism found in nature in that software constructs can change dynamically without affecting the clients, depending on the situations they encounter and the signals or messages they receive. In software design it allows us to hide a variety of implementations behind a common interface and dynamically change the implementation to process based on the message arriving at the interface. How an application calls methods is polymorphism at work, the implementation of code in various classes is polymorphism at work, and the ability to override and overload methods is polymorphism at work. Late binding is also polymorphism at work.

Polymorphic behavior is usually one of the hardest traits of OO software development to grasp, especially if you were brought up in the procedural programming world, where functions and procedures do not belong to objects that "talk" to each other.

Polymorphism can be classified in various ways, but we won't go into it in depth in this book. For a more detailed discussion, see *Visual Basic.NET: The Complete Reference*.

Polymorphism and Methods

Polymorphism provides the ability to change an overridable method's implementation in a descendent class. In this regard, it facilitates your use of inheritance by disallowing methods, or at least their implementations, from being inherited in your subclass. This is useful when you want to create a class that uses some of its parent's implementation, but not all of it. Conversely, a class can seal a method and prevented it from being overridden.

Polymorphism thus lets you provide different implementations of a method, depending on various circumstances that can be decided at runtime and/or during the design time.

Polymorphism Among Objects

In OO programming, you send messages to objects with data that the object can use to perform tasks. This is known as a *method call* or a *method activation*. In an object-oriented system, such as an operating system, objects can load data from databases when they are created and send messages to each other. The objects can perform system checks, operate hardware, and perform a variety of other tasks.

To send a message to an object, you need to *reference* the object by name. For example, to talk to a Web agent object, you would reference the name of the object and its method. Consider the following method call:

```
MyAgent.MoveTo(0, 22)
```

This message communicates to an instance of an agent object, named **MyAgent**, telling it (a method call) to move to the *x, y* coordinates on the monitor. **MyAgent** is the name of the *receiver* object, while the object that sends the message is called the *sender*.

For objects to recognize messages that belong to certain OO languages, the objects and method messages need to conform to a format known as the *message signature*, which comprises the method's parameter list and the types they represent. *Polymorphism* is thus also the "phenomenon" that lets objects intercommunicate and respond to a message.

Assignment of objects is also polymorphism at work. The following code demonstrates a form of polymorphism called *polymorphic assignment*:

```
Dim We1 As New Engineer
Dim We2 As New WarpDrive
We1 = We2 'ahem, this will not work
```

A "Real-World" Scenario

Now let's get back to the business of our spaceship. An engineer needs access to consoles to monitor the warp engine. The engineer activates the login console, and is supposed to provide a user ID and password to the system for authentication. This information is compared against a database record that checks to determine whether the password, voice print, or some other biological evidence that accompanies the engineer's user ID matches what is stored in the database table.

The first question you have to ask about the engineer is the following: "What is the engineer first and foremost aboard the spaceship?" This may seem like an odd call, but stopping to ask what an object *is* before you code facilities for it is a must when designing object-oriented systems. The reason will become more apparent as you read on.

Is the person first a crewmember or an engineer? This type of question is important in all OO design projects, because no matter what object you create, it is *a kind-of-thing*, which is the purpose of a class. In other words, while an engineer *"is an"* individual, it is also *"a kind of crewmember."* Most VB programmers have probably never asked such a question before, and there was good reason for this—because VB has never, until now, been able to represent such relationships.

NOTE

Here's another real-world example: While we consider ourselves to be individuals, we are also members of the human race; we are a kind of species.

Spaceships, thus, are not manned (excuse my political incorrectness) only by engineers. Engineers are actually part of the crew, starting from the captain or commanding officer to the lowest recruit who might do nothing else aboard the ship but peel space potatoes. Thus, like any enterprise, we first need to classify our crewmembers as **Crew**.

If we sketch two use case diagrams to represent our engineer's authentication to the system, we could depict that the crewmember can be an engineer in the one case, and a cook in another. This tells us that to represent an engineer in OO terms, the root class of all crew members is not **Engineer,** but **Crew**—in other words, an **Engineer** *is a* **Crew** (or *is an **Engineer** as well as a **Crew***). Let's now design and create the class (the reasons for creating a base class will become more apparent as you progress through this chapter).

Designing the Application

Given that VB.NET is now a true OO software development language, it is even more important to model your .NET applications and components properly and adequately before you begin to hack out your code. My modeling tool of choice is either Rational Rose or Visio 2002, and several other tools are available as well. Visual Studio.NET Enterprise Edition can reverse-engineer your assemblies and classes and produce Unified Modeling Language (UML) class diagrams for you. Figure 4-9 illustrates our UML class diagram in Visio. If you are lazy, you can export the definitions directly out of Visio as VB.NET class files (*.vb) ready for use in Visual Studio.

I will not be delving into the software development cycle in any depth in this book, nor will I introduce you to visual modeling or the UML, which is the most popular modeling language for software development. I do, however, cover modeling in more detail in *Visual Basic.NET: The Complete Reference* (Osborne/McGraw-Hill, 2002).

NOTE

The Visio UML option is available only in the Enterprise Edition of Visual Basic.NET (and you'll need Visio 2002 as well).

A model allows you to visualize a software system at a high level of abstraction. In our intergalactic space quest, we have modeled our system as completely as possible, but it comprises dozens of use cases and diagrams for all the various parts of the system. And the "system" is not one big application, but various applications, services, components, and algorithms that interoperate.

Before we get too involved in the various components of the system, we need to first design the login and authentication service, as a point of departure for the entire system.

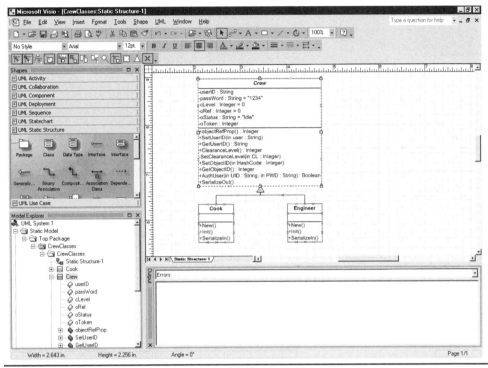

Figure 4-9   *UML class diagram in Visio*

Modeling

To authenticate an engineer and allow access to a system module, we should model the first version of the user authentication and login application as follows:

Authentication and Login, Version 1	
Use Case	Crewmember uses application to authenticate to the system and login for representation in the system.
Actor	Any crewmember.
Purpose	Authenticate member, track time and location logged in, restrict access to unauthorized modules and applications, monitor shift duration. Provide a means of tracking system usage and a means of tracking the progress of a crew member, during shifts and shift transition periods.

Authentication and Login, Version 1	
Synopsis	Before a member can use the system, he or she needs to present authorization credentials to the system in the form of a user ID and a password or biometric information. Credentials can be presented using smart cards, old-fashioned keyboard input, spoken commands, or biometrics devices.
Type	Essential.
Cross Refs	None as of Version 1.

Before you code the **Crew** class, you should model it in UML by first making a list of all the attributes you believe you might need in the class. These attributes, of a parent class, should be the attributes of all crewmembers, no matter their rank, profession, or experience. Eventually, the list will be rather long because we plan to use the class to interact with the database. Figure 4-10 demonstrates a simple use case diagram and sequence diagram depicting the crewmember login scenario.

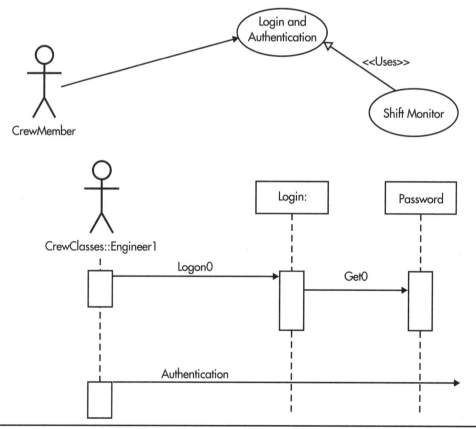

Figure 4-10   *Use case diagram and sequence diagram depicting login and authentication*

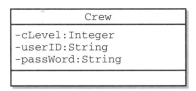

Figure 4-11   *The **Crew** class diagram (UML)*

For this demonstration, we are just going to list the fields we need for authentication, as shown in Figure 4-11.

Creating Classes

At the moment, functionality (methods) has not been included in the class diagram shown in Figure 4-11. That will come a little later in this chapter (see "Adding the Methods"). One of the fundamental differences between procedural programming and OO programming is that procedural programming is computation-centric, while OO programming is data-centric. And as mentioned earlier, the core purpose of an object is to contain or encapsulate data (and the methods are required for manipulating and working with the data). In case you need a refresher on the definition of an object and a class, here's my take:

▶ **Object**   An object represents something in the real world; it is something that is both distinct and physical.

▶ **Class**   A class is first a means of classifying objects with similar attributes and characteristics; it is also a blueprint for an object—a means by which an object can be created, directly or indirectly.

Classes can also be "dynamically linked" (polymorphism again), so that their methods are available at runtime, although that is not an implementation characteristic of all classes but rather a characteristic of a *sealed* (noninheritable) class whose methods can simply be called like an old-fashioned function library. A good example of such a class is **System.IO.File**, which does not get instantiated.

Classes can contain the following key members:

▶ Fields
▶ Methods
▶ Properties
▶ Events

Class Visibility and Role

The visibility of a class is set by one of several visibility modifiers. A class can be declared public, which is the default if you omit any modifier in the class statement. It can also be declared as a "friend," which specifies the level of visibility from outside the assembly.

Classes can also be specified according to *role*. In an *abstract* class, all or several members must be inherited or implemented in a child class—and the class itself cannot be instantiated. An abstract class is also known as a *virtual* class by some languages, such as Java. A *sealed* class, also known as a final class, cannot be derived from and it might not be possible to instantiate it as an object. In other words, its constructor that manifests from **Object** is hidden or declared private—meaning you have no access to **New** and thus no means of constructing an object.

Each of the methods of a sealed class must be implemented in its original class. Table 4-1 lists the class visibility and role as defined by the Common Language Specification (CLS), and the corresponding Visual Basic nomenclature.

Encapsulation at Work

Notice in the class representation, back in Figure 4-11, that every one of the fields in the class is indicated as being private (with the dash UML notation). The CLR supports several access or visibility modifiers (or *specifiers*), but for simplicity's sake, let's first discuss the three you will be using the most. Table 4-2 lists the three modifiers supported by .NET and the scope of access they provide.

CLS Characteristic	Restriction	VB.NET Usage
Sealed (final)	Does not permit child classes.	NotInheritable
Abstract (virtual)	Cannot instantiate this class. To use it, create a child class and provide a constructor for it.	MustInherit
Exported/Not exported	Can be accessed only from the program in which it is declared.	Friend
Public	No restriction on who or what can see this class.	Public (optional, if omitted public, by default)

Table 4-1   *The .NET CLS Class Characteristics Model*

Modifier	UML	Meaning
Public	+	Members (fields and methods) are Public; they can be accessed from any class and the class in which they are defined.
Protected	#	Members are neither visible to the outside world nor accessible from any unrelated classes. Only the class in which it is resident, and any nested classes, can see and use it.
Private	–	The variable or member is visible only to the class in which is resides. The fields and methods of the class (the source file) are not accessible to external classes.

Table 4-2   *The .NET Member Access Modifiers (Represented in UML Notation)*

Creating a Class Others Can Use

To follow along, open Visual Studio.NET and create a new project. To create a project for a class library, perform the following steps:

1. Open VS.NET, and in the File menu, select New Project. The dialog box illustrated in Figure 4-12 appears.

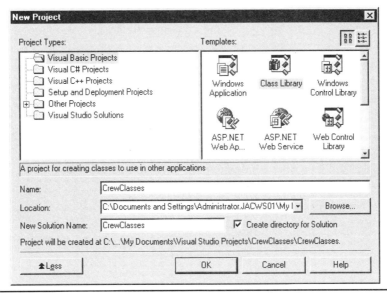

Figure 4-12   *Selecting a new class library project in Visual Studio*

2. Select Visual Basic Projects from the Project Types list, and then select the Class Library option from the collection of templates, as shown in Figure 4-12.

3. Provide a name and location (path) for the project and click OK. (It is easy to overlook this important step—and it's a real pain to change this data later.) VS.NET creates the project for you and creates a new class file (and names the class *Class1* by default).

4. Change the name of the class to **Crew**. At the top of the class, add the **Option** statement, as illustrated in the following code. The **Option** statement is explained in Chapter 3.

```
Option Strict On
Public MustInherit Class Crew
. . .
End Class
```

In this code, the class is declared public using the **Public** keyword, which is optional. This designation indicates that the class can be accessed from all other classes. The keyword **MustInherit** denotes that the class cannot itself be instantiated or linked to and that to use the class, it must be inherited. In other words the class is *abstract*.

NOTE

If you do not provide a visibility modifier, the class is public by default.

Returning to our spaceship model, notice that we want to create a base class that provides a template with implementation for all crewmembers, from which all new crewmember classes can inherit. We have thus set down a specification that *whenever an object representing a crewmember is created, it will inherit base members that need to be manifested in the derived or child class.* In other words, as demonstrated in Chapter 5, in order for consumers of the class to instantiate a crewmember object, they first need to create a new crewmember class and inherit the new class from **Crew**. This inheritance derives class members from two sources: the root **Object** and the class explicitly inherited using the **Inherits** keyword.

Why do we do this? In our case, policy dictates that all data stored in the database is added or changed through the base fields in the **Crew** class. By insisting on deriving from **Crew**, we ensure that the object's fields and methods will correctly connect to the database and be able to read and write data according to the specifications of the classes, policy, and the contract between the class and the class consumer.

If the database tables change, this can be correctly and efficiently coordinated between the database administrator and the individual responsible for the creation and maintenance of the **Crew** class, leaving the consumer safe to implement the feature in a new version of the application that needs to access crew data.

There are several ways to work with a base class like **Crew**. We could make the class 100-percent abstract and not encapsulate any data or implementation in the class. This approach allows the class creator to allow all the methods in the **Crew** class to be overridden. The class thus becomes nothing more than a template for a child class, and the implementation of the methods is carried out in the child or derived class.

As an alternative, we could seal the class and prevent its methods from being inherited, forcing the user to instantiate the class. This would force any derived class to process data by calling the parent's methods. The methods in the parent class would thus be fully implemented, or final.

And, finally, we could do a little of both of the above for methods where it makes sense to allow overriding and in some cases seal the method. This final approach in exactly how **Object** works, and thus the class is abstract. Some of the methods in **Object** can be overridden if the need arises; some of them must be overridden (that have no base implementation) before they can be used; and some of them are sealed, which forces the user to call the base classes method (the constructor is an example). Table 4-3 lists the access characteristics of the methods of **Object**.

We are going to implement an object to represent a crewmember using the latter approach. We want the developer to create a child class from **Crew** and implement the methods in the parent class whenever data needs to be fetched from and saved to the database. This ensures that all database work pertaining to the records of crewmembers gets channeled through the same methods, implemented in **Crew**.

Method	Characteristic
Finalize	Overridable
New (object constructor)	Inherited
Equals	Overloaded
Reference Equals	Inherited
GetHashCode	Overridable
GetType	Sealed
ToString	Overridable
MemberwiseClose	Shallow clone of an object

Table 4-3   *The Methods of **Object***

Here's how to use **Crew**:

1. Create a new class, such as **Engineer;** derive from **Crew** using the **Inherits** keyword.

2. In the derived class, implement the constructor method (**New**) to instantiate the object (thus **New** is public and not hidden).

3. Override methods where necessary, and add new methods to the derived class for additional functionality.

4. Use the implementation inherited from the parent class to manage the data, or further extend in "grandchild" classes.

Next we'll look at the details.

Inheritance at Work

This code and procedure demonstrate the new support for true inheritance in VB.NET, which is supported in its entirety. An example: Let's say that we—the developers responsible for the class creation and upkeep—need to add a transponder ID field to the **Crew** class to record the ID number of the transponder provided to each crew member. By updating the **Crew** class with this new field and a method to access or modify the transponder ID in the database table, we ensure that the next version of any software that needs access to the new field will be able to access this functionality in derived classes.

Version 1.0 of the **Crew** class with its private variable fields should look like this:

```
Public MustInherit Class Crew
  Private userID, passWord As String
  Private cLevel As Integer
'. . .
End Class
```

Before we go and add methods to the **Crew** class, let's check out how VB.NET supports inheritance. To derive a class from **Crew**, your new subclass (add a new class from the Solution Explorer) or child class's code will look like this:

```
Imports CrewClasses
Public Class Engineer
  Inherits Crew
'. . .
End Class
```

And our C# friends might be tempted to write their VB.NET code like this,

```
Imports CrewClasses
Public Class Engineer : Inherits Crew
'. . .
End Class
```

which is also fine by us VB gurus (if you intend to swing both ways, the latter style might be more convenient for you).

NOTE

Visual Basic.NET: The Complete Reference *(Osborne/McGraw-Hill, 2002)* points out a number of grammar, syntax, and style options that can help you close the gap of idiomatic differences between C# and VB.NET.

The critical keyword in the preceding code block is **Imports**, which is a pointer to the **CrewClasses,** which holds the classes from which we wish to inherit (which is a similar modularization to what you might know in Delphi, Java, C++, Eiffel, and so on). In other words, the namespace contains the **Crew** class and possibly any other classes that are closely related.

You can now check inheritance in VB.NET at work. In the new **Crew** class, try and reference the fields of the base class as follows:

```
Imports CrewClasses
Public Class Engineer : Inherits Crew
  Public Sub TestVar
    userID = "  "
  End Sub
End Class
```

You will see that the variable is immediately picked up from the super class, or parent class, because VB.NET (with its marvelous background compiler that keeps chugging away) tells you that the variable **userID** is declared private and "not accessible in this context." If you have been coding these examples in Visual Studio.NET, you can go back to your version of **Crew** and change the access modifier to **Public**, which will unhide the field, and the restriction will go away.

Incidentally, you can also see inheritance at work here because all classes implicitly derive first from **Object**. Your classes thus inherit the constructor method from **Object** (**New**), and the **Finalize** method (which is not actually implemented; that's your job). **Object** also provides a collection of methods you can override or overload in any class you implement. See the section on methods in the Chapter 3 and the section on overloading and overriding in Chapter 1.

At this point, you do not need to build a class, compile (to intermediate language or IL), place it onto the namespace, and drop it an assembly. If you so permit, a consumer of the class can directly reference the source class file in a new library or application, and then use the class directly (as **YourClass.vb**). That's a useful feature if you are writing your own applications and are both the creator and consumer of your own classes.

All applications are *collections* of *classes* (even a module is a type of class with limited powers). But shipping assemblies makes more sense when you do not want the consumer of the class to change the source code or alter the implementation. Remember what we discussed in Chapter 2—you can *strong name* your assemblies and lock them up with digital signatures.

Implementation in the Parent Class

Earlier on we defined three fields, or instance variables, for our object. Now we will use them to hold the data that represents the engineer's data that we are going to load into the object. When we create objects, we usually initialize the data in the fields. This is done using instance constructors.

Adding the Methods

Let's now add a couple of methods to the **Crew** class. The operation is simple. We want to allow the consumer to derive the methods and be able to perform several tasks. First, after instantiation and initialization, the object's owner should be able to pass several arguments to the object's public methods. The interface must allow the user to pass in a user ID and a password. Both variables can be passed to the object by calling a single method, **AuthUser**. The method **AuthUser** looks up the user ID and password passed and confirms that the user ID does indeed have a matching password to the one sent. If confirmation is obtained, the method will return **True** to the client.

A second method to add to the class is the modification method **SetUserID**. This method is called on condition that the password matches the value stored in the database. This means that the object's **userID** field will be set, and anything that can reference the object will be able to query the identity of the user the object now represents. Querying the user ID can be achieved through the **GetUserID** method or a property (for the sake of our Java converts, we are going to show you accessing the value by means of a simple accessor method).

The **Crew** class diagram now looks more complete, as illustrated in Figure 4-13. The diagram does not show the inherited members from **Object**, but they are there nonetheless. We have also not included all the methods of the base class to save a little space and time; these will be developed and added as we progress through this book.

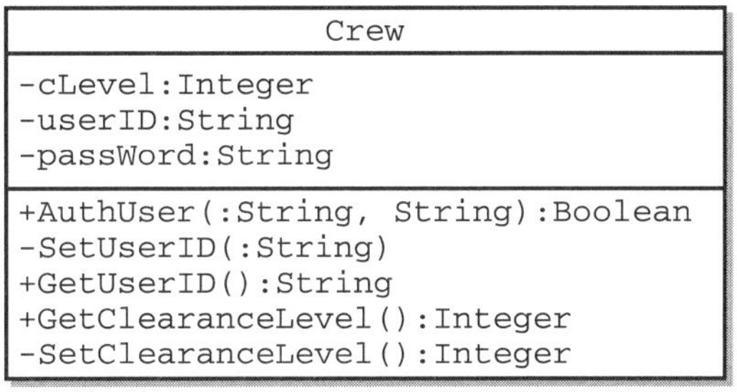

```
                      Crew
       -cLevel:Integer
       -userID:String
       -passWord:String

       +AuthUser(:String, String):Boolean
       -SetUserID(:String)
       +GetUserID():String
       +GetClearanceLevel():Integer
       -SetClearanceLevel():Integer
```

Figure 4-13   *The **Crew** class diagram expanded to include method definitions*

The specification for the **AuthUser** method looks like this:

▶ **Method**   Accessor method **AuthUser**.

▶ **Method Signature**   The method is called **AuthUser** and has a parameter list of two strings. The first string provides the value for the **passWord** lookup parameter, and the second string provides the value for the **userID** parameter that owns the password.

▶ **Preconditions**   None.

▶ **Postconditions**   First, if the method returns True, it must call **SetUserID** to set the **userID** field with the name of the engineer the object represents. Second, the method also obtains the clearance level of the user and applies it to the **ClearanceLevel** field.

▶ **Parameters**   Two. We need to provide both user ID and password when the method is called.

▶ **Exceptions**   One or no arguments supplied. The exception handler returns False to the client (see Chapter 5 for a discussion on exception handling).

So the first version of the **AuthUser** method might look like this:

```
Public Function AuthUser(ByVal UID As String, ByVal PWD As String) As Boolean
  If PWD = passWord Then
    SetUserID(UID)
    SetClearanceLevel(1)
    Return True
  End If
    SetUserID("Not Authorized")
    SetClearanceLevel(0)
    Return False
End Function
```

Let's now add a property to set and retrieve the value of the **cLevel** field.

Properties are a major convenience factor in the .NET languages and as class members have the same standing as methods. So they can be inherited, they can be overridden, they can be sealed and made static, and so on. A property is a construct supported by the compiler that combines an *accessor* method and a *modification* method in one package. Both accessor and modifier methods, also known as *setters* and *getters,* respectively (or just *accessors*), can be accessed via a public reference, which is the name of the property. The name of the property behaves like a variable, but unlike a variable it does not require storage.

The property is exposed as a public property of the class or object, masquerading as a field, an intelligent one at that. The property can also be hidden, which is the default behavior if the property is inherited, and it can be modified as read-only or write-only. Field data is still accessed, but it can remain private, leaving the property to handle field access and modification for you. Using properties ensures that the private data fields stay private. One last plus for using properties is that they are listed in the declarations list of a class. The following is a simple usage for a property called **State** (which we will add to the next version of our class diagram):

```
Public Property State() As Integer
  Get
    Return oState
  End Get
  Set(ByVal Value As Integer)
    oState = Value
  End Set
End Property
```

A property is declared and used as follows in VB.NET:

► If it does not carry modifiers, you must implement both **Set** and **Get** methods.

► If the property is modified as *ReadOnly,* you must drop the **Set** method.

► If the property is modified as *WriteOnly,* you must drop the **Get** method.

The **ClearanceLevel** property can be written as follows:

```
Public ReadOnly Property ClearanceLevel() As Integer
 Get
    Return cLevel
 End Get
End Property
```

The entire first version of our class **Crew** is now demonstrated in the following code:

```
Option Strict On
Imports System
Public MustInherit Class Crew

Private userID As String = "not authorized'
Private passWord As String = "1234"
Private cLevel As Integer = 0

Private Sub SetUserID(ByVal user As String)
  userID = user
End Sub

Public Function GetUserID() As String
  Return userID
End Function

Private Sub SetClearanceLevel(ByVal CL As Integer)
  cLevel = CL
End Sub

Public ReadOnly Property ClearanceLevel() As Integer
  Get
    Return cLevel
  End Get
End Property

Public Function AuthUser(ByVal UID As String, ByVal PWD As String) _
  As Boolean
  If PWD = passWord Then
   SetUserID(UID)
   SetClearanceLevel(1)
   Return True
  End If
   SetUserID("Not Authorized")
   SetClearanceLevel(0)
   Return False
  End Function
End Class
```

What are you seeing here? First, and very simply, the **Crew** class now exposes a number of methods, properties, and fields that you will be able to inherit in your new class. When you need to work with a crewmember's data, the client or consumer of the class will simply need to instantiate the extended class, pass values to the object to set the fields of the class, and call one of the three methods. Now let's work with the object from the consumer or client point of view.

Object-Oriented Development at Work

The **Crew** class was made abstract to allow developers to inherit the class and all of its members and implementation, and to override where necessary. This achieves the objectives of allowing the class to be extended and the implementation code to be reused, and it provides additional functionality required by the adopter, yet still maintains or enforces adoption of key methods that interact with a database and other functionality.

Inheriting the Implementation

Put on your implementor hat and extend the **Crew** class as you need. But alas, for the first version all the code has been inherited for you. There is nothing to do—except provide constructors to instantiate and initialize objects of the child class.

Adding Constructors

You cannot instantiate an object without the inclusion of the **New** method, which is the instance constructor (implicitly or explicitly declared). **New** is inherited from **Crew**'s base class, in this case **Object,** which does two things:

▶ The constructor calls **MyBase.New** (which is not an option, but if you leave out this call, the CLR makes it anyway).

▶ The constructor initializes the data, or it calls a secondary constructor to initialize the data.

  We recommend keeping **New** simple and making it a *no arguments* or *parameterless* constructor. Instead, just call **MyBase.New** and refer the variable initialization to a secondary constructor. Let's document a definition for these constructors:

▶ **Constructor** Instance constructor.

▶ **Constructor Signature** The constructor **New** creates instance of **Engineer** and hands off initialization to a secondary constructor:

```
Public Sub New()
```

▶ **Preconditions** None. We do not need any preconditions at activation.

▶ **Postconditions** The constructor hands off initialization after activation to the **Init** constructor.

▶ **Parameters**   None. We do not need to pass arguments at activation.

▶ **Exceptions**   None.

The instance constructor is very simple. The initialization constructor does a little more work. The specification for the **Init** method is as follows:

▶ **Constructor**   The second constructor initializes fields.

▶ **Constructor Signature**   The constructor **Init** performs the actual initialization of the object's fields. The constructor is a function:

```
Public Sub Init()
```

▶ **Preconditions**   None. We do not need to supply the constructor with any parameters.

▶ **Postconditions**   This constructor performs initialization and returns a Boolean to signify success or failure.

▶ **Parameters**   None.

▶ **Exceptions**   None.

Now let's write some code for the two constructors.

```
Public Sub New()
  MyBase.New()
  Init()
End Sub

Public Sub Init()
  SetUserID("Not Authorized")
End Sub
```

NOTE

If you declare private constructors, consumers of your class will not be able to derive from the class. This behavior can also be useful and further protects a class that has been explicitly sealed for inheritance.

Variable initialization is optional, yet recommended. C# does not provide a default initialization variable and the variables are set to null when the object is instantiated. VB.NET, on the other hand, does provide a default value, and sets integers and decimals to zero, Booleans to FALSE, and strings to null.

NOTE

*If a virtual or abstract class does not require explicit initialization, you can leave out the constructor. On a final class, **New** is implicitly inherited and the CLR makes the call for you. For a more detailed treatise on constructors, see* Visual Basic.NET: The Complete Reference *(Osborne/McGraw-Hill, 2002).*

To create a new class to use in the console application, you will derive from **Crew**. This lets you use the derived class in the console application, and thus you can instantiate the objects numerous times. Properly encapsulated data is fully reentrant, so running more than one console application that instantiates the new **Engineer** object ensures that the data of each object does not interfere with the data of another instance of the same object.

You can derive the new class directly in your project, or by creating a new standalone class library, as demonstrated in the following code:

```
Option Strict On
Imports CrewClasses

Public Class Engineer
    Inherits Crew

Sub New()
  MyBase.New()
  Init()
End Sub

Sub Init()
 SetUserID("Not Authorized")
End Sub

End Class
```

You now have a new class, **Engineer**, to use in your application. The **Init** method is provided here for illustration. You could easily initialize the variable in the parent class and save the implementers more time. Let's now look at what we have done in UML.

To export the classes in UML open the Project menu and choose Visio UML, Reverse Engineer. A target folder for the new Visio (VSD) files is created. Visio activates, and in a jiffy you have your VB.NET code represented as UML class diagrams. The result should be identical to the class diagrams illustrated earlier in this chapter.

Using the Classes

Classes can be used in many different ways. So to demonstrate using the **Engineer** class, we can build a console application to test each method. Console-based applications are useful for testing classes, although you can also use diagnostics classes, as demonstrated in Chapter 3. Console applications are convenient because you do not have to waste time building forms and coding events under button clicks, handlers, and so on.

To create a project for a console-based application, perform the following steps:

1. In the File menu in VS.NET, select New Project. The dialog box illustrated in Figure 4-14 appears.

2. Select Visual Basic Projects from the Project Types list, and then select Console Application from the templates (as shown in Figure 4-14).

3. Provide a name and location (path) for your project and click OK. (Remember to provide a name and location at this point because changing this information later is unpleasant.) VS.NET creates the project for you and loads a module for the application shell. The **Sub Main** method is also automatically inserted for you.

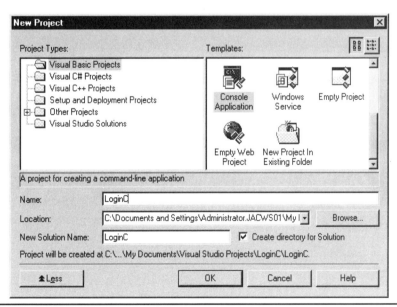

Figure 4-14 *Choosing to create a console application*

To use the source file in your new project, follow these steps:

1. In the VS.NET Project menu, choose Add Exiting Items. A standard dialog box will let you browse for the class files.

2. Locate the file and click OK. (You can also right-click the Project node in the Solution Explorer and choose Add, Add Exiting Items from the context menu.) The source file now appears in the Solution Explorer, under your project node.

3. Before you can use the class to inherit from, include the **Imports CrewClasses.Engineer** statement immediately after the options directives (which always come first), as follows:

```
Option Strict On
Imports CrewClasses.Engineer

Module Module1
    Sub Main()
    . . .
```

If you want to use the assembly containing the **Engineer** class, follow these steps:

1. In the VS.NET Project menu, choose Add Reference. The dialog box illustrated in Figure 4-15 appears.

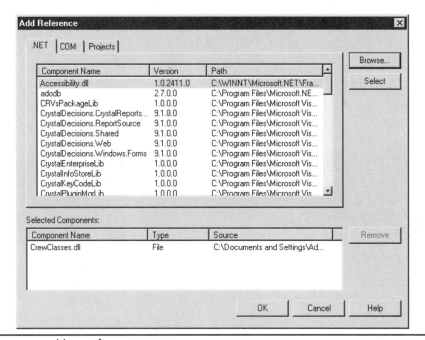

Figure 4-15 *Adding references*

2. Locate the assembly and add it as a reference; then click OK. The source file now appears in the Solution Explorer, under your project node. (You can also expand the Project node in the Solution Explorer by right-clicking the References node and choosing Add Reference from the context menu.)

3. Before you can use the assembly, include the **Imports CrewClasses.Engineer** statement immediately after the options directives, as follows:

```
Option Strict On
Imports CrewClasses.Engineer

Module Module1
    Sub Main()
    . . .
```

Now, let's create an application that instantiates **CrewClasses.Engineer**.

Instantiation

Declaring and using more than one object of the same type is not uncommon. If the class allows this, you can activate as many **Engineer** objects as you need to in the application or execute more than one application. While there might be no reason to create multiple objects of the same type, you will often be working with solutions that require you to create more than one instance of the same object. The following code demonstrates the instantiation of one **Engineer** object:

```
Option Strict On
Imports CrewClasses.Engineer
Module Module1
  Sub Main()
      Dim cUserID, cPassWord As String
      Dim cLevel As Integer
      Dim itsaGo As Boolean
      Dim E1 As New Engineer()

      Console.WriteLine("Please enter a user ID")
      cUserID = Console.ReadLine
      Console.WriteLine("Please enter a password")
      cPassWord = Console.ReadLine

      itsaGo = E1.AuthUser(cUserID, cPassWord)
      If ItsAGo Then
         Console.WriteLine("User: " + E1.GetUserID + " you may proceed.")
         Console.WriteLine("Your clearance level is: " +
         CStr(E1.ClearanceLevel))
         Console.ReadLine()
```

```
        End If

        If Not itsaGo Then
            Console.WriteLine("Authorization Failed")
            Console.ReadLine()
        End If
    End Sub
End Module
```

Compile and execute the console application and it will instantiate **Engineer** as object **E1**.

Creating more than one object of the same type requires nothing more than another call to the **Engineer** class's constructor. All you need is a new name, as shown here:

```
Dim E1 As New Engineer()
Dim E2 As New Engineer()
```

You can now reference each object independently through the variables **E1** and **E2**.

The data in each object is encapsulated in its own field; trying to modify data by calling **E1.SetUserID** will not work because the method is private.

Remember that you have created two distinct variables: **E1** and **E2**. But you have also explicitly created two **Engineer** objects, and each variable references its own object. So what happens when **E1** and **E2** reference the same object? You can alter the reference **E2** has to an object like this:

```
E2 = E1
```

As explained earlier in the section "The .NET Object Reference Model," **E2** references **E1**'s object instead of its original object. With the object that **E2** referred to now cut loose, the GC will free the resources accordingly, because it will see it as an object that no one refers to.

Now **E1** and **E2** refer to the same object. In other words, if you set the **userID** by authenticating to **E1** and then call **E2.GetUserID**, the return value will be the same, because **E1** and **E2** refer to the same object. If you had trouble understanding the difference between the value types and reference at the beginning of this chapter, it should now be more clear. However, if you now run several instances of the console application, you will see that the **Engineer** object **E1** is fully reentrant and the fields in each console application are completely isolated one from the other.

The code demonstrated has been kept simple and the parent class **Crew** can now be further expanded to include database lookup routines, encryption, and so on. We will return to this in Chapter 5, where we'll show you a more advanced implementation of **Crew** extended as **Engineer**, used in forms and more.

Observations

By encapsulating the data and functionality in an object and wisely using inheritance, an entirely new "deal" has emerged for Visual Basic programmers. The code that controls the database does not have to be embedded in a form. And reuse of code is no longer a kluge that requires you to expose public class modules.

Polymorphism allows for a ton of flexibility in the design and implementation of the algorithm. The object can be created from a classic form, and the user can work with the data in the standard Windows graphical user interface. Or the object can be instantiated remotely from a Web form and called over the network. It can also be called from the command console (as demonstrated). And the object is small and flexible enough to be accessed from a mobile device (like a tricorder or a mobile emitter).

The object can also be serialized in such a way that its data can be persisted, rolled back, or even stored in a flat file in XML form before being committed to the database (and we will deal with that and much more in Chapter 5).

This chapter provided some general discussions of object-oriented technology and software development. You might go so far as to say that the .NET Framework, and thus Visual Basic.NET, is "radically" object-oriented. Now ask yourself again, "Do you feel lucky?"

VB.NET in Action

IN THIS CHAPTER:

Exception Handling

Serialization

File I/O

Data Access

Interfaces

Fat Forms

Thin Forms and ASP.NET

Web Services

I n the previous chapter, we went through the process of creating a class that could be derived from and how the derived class could be further developed and extended to be used by consumer applications. This was just one of a myriad of different ways to design an application or algorithm. As long as your classes and objects obtain maximum reuse, scalability, encapsulation, atomicity, concurrency, isolation and reentrance, recoverability, and, of course, durability, you're in the commander's seat.

The flexibility of VB.NET and the Common Type System (CTS) provides you with many options. In this chapter, you'll see a little more of the advanced capabilities of VB.NET. But before we get too carried away, the first subject, .NET exception handling, cannot wait any longer.

.NET Exception Handling

Structured exception handling (SEH) has finally been added to the Visual Basic language (about a decade late!). In the past, error handling in VB revolved around the **On Error GoTo** statement, a rigid and narrow form of unstructured error handling that combined an error-detection event with the archaic and notorious **GoTo** construct.

The **On Error** statement is placed at the head of a block of code and covers any error-event occurring in the block. When an error is detected, execution is transferred to a *label*, where the error is handled. As soon as execution encounters another **On Error** statement, coverage is transferred to the current handler.

Unfortunately, this is not too suitable a model for complex algorithms and data structures, and a number of problems exist with this form of unstructured error handling. First, the excessive use of **GoTo** makes the code hard to maintain and difficult to debug. Second, the entire **On Error GoTo** mechanism is a performance hog (in comparison to SEH). Third, error detection and interpretation is based on an error code that bubbles up from the operating system, and it is difficult to use the information as a means of interacting with the user, controlling execution flow, or properly handling the error.

Finally, the error architecture precluded any form of custom exception handling or extension of the error handling system that other languages like Java, Delphi, and C++ have enjoyed for so many years. All of the above reasons often meant that no error detection was provided by an application's developers. It is not possible to ignore .NET exception events, because SEH is built into the Common Language Runtime (CLR), and any exception that is not handled terminates the thread that caused it, or the entire application. This process forces the developer to handle errors properly, or be doomed to the wrath of users.

NOTE

SEH in the managed world is a lot less resource intensive than SEH in the unmanaged world, because in the former, used exception objects are tracked and disposed of by the garbage collector (GC).

In structured exception handling, a block of code is placed within a protected section. The protection starts with the first line of code after the **Try** keyword and ends at the last line of code before the first **Catch** keyword. The **Try...Catch** section look like this:

```
Try
  Protected code goes here...
Catch Instantiate exception object here
  Exception handler code goes here...
End Try
```

As soon as an error is detected within the protected section, execution is immediately transferred to a "catchment" area, where an exception class to handle the exception is searched. Once the exception is found and an exception object is created, information may be passed to its parameters and the exception object is then "thrown" up to the point where the error occurred. How, you might ask, is the exception handled? The best way to answer that question is to examine what an exception is.

If you're like most programmers, you can recall a time when, while reworking an application at 4 A.M., you wanted nothing more than to throw your monitor out the window. An exception works in a similar way, only a lot less costly. Instead of throwing your monitor, the system creates an exception object capable of handling the error—this "throws" the object. As soon as the error is detected, further execution is suspended in the **Try** block.

The brilliance of the thrown exception, however, is that because an exception is a class, it can implement a variety of methods and data structures to handle the error. For example, it might report an error number, or it can translate the error number into something more meaningful, or it can examine the call stack to look for the problem and take the appropriate action. The exception class can also "roll back" execution in your application, thus preventing it from being terminated or doing something dastardly that will get you into a lot of trouble.

The actual errors that cause your code to throw fits occur in a number of specific areas of your code. *Syntax* errors occur because something might be declared incorrectly, and the compiler does not realize it. *Runtime* errors occur when a program is executed. They can be produced by some of the simplest problems that may arise during runtime, but the errors do not normally mean the algorithm or application is flawed. An example of such an error is an attempt to open a file or database that does not exist. If the file existed, normal execution would ensue; the code is not the problem here. Other examples include trying to dial a telephone number with no modem attached, serializing an object to a full disk, and processing a lengthy sort with no memory. In all these cases, if the resources existed, no errors would result and no exceptions would be thrown. Runtime errors usually come from the operating system, which detects the violations.

Logic errors also occur at runtime and cannot be seen by any preprocessor or the compiler. A *divide-by-zero* error is a classic example. This is not seen as an error until the program finds itself in a divide-by-zero situation—the logic of the algorithm leads the program to code that is essentially flawed. Other examples include trying to access an element in an array that exceeds its upper boundary, reading beyond the end of a stream, trying to close a file that has not yet been opened, or trying to reference an object that has been terminated. Logic errors usually come from the operating system, which detects the violations. You may also provide custom exception classes to deal with your own logic errors.

Conditional errors occur for custom exceptions you create by extending the base exception class. You can raise error exceptions on these errors if a certain precondition or postcondition exists in your code. For example, if a value is not 0 at the start of an algorithm, you could raise a custom **ArgumentNotZeroException** exception to trap the condition. A postcondition exception would be raised if a condition you specify in the exception handler does not exist after the algorithm is processed. For example, if your code is supposed to leave the application in a certain condition before continuing, you could provide an exception facility right then and there—in a postcondition exception handler.

You can also create custom exceptions to cater to anything you believe should be considered an error and that is not provided by the default exception classes provided in the base class library. Such errors could result in an alternative course of execution or the shutting down of the application.

Why place exception handlers in VB.NET programs?

▶ To catch a method's inability to complete a task for some reason.

▶ To process errors caused by a process accessing any functionality in methods, libraries, or classes where those elements are unable to directly handle any error that arises as a result of the access and the ensuing computation.

▶ To deal with errors caused by components that are not able to handle any particular error in their own processing space.

▶ To ensure that a large and complex program (actually any VB.NET program) can consistently and holistically provide programwide error-handling facility.

When don't you use an exception handler? For any code segment that is unlikely to ever cause an error. SEH is resource intensive, so use common sense and don't go throwing everything into **Try** blocks. The following example demonstrates a silly use for SEH:

```
Try
 NameLabel.Text = "First Name"
Catch E As Exception
 'Catch what?
Finally
 'Nothing to do
End Try
```

An exception hander is used to trap the error and handle the ensuing events. Handling the exception sustains the application and makes sure the data and the application remain in a consistent state. Some handlers can simply roll back an error and continue silently, such as an array bounds exception, while others require advising the user what's happening and provide new execution flow, such as resetting values.

NOTE

If an exception is not handled, the standard course of action is to close down the application. Some "unhandled" exceptions can leave the application standing, but it might not be in a stable state.

Now that you know what an exception is, let's talk about how your code catches it after it is thrown and what it does with it once it's caught.

The Exception Handler

The exception handler is your entire catch block, which contains a single exception "filter" that might apply to the error at hand. If the first catch block does not apply to the error, the code moves to the next one, if you provided it, and so on until the correct catch block, or exception handler, is found. This is demonstrated in the following code, where the so-called filters are represented in boldface:

```
Try
 Protected code goes here...
Catch oyVey As EndOfStreamException
 'handle this exception here
Catch oyVey As PasswordException When passWord = ""
 'handle this exception here
Catch When passWord = ""
 'handle this exception here
Catch oyVey As ArgumentException
 'handle this exception here
End Try
```

The exception-handling filter mechanism is flexible. In the preceding code, **oyVey** is used repeatedly as an instantiation target for the exception class. In other words, in the first catch block, **oyVey** is instantiated as an **EndOfStreamException** object if the code indeed blew up on the unexpected encountering of the end of a stream.

It is also possible to raise an exception when something is **True**. Here's an example (a custom exception class) from the preceding code:

```
Catch oyVey As PasswordException When passWord = ""
'handle this exception here
```

Here, an exception is raised when something becomes **True**. In this example, the **passWord** argument was passed without a value, a precondition exception.

The use of **When** in the catch block also allows you to test for an error number. This is demonstrated as follows:

```
Catch When ErrNum = Err_EndOfStreamException
'handle this exception here
```

If no handler is found for the exception, it is referred to the previous caller to look for the correct exception handler to deal with the exception. The exception will continue to be passed up the call stack until an exception class is found, or until the generic exception code is used to process the exception. If no exception class is found, the program will terminate with an "unhandled exception" message.

Usually, the caller of a method handles the exception. It might also be necessary for the caller of the caller to handle the exception, which might go quite far back up the call stack before the exception is handled. You can also catch all exceptions in the method that caused them with a default handler called **Exception.** This is a useful technique if something happens that you did not write handler code for; just remember to station the default as the last exception handler in your list—otherwise, it will catch and dispose of any thrown exceptions before the intended handlers are reached.

The **Finally** keyword is optional and its code is always executed, no matter how much **Catch** processing is performed. This section of the entire construct is useful for checking postconditions and providing some housekeeping.

You can also specify the exact exception to throw in the body of your **Try** block using the **Throw** keyword. The following code demonstrates this:

```
Try
  If (UID = "")Then
    Throw New BadBoyException
  End If
```

```
Catch E As BadBoyException
 Me.oState = "Last Error: Password null"
End Try
```

If you're new to writing code inside **Try...Catch** blocks, it can take some time to get into the habit of doing so. While you can easily compile VB.NET code without a **Try...Catch** (and **Finally**) block, good VB.NET code technique means writing **Try...Catch** blocks as if the language absolutely depended on them—because it does. When you write error-potential code without a **Try...Catch** block, you are relying on the runtime system to serve up the default exception handler. But that's like flying on autopilot—eventually you have to take control to land the plane. And if the exception goes unhandled, that's like exploding in midair.

When you have been writing VB.NET code for a while, you'll begin to think in terms of **Try...Catch...Finally** in the same way you think in terms of objects and classes, or methods and their members—the inherent makeup of an object-oriented program. It becomes natural to build blocks of functionality with the **Try** keyword, at least if there is the slightest chance that the algorithm might take *exception* to something you are trying to do in the code. The following code demonstrates this philosophy (also notice the alternative usage in the **Catch** handler, which displays the error message generated down below.

```
Sub LookInRoot()
 Try
   Dim Fldrs As New DirectoryInfo("X:\")
   '...horrifying code here
 Catch e As DirectoryNotFoundException
   Debug.WriteLine(e, "Error")
 Catch e As Exception
   Debug.WriteLine(e, "Error")
 End Try
End Sub
```

Exit Try and Finally

You can use the **Exit Try** keyword combination to "break out" of a **Try...Catch** block (it works in both the **Try** section and the **Catch** section). Execution resumes with the code that immediately follows the **End Try** terminator. You cannot use **Exit Try** in a **Try...Catch...Finally** combination. **Finally** code is always executed, so breaking out would defeat its purpose. Here is a simple example:

```
Try
  If File.Exists(persistFile) Then
```

```
        Exit Try
    End If
Catch
```

Nesting Exception Handlers

It is considered good exception-handling design to add **Try...Catch** blocks inside your outer ones rather than providing a long collection of catch filters. In other words, you'll find that as a matter of course you'll be nesting your **Try...Catch** blocks—sometimes to several levels.

When the code being executed enters a **Try** block, the so-called *context* of that exception is pushed onto the stack. When something goes wrong and the current exception does not have the correct handler, the code reverses back up the stack and the next **Catch** statement is scanned for a handler. The code continues to back out of the stack until a handler is found or the runtime system is forced to handle the exception.

Observe the following (with **Option Strict Off**):

```
Private Sub Main()
Dim D(20) As Integer
Dim Result As Integer
  Try
    D(1) = 0
    D(15) = 100
      Try
        Result = D(15) / D(1)
      Catch e As OverflowException
        Debug.WriteLine(e.Message)
      End Try
    Catch e As IndexOutOfRangeException
      Debug.WriteLine(e.Message)
    Finally
      Debug.WriteLine("You screwed up bozo")
  End Try
End Sub
```

What's happening here? This code nests one **Try...Catch** block within another. If **D(15)** was **D(25)** we would first encounter the **IndexOutOfRangeException** and the code would jump directly to the outer catch and be done. But the example lets the code go down to the next **Try...Catch** block, which causes an **OverflowException**, and it gets caught by the inner **Catch.** If the inner **Catch** was not present or did not specify the overflow error, the application would have died then and there. Instead, it proceeds to the **Finally** section and prints the "bozo" message.

Nesting **Try** statements is not easy, and you can often waste a lot of time with misplaced **End Try** statements and the like (closing curly braces for C#-ists), and out-of-position **Catch** statements, which result in a compiler error reporting that the **Try** is "catchless." Here's a tip: First create and complete the outer **Try** with its **Catch** and even a **Finally** block. Then go into the outer **Try** block and code the new inner **Try...Catch** from start to finish. Do not leave out all the **Catch** blocks until after all the **Try** blocks are done. You'll tear your hair out trying to properly place the **Catch** blocks after the fact. VB.NET's "code complete" and IntelliSense mechanisms, however, go a long way to helping make sense of your nests.

Creating Your Own Exception Classes

We've spoken at length about the VB.NET built-in, or runtime, exception objects. But solid exception-handling code often requires you to provide custom exception classes. Creating your own exception classes is not a difficult task. These exceptions need to be derived from class **Exception.** But you typically inherit from **ApplicationException,** which provides a lot more utility for you to use. Your class inherits the necessary methods of a "throwable" object and shields you from its complexities and implementation. To create your own exception class, you can override the methods of **Exception** as needed, and provide the necessary custom functionality or your own new methods.

Examining your class, you can come up with a list of errors that are not catered to by any base exception classes. Your method preconditions will probably be the first exception handlers you will want to create, because preconditions might be essential to achieving the objective of the algorithm.

You can create a new exception class for the **CrewClasses** classes as follows:

```
Public Class BadArgsException
  Inherits ApplicationException

  Public Function BadArgsException(ByVal message As String) As String
    'Add code and return Message string here
  End Function
End Class
```

This represents a complete subclass of **ApplicationException** to be used as a custom exception class to go with our **CrewClasses** namespace. You can use the new exception class as follows:

```
Private Sub TestNew()
 Try
    'code here that might cause an exception of BadArgsException
```

```
Catch e As BadArgException
    'get e.message here
End Try
End Sub
```

You can then reference the custom exception with the **Throw** keyword in the **Try** block if a test finds the precondition does not exist.

A more advanced chapter devoted to exception handling, specifically building custom exception handlers, can be found in *Visual Basic.NET: The Complete Reference* (Osborne/McGraw-Hill, 2001). The following tips will add to continued development in this area:

▶ Avoid using VB.NET exception handling for anything other than exception handling. Often developers will find that **Try...Catch...Finally** blocks make for interesting flow-control structures, but this only serves to damage the structural integrity of the program and consume resources.

▶ Despite the discussion on custom handlers, it does not make sense to create custom exception classes for every error you might encounter. Creating equivalents of the runtime exception classes only wastes time and resources.

▶ Notwithstanding the usefulness of the **Throw** feature, you should handle exceptions, as far as possible, at the point where they were raised. This too conserves resources and makes your code easier to follow.

▶ When using nested **Try** blocks or multiple **Catch** blocks, remember to place the default **Catch E As Exception** as the last **Catch** block, because placing it earlier will prevent any later exception classes (both custom or built-in) from ever getting executed.

▶ Handle all exceptions and do not simply **Catch** exceptions and then do nothing with them. Providing "sterile" exception-handling code does not mean you do not have to deal with the exceptions, and they should not merely be swept under the proverbial carpet. The **resume** keyword of VB 6 and earlier will be a habit hard to break, but it has no place in VB.NET.

▶ While **On Error GoTo** has been retained for backward compatibility, you should strive to replace all of these unstructured error-handling blocks of code with the new SEH support.

Now that we have exception handling ready and waiting, let's get back to enhancing the **Crew** class.

Extending the Base Class

What have we done so far? We created a simple class called **Crew** that we intended to be reused in a number of circumstances. Once such circumstance involved using the class to beget a child class that could be instantiated or activated in a number of situations. The previous chapter showed us that we can derive a host of functionality from the parent, which itself does not get instantiated, and then add some custom implementation to the child class.

We should further extend the parent in the child class to allow us to do certain things that make more sense in a child class and certain things that are possible only with object activation at runtime. Our class design, inheritance, and instantiation features allow us to reuse the code in many different situations. Here we will use the classes to provide a login authentication facility from any Windows-based process—graphical, character-based, or user interface-less. Figure 5-1 illustrates the number of different applications that will have use for our classes by the end of the chapter. And each facility will make use of the classes without requiring any modification of the base class code for each facility.

Now let's get back to the development of the **Crew** class. What do we have so far in this "super" class? Looking back at our specification and class diagram, we can make a short list:

▶   A collection of four fields (variables), which are kept private (*shhh*)

▶   *Accessor* and *modification* methods that read and write the variables, and a sprinkling of properties

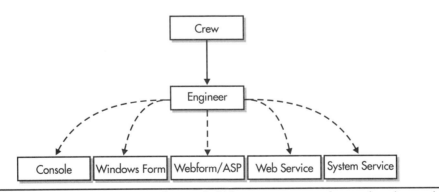

Figure 5-1   *The base class* **Crew** *and extended class* **Engineer** *can be used unchanged across the entire spectrum of Windows applications and services.*

That's not a lot of functionality for a base class. What else can be comfortably jammed into the base class, so that consumers of the class have (a) less work to do, and (b) less to worry about? Think about what else is common among all crewmembers—engineers or otherwise? For starters, they all have names and addresses, job descriptions, paychecks, ranks, and so on. That makes sense; we could add support for this type of data quite easily, because all descendent classes would use these fields—remember everyone *is a* crewmember first, an engineer, cook, or pilot second.

If we provide such support for the **Crew** class, we thus provide much more utility for reuse. But we are also opening ourselves up to attack, data loss, error problems, and so on. Before we go nuts adding the support for the additional data, we need to build a little more of a support structure in the class—prop it up a little more, so to speak. What do we then need to do?

First, if we are going to populate the object with runtime data and reliable settings, we need to save the data in the object to a persistent storage location from time to time. We do this because we could lose the object, or lose access to it, for a number of reasons. We might lose power on the machine where the object is running. Or our application might crash due to some catastrophic error (caused by hardware or the OS of course). Or the end user might just decide to close the application abnormally. The latter scenario is typical of Internet and Web applications, where we might have to rebuild an object and recover its data from time to time. So make that the first item to add to the class as follows:

> 1. To do: provide support to persist the object's data.

Now *persistence* implies use of the file systems, creating and deleting files, or possibly streaming data in storage locations, which means we also need to build I/O support into the base class.

What else? We also noted that the password field was exposed in plain text and that it was stored in the object itself. Both would not work in real-life scenarios. We basically have an object floating around in space that has a password in it that is stored in plain text. So make that the second item to fix in the class as follows:

> 2. To do: get rid of password field, and encrypt the data streams going into and out of the object.

This would imply creating support to look up passwords somewhere. A typical source for storing passwords would be a database. Since we want to add database fields and give the **Crew** class a wider audience, database lookups of the password would be a good start to adding database support in the base object.

Can you think of what else might be missing in the base class? Now that we are going to add a bunch of new functionality—persistence, I/O, database support—there is room for errors. Notice that the work we did in the previous chapter was very straightforward, but now a lot more can go wrong. We could run out of memory, hard disk space, and other resources. Files we are expecting to be waiting for us on the hard disk might not be there. Database connections might be lost, arguments missing, and so on. We thus need to provide some decent exception handling in the class.

Let's also add the exception-handling code as we create all the new functionality. And we'll add some debugging code using the **Debug.WriteLine** method from time to time to check how the object and its inherited functionality perform during our tests. A field to store current state or status—like a built-in event log—and a token field (a place to store session tokens, security IDs, and so on) may also come in handy, and we can expose those as properties.

Before we do anything, we must update our docs and the model with a synopsis of the new support. We also need to create the necessary class diagrams, sequence diagrams, and so on to support the expanded base class, and we need to document the various roles that child classes will play. We don't have the latitude to do too much in this book, but let's at least update the UML class object with the new definitions so that we can see a snapshot of what the updated class will shortly look like. This is demonstrated in Figure 5-2.

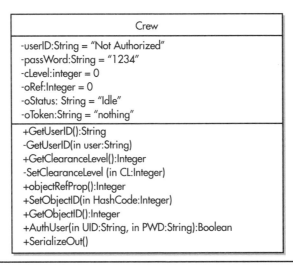

Figure 5-2   *The **Crew** base class version 2.0*

Object Serialization and .NET I/O

As discussed in the previous chapter, an object is stored in memory on a local or remote computer. That representation of the object in memory is called an *object graph*. When you instantiate the **Engineer** object, as demonstrated in the previous chapter, it becomes necessary to persist its data periodically. While we currently have only a few fields in the object, the more data you place into an object, and the more you depend on it, the more critical it becomes to persist the object's data.

There are two ways to do this. First you could transmit the data back to the database, which you would want to do from time to time, but not so often that you hog bandwidth and use up valuable connections. But you would also want to persist the data in the object to a disk or storage location other than the database for a number of reasons.

It makes no sense to keep transferring or uploading data to the database. The information in the object might be in a constant state of transition or flux, and until such time as the data is ready for saving, the user would not want to keep writing it to the database. Besides, constant writing to the database merely wastes resources and connections.

There is also a possibility that data is not yet ready to be saved to the database; then it has to be stored somewhere else. You want to persist data locally to protect the user and the application against data loss should the user experience power loss, system faults, or some other failure that causes the object to either be destroyed, go out of scope, or otherwise explode. The process of saving the data is not unlike writing to the old .ini files of yesteryear or saving data in registry keys from time to time.

And you might have data fields in the object that are useful only to the object, and any time it is resurrected—like a security token or state information—that type of information does not need to be stored at the database.

You, as the class developer, would want to code two areas of additional support into the **Crew** class: database connectivity and database integration, and persistence of the object's data. But just recovering the data is not always enough. In our examples, we would want to re-create the "naked" object and its data.

How can we do this? In the past, you probably "walked" the fields of your object and saved its data to a local file. But writing the code for this is cumbersome and hard to reuse or inherit, plus you have the problem of *recursion* to take care of. Recursion problems occur because you want to save the data of the current object you are referencing as well as any objects being referenced by the current object. Unless you specifically write code to detect the recursion, you'll end up going around in circles until the hard disk says "no more."

One of the first of the powerful features of Visual Basic.NET we are going to work on takes care of persisting object data (and then some) for you. It is achieved using a process called *serialization*. The framework's support for serialization is extensive, but what is it? And how does it let us persist an object's data?

NOTE

A number of software languages have support for sophisticated serialization, implemented in a similar fashion to .NET serialization. Most noted for its support for serialization is Java.

What is serialization? The answer to this question is in the word serialization. An analogy we can all visualize is the transporter technology on a starship. The crewmember stands on the transporter platform and then gets serialized into a stream of "bits" that are stored in the transporter's pattern matrix. The stream is then transmitted to the new location, where it is reconstituted as a crewmember, still alive and kicking. Of course, if the crewmember stays serialized for too long he or she can die, and that problem is known as a *serial* killer.

Serialization is a similar process, although not as life threatening. The *serializer* walks the object graph and converts the object and its data into a serial stream of binary or textual data. In other words, it goes into the serializer as an object and field data, and comes out the other end as a stream of bytes that can be persisted to disk or channeled down the network pipe. The data that emerges from the serialization process can now be saved somewhere or reconstituted as an object with data.

To regenerate the object's data, you simply reverse the process and feed the serialized data back into a stream and reconstitute the object. The reverse process is known as *deserialization*.

Let's now write the code to serialize our objects. The following procedures will let you save the object and its data to a persistent storage facility:

▶ Return to the base class **Crew** of the previous chapter to build the support for the serialization.

▶ Reference the serialization classes in the base and the descendent classes.

▶ Code the events that allow for the periodic serialization of the object data.

To serialize the object, it makes sense to go back to the parent class of **Engineer**, which is **Crew**, and place support for the serialization process in the parent class first. Then this functionality can be inherited for every object that is instantiated by implementing classes. In other words, you simply have to create **Engineer**, derive from **Crew**, and you have a new child class with serialization support.

Serialization Part I

Before we write the serialization/deserialization code, let's investigate the serialization support further. Figure 5-3 provides a representation of the serialization namespaces. Notice that the figure shows five namespaces: three of them are located in the **Mscorlib** assembly, the fourth one that we are going to fiddle with currently has its own assembly **System...Soap** as illustrated, as do the XML serialization classes (which are in the **System.XML** assembly as **System.XML.Serialization**). The serialization assemblies and namespaces are likely to be consolidated by final release of Visual Basic.NET, so check the Osborne Web site for new reference data.

Serialization support in .NET is extensive. The base implementations and interfaces are derived from **System.Runtime.Serialization**. The **System.Runtime.Serialization.Formatters** namespace provides enumeration support and the base classes for the serialization formatting. Then we have access to two namespaces that provide the actual implementation and formatting. One class provides binary formatting (**Formatters.Binary**) and the other, which we are going to use, provides text formatting in Simple Object Access Protocol (SOAP) format (**Formatters.Soap**). The **Soap** class is useful for serializing across and through network boundaries, because the data, XML, is encapsulated in a SOAP envelope. The framework also provides a namespace specializing in pure XML serialization streams, essentially serializing into and out of XML documents.

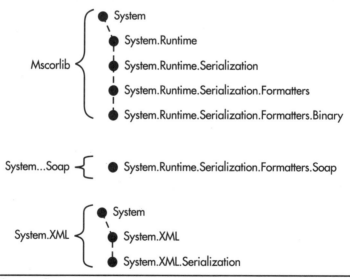

Figure 5-3   *The serialization namespace*

Before we can use the serialization classes, we have to mark the classes we want to serialize as being serializable. This entails providing serialization attributes for the base class. This is done with the following code, some of which has been set in boldface so that you can easily see the changes from the earlier provided code:

```
Option Explicit On

Imports System
Imports System.Runtime.Serialization

<Serializable()> Public MustInherit Class Crew
```

What's now different about the class in this code compared to the version in the previous chapter? For starters, the class makes a reference to the **Serializaton** classes by importing the **System.Runtime.Serialization** namespace. In addition it marks the **Crew** class as serializable. This is done using the **Serializable()** attribute and the VB.NET attributes indicators (<>).

You will next need to provide a method in this class that performs the actual serialization. But before you can do that, you need to build file and stream support into the **Crew** class to get the data in the object to the file system, and store it in a folder somewhere. This is done using the extensive I/O support provided by the framework's base class libraries. Before we continue coding serialization support, let's take a break from the serialization lesson and have a look at this powerful I/O support.

I/O Support in .NET

The **System.IO** namespace, illustrated in Figure 5-4, contains an extensive collection of classes that let you code asynchronous and synchronous reading and writing on data streams and files. Figure 5-4 provides a representation of the I/O namespaces, which are currently partitioned into the **Mscorlib** and **System** assemblies.

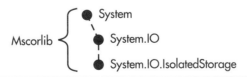

Figure 5-4   *The **System.IO** namespace*

While files are ordered collections of bytes on a file system and remain static, data streams are continuous feeds of data. Streams can originate from hard disks and other means of persistent storage, such as tape drives and optical disks. Streaming data moves across networks, feeds into and out of memory, and so on.

The base classes library (BCL) proves a base class called **Stream** that supports the reading and writing of bytes. When you need to implement stream I/O functionality, you'll need to instantiate objects from a collection of classes inherited from the **Stream** class. **Stream** is thus a pure abstract class and has to be extended in a collection of child classes. Using the **Stream** class and its derivatives allows you to program streams without as much as a hint of what's going on under the hood of the operating system.

The following sealed I/O classes derive from **Stream**:

▶ **BinaryReader** and **BinaryWriter**   These classes let you read and write encoded strings and primitive data to and from stream objects.

▶ **File**   This class lets you work with files. You can create, delete, open, close, copy, and move files. The **File** class also lets you create **FileStream** objects. **File** doesn't have to be instantiated before you can use its methods.

▶ **Directory**   This class lets you work with folders and subfolders on the operating system. You would use this class to iterate through directories and enumerate their contents, move files between directories, and otherwise manage the files in the directories. **Directory** must also be instantiated before you can use its methods.

▶ **Path**   This class provides a collection of methods that let you process directory strings across multiple platforms. **Path** must also be instantiated before you can use its methods.

In addition to the above classes, a number of sealed classes derive from **Stream** to provide additional file and directory utilities. These include **FileSystemInfo**, **FileInfo**, and **DirectoryInfo** and provide a collection of advanced directory and file manipulation methods.

The **FileStream** class gives you the ability to obtain random access to files through the use of a **Seek** method. The namespace also provides a **MemoryStream** class that supports access to a nonbuffered stream that encapsulates data directly accessible in memory. The stream has no backing store and can thus be used as a temporary buffer.

To code against network streams you can use the **NetworkStream** class. Interestingly though, while **NetworkStream** derives from **Stream**, it has been placed into the **System.Net.Sockets** namespace.

Another **Stream** derivative you will find useful is **CryptoStream.** This class is also not included in the **System.IO** namespace but has been added to the **System.Security.Cryptography** namespace. The **BufferedStream** class provides buffering utility to other streams, such as **NetworkStream.** The buffer stores the stream data in memory in a byte cache, which cuts down on the number of calls that need to be made to the OS.

A number of text readers and writers allow you to work with streams of textual data. Table 5-1 lists a partial collection of I/O classes.

Class	Functionality
BinaryReader, **BinaryWriter**	Reads and writes primitive data to streams
File, **FileStream**	Static methods for creation and manipulation of files; exposes a stream around a file
Directory, **DirectoryInfo**	Static methods for creation, manipulation, and iteration of directories and subdirectories
Path	Processes cross-platform directory paths
FileInfo	Instance methods for creation and management of files
MemoryStream	Creates a stream in memory
NetworkStream	Support for network streams
CryptoStream	Support for encrypted data
BufferedStream	Reads and writes to other streams
TextReader, **TextWriter**	Reads and writes a sequential series of characters
StreamReader, **StreamWriter**	Implements the text readers and text writers for characters and supports encoding
StringReader, **StringWriter**	Implements **TextReader** to read from a Stream
FileAccess (Enumeration)	Constants for read, write, and read/write access to a file
FileMode (Enumeration)	Specifies how the OS should open the file
FileShare (Enumeration)	Constants for controlling the access file streams can have to the file
IsolatedStorageFileStream	Stream support for isolated storage

Table 5-1 *The File I/O and Collateral Support Classes (Abridged)*

One of the classes you will find especially interesting is **IsolatedStorageFileStream**. This supports the streaming of data to isolated storage units, which are a form of private file systems that can contain files and that can only be accessed by its owner, an application, or user. See *Visual Basic.NET: The Complete Reference* (Osborne/McGraw-Hill, 2002) for extensive coverage of the isolated storage classes.

Using the stream classes is simply a matter of calling methods directly in some cases and instantiating the objects you need and working with their methods in other cases. The following example creates a listing of folders on the Windows 2000 file system using several of the above-mentioned classes:

```
Sub GetRoot()
 Try
   Dim Fldrs As New DirectoryInfo("F:\") ' the root to search
   Dim listFiles As FileInfo
   For Each listFiles In Fldrs.GetFiles("*.*") ' the search pattern
    'retrieve the full path of file or folder
   Dim fNames As [String] = listFiles.FullName
   'the length of the files (a long)
   Dim size As Long = listFiles.Length
   'the creation times of the files
   Dim createTime As DateTime = listFiles.CreationTime
   Console.WriteLine("{0,-12:N0} {1, -20:g} {2}", size, _
    createTime, fNames)
   Next listFiles
   Console.ReadLine()
 Catch e As DirectoryNotFoundException
   Debug.WriteLine(e, "Error")
 Catch e As Exception
   Debug.WriteLine(e, "Error")
 End Try
End Sub
```

Creating a file and opening it is also quite simple. Here is an example:

```
Dim newFile As New FileStream("C:\testbench\tester.txt", IO.FileMode.Create)
newFile.Open
```

And working with a single file is a no-brainer using the **File** class and its static methods (such as **Exists**, **Open**, and **Delete**). Here's another example:

```
If File.Exists("C:\testbench\tester.txt") Then . . .
```

To build in the file I/O and streaming support, all we need to do is simply add a new **Imports** directive in the **Crew** class to reference the **System.IO** namespace, because that's where we are going to find support for creating a file and saving the object's data into it.

Now back to our little demonstration of serialization before we get too carried away with I/O.

Serialization Part II

To do the object serializing and then save it to disk, you will need to create a method that walks the graph, serializes the data in the SOAP format, and then saves the stream into a file. This method achieves that objective:

```
Public Sub SerializeOut()
 Dim meData As New SoapFormatter()
  Try
   Dim persistFile As String = "C:\temp\" & objectRef & ".txt"
    If File.Exists(persistFile) Then
      File.Delete(persistFile)
    End If
    If (Not File.Exists(persistFile)) Then
      Dim fileForObject As New FileStream(persistFile, IO.FileMode.Create)
      meData.Serialize(fileForObject, Me)
      fileForObject.Close()
    End If
  Catch e As DirectoryNotFoundException
    Me.oState = e.Message
  Catch e As FileNotFoundException
    Me.oState = e.Message
  Catch e As Exception
    Me.State = e.Message
  End Try
End Sub
```

The first step in actually implementing serialization using the SOAP format is to create a new **SoapFormatter** object to process the SOAP stream, and this was done using the following line:

```
Dim meData As New SoapFormatter()
```

However, to instantiate **SoapFormatter** as **meData**, we need to reference the **SoapFormatter** class. This should be done using an **Imports** directive, as follows:

```
Imports System.Runtime.Serialization.Formatters.Soap
```

Next it would be a good idea to create the stream and file support, or our object will be going nowhere in a hurry. And this was achieved using the following code:

```
Dim persistFile As String = "C:\temp\" & objectRef & ".txt"
  If File.Exists(persistFile) Then
    File.Delete(persistFile)
  End If
```

So what have we done here so far? In the **SerializeOut** method, we created a **SoapFormatting** object that provides the necessary transport to move the data from the object's location in memory to storage. We could have used TCP or some other transport mechanism, but SOAP is an excellent protocol to use and allows us to support the serialization of the object across machine and even process boundaries.

Notice the variable **objectRef** in the **persistFile** string in the earlier code. This variable gives us a unique string to use as a file name for the current object to be serialized. There are a number of ways to get the file name. In this method, I have simply overwritten the **GetHashCode** method that bubbles down from **Object** and used the key for a file name. You will need to overwrite the method as well to get something with a little more substance than the default ordinal that the root **GetHashCode** method delivers.

Finally, we call the **Serialize** method on the **FileStream** object and reference the current object's data via the **Me** keyword. Here's the code that achieves this:

```
If (Not File.Exists(persistFile)) Then
  Dim fileForObject As New FileStream(persistFile, IO.FileMode.Create)
  meData.Serialize(fileForObject, Me)
  fileForObject.Close()
End If
```

First we created a new file to receive the SOAP stream. Then we called the **Serialize** method on **Me** and pointed it to the persist file. After the job is done, it would be a good idea to close down the **FileStream** object with a simple call to its **Close** method. You can check the serialized data in the file. If everything worked according to plan, the saved file will contain data that looks like this:

```
<SOAP-ENV:Envelope xmlns:xsi="http://www.w3.org/2001/XMLSchema-instance"
xmlns:xsd="http://www.w3.org/2001/XMLSchema" xmlns:SOAP-
ENC="http://schemas.xmlsoap.org/soap/encoding/" xmlns:SOAP-
ENV="http://schemas.xmlsoap.org/soap/envelope/" SOAP-
ENV:encodingStyle="http://schemas.xmlsoap.org/soap/encoding/"
xmlns:a1="http://schemas.microsoft.com/clr/nsassem/CrewClasses/CrewClasses">

<SOAP-ENV:Body>
<a1:Engineer id="ref-1">
```

```
<Crew_x002B_userID id="ref-3">Jeffrey Shapiro</Crew_x002B_userID>
<Crew_x002B_passWord id="ref-4">125280</Crew_x002B_passWord>
<Crew_x002B_clearanceLevel>1</Crew_x002B_clearanceLevel>
<Crew_x002B_objectRef>234654</Crew_x002B_objectRef>
<Crew_x002B_objectStatus id="ref-5">Idle</Crew_x002B_objectStatus>

</a1:Engineer>
</SOAP-ENV:Body>
</SOAP-ENV:Envelope>
```

That's all there is to serializing object data out to some persistent storage location. Instantiating **Engineer** now automatically provides the serialization support in the **Crew** class.

Activating Serialization at Runtime

There is no code here that fires serialization events (that automatically calls the **SerializeOut** method), so we will have to do it manually from the console application we created in the previous chapter. Later, we could easily add a timed interval event that calls the method every few seconds or minutes.

To fire the serialization manually, we need to add a method to the console application we created. Let's look at that code again, repeated here so that you do not have to keep flipping back to Chapter 4 to see what's different:

```
Option Strict On
Imports CrewClasses.Engineer

Module Module1
    Sub Main()
      Dim cUserID, cPassWord As String
      Dim cClearanceLevel As Integer
      Dim ItsAGo As Boolean
      Dim E1 As New Engineer()
      Console.WriteLine("Please enter a user ID")
      cUserID = Console.ReadLine
      Console.WriteLine("Please enter a password")
      cPassWord = Console.ReadLine
      ItsAGo = E1.AuthUser(cUserID, cPassWord)
        If ItsAGo Then
           Console.WriteLine("User: " + E1.GetUserID + " you may proceed.")
           Console.WriteLine("Your clearance level is: " _
             CStr(E1.ClearanceLevel))
           E1.SerializeOut()
           Console.ReadLine()
        End If
        If Not ItsAGo Then
```

```
        Console.WriteLine("Authorization Failed")
        Console.ReadLine()
    End If
  End Sub
End Module
```

The code in boldface is the only code that is different or new in the console code. We simply call the method **SerializeOut** in the **E1** object, which is an instant of the **Engineer** class. This method then invokes the serialization process inherited from **Crew**, and that all there is to it.

The instantiated class must also be marked as serializable, as demonstrated with this code:

```
Option Strict On
Imports System
Imports System.IO
Imports CrewClasses
Imports System.Runtime.Serialization
Imports System.Runtime.Serialization.Formatters.Soap


<Serializable()> Public Class Engineer : Inherits Crew
```

Serialization Part III

Now what happens if the console crashes or the machine shuts down abnormally (a power failure or some other disaster)? How do we get the data we had back when we create a new console application? Reconstituting the object can be a little tricky. We need to create a method to implement the deserialization. In this case, I implemented the deserializing method in the child class and not the base class. Follow these steps to provide this:

1. Check whether an object was serialized to disk. This could be as simple as checking for a persist file.
2. Create a holding object of the type to receive the data from the file.
3. Create a SOAP formatter to recover the data from the file.
4. Open the file.
5. Deserialize into the holding object.

This process is demonstrated in the followed deserializer method:

```
Public Sub SerializeIn()
  Try
  Dim recoverFile As String = "C:\temp\" & GetObjectID() & ".txt"
  If File.Exists(recoverFile) Then
```

```
      Dim fileForRecover As Stream = File.OpenRead(recoverFile)
      Dim aClone As New Engineer()
      Dim meData As New SoapFormatter()
      aClone = CType(meData.Deserialize(fileForRecover), _
        CrewClasses.Engineer)
      fileForRecover.Close()
      SetUserID(aClone.GetUserID)
    End If
  Catch e As DirectoryNotFoundException
    Me.State = e.Message
  Catch e As FileNotFoundException
    Me.State = e.Message
  Catch e As Exception
    Me.State = e.Message
  End Try
End Sub
```

What's cooking in this code? First we needed to create a new **Stream** to open the file in the **C:\temp** folder. The code that achieves this can be written as follows:

```
Dim fileForRecover As Stream = File.OpenRead(recoverFile)
```

TIP

*Notice how we can simply call **File.OpenRead** and feed it to the stream.*

Next we have to create a new **SoapFormatter** just as we did earlier. The code that achieved this is as follows:

```
Dim meData As New SoapFormatter()
```

Finally, we call the **Deserialize** method and close the file. Notice that we used **CType** to explicitly convert the holder type to the type represented in deserialized data.

```
aClone = CType(meData.Deserialize(fileForRecover), _
 CrewClasses.Engineer)
fileForRecover.Close()
```

At this point, our job is not yet done. We got the data back, but it is in an object that is not currently being referenced by our application. However, all that's left to do is to copy the data in one object to the other, which is illustrated in Figure 5-5. I did it this way so that I could pick out what I needed to restore the data. There are a million different ways to recover the data.

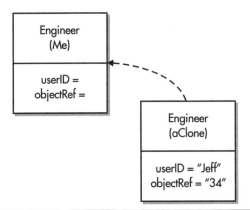

Figure 5-5   *The object is reconstituted as a new object of the same type, and its data can be restored to the current object (**Me**).*

Activating Serialization at Runtime

To call the deserializer method at runtime is not difficult to achieve. You could call it shortly after startup, as demonstrated in the following code to enhance the console application:

```
Module Module1
  Sub Main()
  Dim cUserID, cPassWord As String
  Dim cClearanceLevel As Integer
  Dim ItsAGo As Boolean
  Dim E1 As New Engineer()
  E1.SerializeIn()
```

So how do we "see" for ourselves that we indeed have the serialized data back in the object? We can simply check the data in the object we have a reference to as follows:

```
Console.WriteLine("Houston: " + E1.GetUserID + " is back in business. . .")
```

That's some of the framework's serialization for you. And we landed on only one class in the collection of namespaces.

NOTE

For local applications that do not need to serialize across network streams, it would be better and more secure to use the binary formatter class.

ADO.NET

ADO.NET is the new database technology that Microsoft has created for the .NET Framework. While it is a successor to ADO (Active Data Objects), it does not really replace ADO. The ADO library is a collection of COM components encapsulating the functionality of OLE DB, which has been the key provider to Microsoft's database technology for a number of years. ADO encapsulates the functionality to access the OLE DB provider easily, which at the lower level sports a very difficult API to program against.

ADO.NET, on the other hand, is not based on COM at all, but rather on XML. So ADO is a *binary* model while ADO.NET is a *text* model. ADO.NET also supports a new native access data provider, the SQL Server .NET provider, which we will discuss in the "Connection Architecture" section. In addition to the COM/XML or binary/text difference, ADO.NET also provides a new collection of data access and manipulation objects. Let's go over the differences between these two collections of objects.

ADO Revisited

The chief protagonists in the ADO model are the **Recordset** and the **Connection** objects. ADO achieves its mission by allowing you to create the **Connection** objects to establish connections to databases. Once a connection is established, data can be retrieved or manipulated by transmitting SQL query commands (T-SQL to SQL Server) or by executing stored procedures through the connections. Data is returned as a resultset, in a tabular data stream, which is received to the ADO **Recordset** object. Figure 5-6 illustrates the ADO object model.

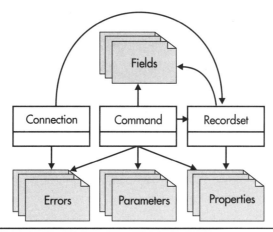

Figure 5-6   *The ADO object model*

ADO technology was primarily designed for applications that typically remained connected to their data sources. And you could create client-side cursors with ADO or work with server-side cursors as necessary. While you can work with ADO data in a disconnected state, maintaining the recordsets is not an ideal model. The data needs to be used and the recordset disposed of as soon as possible.

ADO recordsets encapsulate only a *single* table representing the resultset returned from a database. To get to data that resides in more than one table, the SQL command or stored procedure on the database must perform a **JOIN** query and return a single resultset to the client. To navigate across the rows of a recordset, you iterate through the data sequentially using the **MoveNext** method.

ADO is still a viable technology, and with .NET interoperability, ADO can be comfortably used in VB.NET applications. However, the ADO model is old technology and does not work well in the modern era of widely distributed applications, Web services, and the Internet.

Being a binary standard based on COM, the ADO recordsets cannot be easily interchanged between applications. To pass ADO objects between applications and process boundaries requires COM marshaling.

ADO objects also do not live well in the world of distributed applications. Firewalls, for example, usually block binary traffic. If you send a recordset's data to a destination protected by a firewall, you are sending it to its death.

Enter ADO.NET

In the new era of distributed applications, the chief protagonists in the ADO.NET model are the **DataSet**, **DataAdapter**, and **Connection** objects, and the entire object model is underpinned by (you guessed it) XML. This new object model is illustrated in Figure 5-7.

The **DataSet** object implements **DataTableCollection** (see Figure 5-7), which means that the dataset can represent a collection of tables that can represent a referential schema. The ADO.NET namespace is illustrated in Figure 5-8.

NOTE

Foreign-key relationships enforce referential integrity and also provide a schema of one-to-many and many-to-many relationships.

Datasets store their data in the table collections as XML. The collections are actually standard data structures, so you can loop through a collection of rows as you do with an array. You can thus reference row positions using the data structure's ordinals (0 and higher) or the table's primary key index. You can also navigate

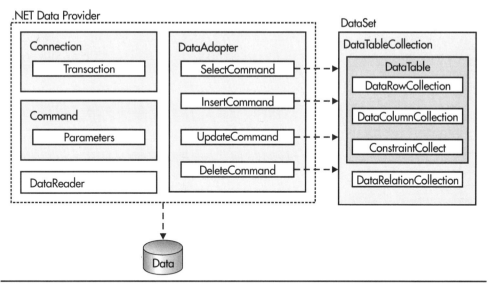

Figure 5-7   *The ADO.NET object model*

across the hierarchical collection of tables via methods implemented in a **DataRelationCollection** object. In other words, you can look up Joe Brown's order numbers in one table, and then associate them with the items in each order in another table, and find payment information in a third table.

The **DataSet** objects come equipped with a number of data access and data manipulation methods, but because XML provides the definition, schema, and representation of the data the dataset can be traversed, iterated, and manipulated as if it was an actual collection of tables on the database.

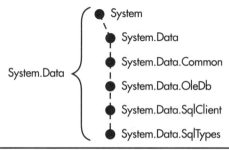

Figure 5-8   *The **System.Data** namespace*

One of the key differences between **DataSet** and **RecordSet** is that **DataSet**s cannot maintain cursors, client side, or server side on the database. Their disconnected architecture precludes cursors by design. However, if you still need to use cursors, you can go back to an ADO **RecordSet**, which can be easily accessed through .NET's COM interop support, as discussed in Chapter 6.

Connection Architecture

In the not too foggy past, when you needed to work with data, you connected to the database and then maintained the connection. Components, such as so-called *databound* controls, maintained connections, and data manipulation in the control (usually a grid) resulted in the direct real-time manipulation of the data on the database. ADO changed that model somewhat by allowing you to disconnect from a database and still work with the data offline; however, it was still very much a connection-oriented architecture.

Maintaining connections to databases is a "no-no" in modern distributed application design. You must connect, query, and then get the heck out. The less time you spend docked to the database, the more connections can be served and the better the scalability, which is essential for Web applications when connections can be suddenly opened up to a server by an order of magnitude. The new **DataSet** object has been precisely designed to allow you to get in, suck up data from a couple of tables, and then work with them offline.

Each **DataTable** object in the **DataSet**'s **DataTableCollection** includes **DataRowCollection**, **DataColumnCollection**, and **ConstraintCollect**. This means that any referential constraint enforced at the server is mirrored in the disconnected **DataSet** object's collection of tables. If the server enforces a cascading delete, the cascading delete will be maintained at the dataset.

NOTE

To cascade deletes or cascade updates means that if you change data in a primary key record, or delete the primary key record, records linked to the primary key by foreign key are also updated or deleted (see SQL Server 2000: The Complete Reference, Osborne/McGraw-Hill, 2001).

But the connection architecture goes even further. Using ADO objects in the middle tier, VB developers received data from the OLE DB provider or transmitted data down to the OLE DB provider, which in turn streamed that data in tabular data stream (TDS) format to and from SQL Server.

While SQL Server still supports TDS, a much better means of transmitting data to SQL Server, encrypted or otherwise, has been implemented. Instead of talking to OLE DB (through ADO), a new .NET data provider can talk to SQL Server directly.

(A new .NET data provider for OLE DB has also been introduced to support continuing OLE DB access to SQL Server, Oracle, and any Jet databases.)

The new SQL Server .NET provider includes the following facilities:

▶ **Connection**   This object establishes a connection to a data source, using a connection string the database server will understand.

▶ **Command**   The command is a SQL query that is executed at the database server. The command also allows you to pass parameters for server-side stored procedures and functions. You can also use **Command** to enlist a transaction on the connection automatically.

▶ **DataReader**   This object is used to read an XML stream representing data returned from a server (we will be using this object in an example shortly).

▶ **DataAdapter**   This object is used to populate a dataset, and it implements a collection of data manipulation language (DML) procedures you use to work with the data in the dataset's **DataTable** object. The four commands in the **DataAdapter** object are **SelectCommand**, **InsertCommand**, **UpdateCommand**, and **DeleteCommand**.

XML

In ADO.NET, data moves from component to component and from place to place in XML format. If you need to serialize data from a **DataTable** object, it can be easily done using the XML serialization classes, which store the data in files as XML. The process is the same as discussed in the earlier sections on serialization.

ADO.NET components can be easily interchanged between both .NET components and components from other platforms, even across process and operation system boundaries. The power that allows this is XML, because it is an industry standard and thus the XML data stream can be easily read, understood, and reconstituted.

XML is *text based*, which means that schema and the data travel together and can thus be transmitted through any protocol, because no binary information is included. This allows your data not only to be transmitted in a disconnected state to SQL Server, which parses it and takes care of it on the server, but it means that data can freely be transmitted through firewalls, because it passes through as text.

The caveat with all this naked text flying around is that it looks very inviting to hackers and other angels of evil. So implementing network, data, and stream encryption is a good idea. Of course Virtual Private Networks (VPNs) can do the trick for private networks; but over the Internet it's a good idea to encrypt data that travels between a client and a server.

Implementing Database Integration with ADO.NET

So, what do we need to do to build ADO.NET support into our **Crew** class? To begin with, we decided that storing the password in the object is a temporary thing and that to implement a login facility we need to compare a password presented with a password stored on the database. Now we surely don't need a dataset just to compare two strings. The **DataReader** object will do the trick for us. Here's what we need to do.

1. Create a **Connection** object and open a connection to the data source.
2. Create a **Command** object and command to send a query to the server, through the connection.
3. Create a **DataReader** object to read the returned stream from the data source.

Let's go back to the **Crew** class now to code the database support using the .NET classes for data, or ADO.NET. First, to use the new SQL Server .NET provider, we need to point the class to the **System.Data.SqlClient** namespaces as demonstrated in the following code (the lines in boldface are the new lines of code added to the **Crew** class):

```
Option Strict On
Imports System System
Imports System.Runtime.Serialization
Imports System.Data.SqlClient
```

Now we can extend the **Crew** class with the following function:

```
Public Function AuthUser(ByVal UID As String, ByVal PWD As String) As Boolean

Dim crewConnectString As String = "Data Source=SQL;" & _
   "Integrated Security=SSPI;Initial Catalog=PN"
'overloaded, can be just new or it can take the connect string as an argument
Dim crewConnection As New SqlConnection(crewConnectString)
'create the command to fetch the password
Dim crewCommand As SqlCommand = crewConnection.CreateCommand()
crewCommand.CommandText = "Select LoginPassword FROM UserLogin" &_
"WHERE UserID = " & UID
Try
  crewConnection.Open()
  'declare a simple data reader to receive the password
  Dim pwReader As SqlDataReader = crewCommand.ExecuteReader
    Do While pwReader.Read()
      passWord = pwReader.GetString(0)
```

```
      Loop
      If PWD = passWord Then
        SetUserID(UID)
        SetClearanceLevel(1)
        crewConnection.Close()
        Return True 'this short circuits the rest of the code
      End If
        SetUserID("Not Authorized")
        SetClearanceLevel(0)
        crewConnection.Close()
        Return False
  Catch e As SqlException
      Me.State = e.Message
  Finally
    End Try
  End Function
```

We have now added quite a bit more code, which will be reused in the derived classes, so whomever derives from the **Crew** class will get all this implementation to go right ahead and use it to process password authentication. In this example, we fetched a string from the database and compared the values at the client. We could have just as easily sent the string to a stored procedure and had SQL Server do the comparing, returning 1 for True and 0 for False. The latter would also work if SQL Server received an encrypted string and then decrypted it to make the comparison. But it might better suite you to receive an encrypted string and have the client decrypt it.

What did we add here? First, we referenced the ADO.NET namespace and the SQL Server .NET provider through the **Imports** statement (**Imports System.Data.SqlClient**). This allowed our base class to instantiate the necessary objects to connect, query, and read the resultset from the server.

In the preceding function, you can do some debugging using the **System.Diagnostics** namespace, which is represented in Figure 5-9.

The ADO.NET classes are rather extensive, and there is lots more we could do. In later, and I am sure, much improved versions of **Crew**, we can implement datasets and datatables for a variety of database support. But further discussion is beyond the scope of this book, so let's continue with more insight into the advanced power of .NET.

Figure 5-9 *The System.Diagnostics namespace*

Interfaces

The subject of interfaces is very extensive, and we don't really have the scope to go into interfaces in any detail in this volume. However, interfaces are very important to you as a .NET programmer for a number of reasons. There are quite a number of interfaces supplied with the base classes library (BCL). So you need to know how to inherit interfaces and how to implement them. In addition to being a consumer for interfaces, you will often have cause to create interfaces, for your own use and for your clients and customers, or members of your development team.

An interface is like an abstract class. In fact, to the Common Type System *it is* a class. Abstract classes have no implementation and thus their methods must be implemented in the classes that implement them. Interfaces also have no implementation (it's expressly forbidden). The code is "postponed" for you to add when the interface is implemented in your class.

There are several key and fundamental differences between classes and interfaces. For starters they do not behave like classes. You cannot inherit any implementation from them and they cannot be instantiated (for that matter nor can abstract classes). The class in which you are implementing an interface can also implement the definitions of more than one interface. You are not restricted from implementing more than one interface as you are from inheriting from more than one base class. The reason for this is in the code of the interface ... because there isn't any.

So when do you inherit classes and when do you implement interfaces? The answer is in the simple *"is a kind of"* test we did when we first extended **Crew** as the **Engineer** class. If the new class you are creating is a natural extension of its parent then you inherit. But if the class is required to *"do other things"* that are of a general nature or *"play the role of"* then it can implement an interface. An interface is useful for allowing classes to do things that the "family" does not care for. For example, if a descendant class of **Engineer**, say **WarpEngineer**, needs to do something that no other class or object will do, implementing an interface and providing the code works.

There will be many occasions when you will need to work with interfaces, because once you have inherited a base class other than **Object**, inheriting functionality from other classes is out of the question.

You can also create interfaces to implement in your base classes, where you would create the definition in the interface and then implement in the base class, and then allow both the interface definition and the implementation to be inherited by new child classes. But enough talking; let's do a bit of this here as well.

To create an interface, add a new class to your class library solution or create a new solution. In the example here we are going to create the encryption support we promised at the beginning of this chapter and create an interface to encrypt/decrypt the password data we send to and receive from the database. There are a number of classes and libraries that provide good encryption/decryption algorithms and techniques (in fact a few good ones are lying around on Java Web sites around the world (*shshsh*) and they easily be adapted in VB.NET).

To create the interface change the declaration in the class file from **Class** to **Interface.** You will also need to change **End Class** to **End Interface.** This is demonstrated in the following code:

```
Public Interface ICrewSecurity
  'other declarations
  Function EnCrypt(ByVal enCString As String) As String
  Function DeCrypt(ByVal deCString As String) As String
End Interface
```

What have we here? There are two function definitions. One passes in a string for encryption and returns an encrypted string and the other passes in a string for decryption and returns the string in plain text.

How do we use these functions? When implemented in the base **Crew** class every time we receive a password from the database to compare to the password provided by the user we first have to decrypt the password from the database before we can compare it to the one supplied by the user. (We don't have to worry about the plain text password being seen because the browser connection and the entire session is already sending data up and down in an encrypted data stream. The whole idea behind implementing this is to store the passwords on the database safely).

NOTE

It goes without saying that someone else can create an interface that might have an identical method definition to one in the interface you are currently using, If you implement both there is going to be a clash (an ambiguity). There are ways to avoid the ambiguities, but that discussion is beyond the scope of this book.

That's all there is to the interface. The real work comes in the implementation. By the way, the paradigm of code reuse is still sound because the code is going into a base class ("shaped" by the interface) and inherited by all child classes. Most interface providers (developers) provide example implementations that give you less work to do. So in many respects your fingers are doing the inheriting for you; it's called "writing code."

OK, now to implement this baby. We go back to **Crew** class and add the **Implements** directive to the class definition. We also need to add the member definitions from the interface. By adding the **Implements** statement you are now setting the class up to "contract" with the interface. The term **contract** is a good choice because you have to implement the entire interface exactly as defined. The following code shows how this is done:

```
<Serializable()> Public MustInherit Class Crew
    Implements ICrewSecurity
    Private userID As String
    Private passWord As String = "1234"
    Private cLevel As Integer = 0
    Private oRef As Integer = 0
    Private oStatus As String = "Idle"

Public Function EnCrypt(ByVal estring As String) As String _
    Implements ICrewSecurity.EnCrypt
    'Encrypt code goes here
End Function
Function DeCrypt(ByVal dstring As String) As String _
    Implements ICrewSecurity.DeCrypt
    'Decrypt code goes here
End Function
```

The code emphasized in bold is all the new code added to the **Crew** class. We are now ready to implement an encryption algorithm. Unfortunately we are out of time and I just got a word from my editor that we might have to go out and get more paper as well. But you can "logon" to the Osborne Web site at **http://www.osborne.com** (no encryption required) and download an example implementation.

One last test. Open the extended **Engineer** class. Has it inherited the encryption/decryption methods? It has. Hallelujah.

Forms

Finally, after all this time we arrive at the subject of the .NET Forms technology and user interfaces—but why now after more than one hundred pages? Why did we not look at forms as early as Chapter 1, which just about every Visual Basic book has done since the word *Visual* was added to the language? As mentioned back in Chapter 1, the objective in this book is to offer an alternative style of programming to the one that VB programmers are accustomed to.

In the past, the model of programming was forms-centric or forms-oriented. And most VB books started out at the form. In fact, everything we taught in books for the earlier versions of VB was centered on forms because little could be done without a form in the picture. All VB applications started and ended with forms.

But now it makes more sense to program to an object-oriented model. The **Crew** class we developed in the past chapters provides all the functionality and code that can be reused in a variety of ways. It can sit behind console applications, as has been the case in the past two chapters. It can sit behind a Web page, and it can sit behind a Web service.

The **Crew** class can also be used in mobile application with no modification. And it can also be used in remote applications and passed as an argument required by a method. Why? The entire implementation has been provided in an object that is not dependent on any visual interface or presentation technology. Consumers of the **Crew** class can simply instantiate an object that inherits it and use it in a variety of ways, as we are now going to do.

As you have realized, the console application has begun to outlive its usefulness. And as we start to improve and extend the **Crew** class, we notice that it is becoming more difficult to provide an event-driven, user-friendly interface to the **Crew** object, in its derived state. So it now makes perfect sense to provide a form to interface to the object. This is simple to do. We merely unhinge the console application and throw it away. And then we create a form that instantiates the child class of **Crew** supported by the application.

There is also another reason that we went to all that effort to code the **Crew** class and demonstrate deriving it as the **Engineer** class, besides shielding you from all that OO stuff as illustrated in Chapter 4. You see, Windows Forms inherit from a very powerful set of classes. By the time you have derived your Windows Form class, you have inherited an extensive amount of class members—methods, fields, properties, and so on. To serialize the form object takes a lot of effort and would actually be pointless for a lot of data that resides in the form. So Microsoft decided it would not make sense to allow form objects to be serialized.

But the data you need to persist in a class such as **Crew** or **Engineer** should be serializable, and luckily it's pretty easy and straightforward to do this. Had you built the implementation of the **Crew** class directly onto a form, you would have lost the ability to serialize the data out to disk or some remote storage.

Let's get cracking and create a Windows Form to provide a user interface to our **Engineer** object. But first let's take a look at the new forms technology offered in .NET.

Windows Forms and Web Forms

The two principal technologies offered in .NET are Windows Forms and Web Forms. Windows Forms more closely resemble the forms technology offered in the classic Win32 libraries. Windows Forms provide user interfaces and forms to cater to the needs of rich or thick-client applications, where most of the processing is done on the client or server machine.

Windows Forms in Perspective

The new Windows Forms technology is much more powerful than its Win32 predecessor. It is in fact derived from the work done for the Windows Foundation Classes (WFC), which were created for Visual J++. Adopted for .NET, Windows Forms provide powerful forms implementation—allowing positioning, advanced docking, exceptional resizing ability, transparency, and other features.

Windows Forms are typically used for creating client applications such as database and data entry programs, business applications, ERP applications, graphics applications, and any application requiring a substantial amount of user interaction on a local machine. Windows Forms applications typically have access to local and network printers, local and network files systems and folders, the registry, Active Directory, and so on. Windows Forms also have sophisticated access to GDI+ for rich and graphical gaming applications.

Web Forms in Perspective

Web Forms are the low-fat version of standard Windows Forms. They are also known as ASP.NET forms. They are used in situations where the primary user interface or the so-called launch pad of functionality is the browser. Over the years, Web Forms applications have become popular for simple data access and data-driven applications. A good example of such an application is a call-center application in which the agent can be positioned anywhere to interact with callers and databases and provide data input.

One significant advantage that Web Forms have over Windows Forms is that deployment is practically nonexistent on the Web Forms client machine. All users have the necessary resources on their machines already—the browser. Web Form applications are much easier to support for the clients because you do not have to deploy any code to the client machine. Everything is driven through the browser.

In the past, DLL hell and other deployment problems that plagued classic Windows applications led to a surge in popularity of Web Form applications. However, we should expect a return to the rich-client application, driven by the more advanced and powerful Windows Forms technology, because .NET XCOPY deployment (see Chapter 1), side-by-side execution, and so forth make it much easier to deploy and maintain Windows Forms applications than in the Windows DNA era. We will get back to Web Forms in our discussion of ASP.NET in the next section.

The Graphical Login

As promised, let's now replace the console application that we had floating above the **Engineer** object with a classical Windows GUI dialog box instead. To create the Windows application, select File | New, Project. The New Project dialog box illustrated in Figure 5-10 is displayed. Select the Windows Application icon and then provide a name for the project. In our example here, the application is called **LoginWF**.

Once the application is created, you can create the login dialog using the Visual Studio.NET designer, as illustrated in Figure 5-11.

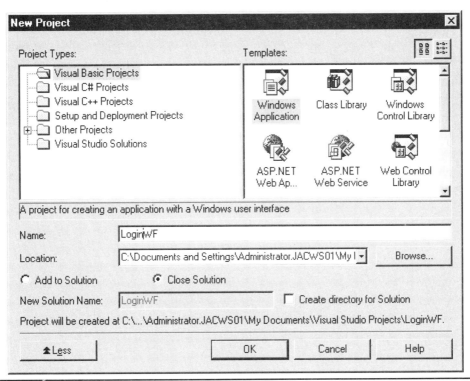

Figure 5-10 *Creating a classic Windows application*

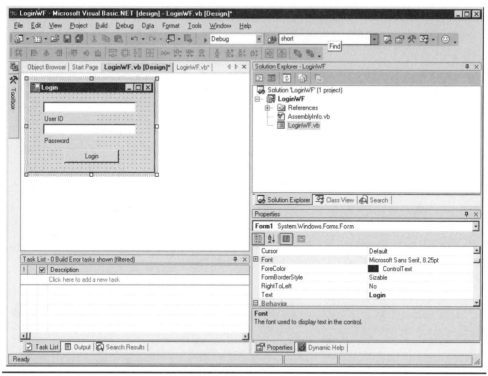

Figure 5-11   *Creating the graphical login form using the Visual Studio.NET designer*

Add two text boxes and a button to the form. Now all we need to do is go to the code behind the form. We can collapse the "Windows Form Designer generated code" section and add the following code:

```
Imports System
Imports CrewClasses

Public Class LoginW : Inherits System.Windows.Forms.Form
    Dim E1 As New Engineer()
    Dim cUserID, cPassWord As String
    Dim cClearanceLevel As Integer
    Dim ItsAGo As Boolean
```

Remember that we need to add a reference to the **CrewClasses** assembly in the Solution Explorer. Next we need to double-click the button and add the following code into the button's subprocedure:

```
Private Sub Button1_Click(ByVal sender As System.Object, ByVal e As
System.EventArgs) Handles Button1.Click
  cUserID = TextBox2.Text
  cPassWord = TextBox1.Text
  ItsAGo = E1.AuthUser(cUserID, cPassWord)
  If ItsAGo Then
   E1.SerializeOut()
   MessageBox.Show(E1.State, "Login Information")
  End If
  If Not ItsAGo Then
   MessageBox.Show(E1.State, "Login Information")
  End If
End Sub
```

That's all there is to using the **Engineer** object to obtain authorization to login. If authorization fails, we can read the object's state property to check the result of the failure and determine whether any exceptions were the cause of the failure.

One last bit of code. We can put the **Engineer** object's last user ID information into the form upon startup. The best place to do this is in the form's **LoginW_Load** method, as follows:

```
Private Sub LoginW_Load(ByVal sender As System.Object, ByVal e As
System.EventArgs) Handles MyBase.Load

  E1.SerializeIn()
  TextBox2.Text = E1.UserID
End Sub
```

So now when the form first loads, the user ID of the last user is displayed in the appropriate TextBox.

ASP.NET

The ASP subject is huge, and thus deserves (and often is) a book of its own. This section is a short introduction to get your feet wet and to demonstrate how our **Crew** class is just as accessible from an ASP.NET application and a Web Form as a classic Windows application or the console. To get you familiar with the new environment and features of ASP.NET, we'll build a sample Web application. The best way to introduce you to ASP.NET is to show you how quick and easy it is to get an ASP.NET application up and running. Of course, our **Engineer** object will be used to provide a login and authentication facility over the Web.

ASP.NET in Action

In this sample application, we are going to design a page that will allow our engineer to enter a user ID and password in a Web browser and get authenticated over the Internet.

1. Open Visual Studio and Start a New Project. This will bring up the New Project window shown in Figure 5-12. Notice the integration of the three Web project types with the regular Visual Basic projects types.

2. Select ASP.NET Web Application and enter **LoginWebF** for the name of the application. You will also need to choose a folder for the application.

NOTE

You need to make sure you have Internet Information Server (IIS) or Personal Web Services running on the machine you are developing on.

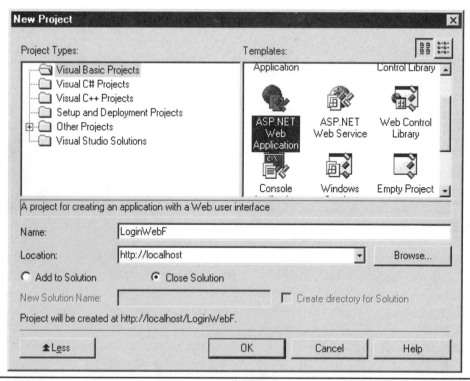

Figure 5-12   *Creating a new ASP.NET application*

3. Open the toolbox and click on the webForms tab. Add a button, two edit boxes, and a label to the form. Arrange the items so that you can see them all, and double-click one of the labels to change the text. If you look closely at the controls you placed on the page you will see that the textbox and the dropdown list have a little green arrow in the upper-left corner, indicating that it is a server control.

    The designer works the same way as building a Windows Form, and when you double-click on a control, it takes you to the code view so you can modify the event code. Server controls can have code attached to them, unlike HTML controls, in which basically the designer generates the HTML for you. ASP.NET gets its power from the server controls, allowing your Web pages to be event driven.

4. Click OK and modify the text of the label to show nothing (""). Repeat this operation for the two text boxes and rename the button's label **Login**. After Visual Studio creates the initial files for the project, go ahead and change the name of the default WebForm1.aspx file to **LoginA.aspx**.

    When creating ASP.NET pages, there are two types of page layout: GridLayout and FlowLayout. Using the grid layout, you can position items in the design window by moving them where you want them to be, ala WYSIWYG. Flow layout is basically a top to bottom layout. Use the SPACEBAR and ENTER key to position elements on the form. The default is GridLayout, but this can be changed in the document properties window.

5. Now that the controls are all labeled and ready to go, let's add some code behind this baby. Well, guess what? There's nothing new for us to do here. We can take the code for the previous example using the traditional Windows Form and drop it right into the Web Form. There is even a **Page_Load** method that works just like the Windows Form's loader method.

Since this is a Web Form, the most important feature you need to pay attention to is the **IsPostBack** keyword. ASP.NET keeps track of whether or not this is the first time the page is loaded or if it is a response to a client postback. This is demonstrated in the following code:

```
Private Sub Page_Load(ByVal sender As System.Object, ByVal _
 e As System.EventArgs) Handles MyBase.Load
'Put user code to initialize the page here
  If Not IsPostBack Then 'will be true first time page is loaded
    E1.SerializeIn()
    Text2.Text = E1.UserID
  End If
End Sub
```

If you recompile and view the page, it acts the way you anticipated, just like the graphical login or the console application before it, as illustrated in Figure 5-13.

This is a simple example of how ASP.NET will save you time during the development cycle. ASP.NET now takes care of tons of details behind the scenes so that we no longer have to.

Many Web controls included with Visual Studio.NET are designed to save you time. Take the Validator controls, for example: Suppose you want to designate a field as a required field. You can place **RequiredFieldValidator** on the form and set the **ControlToValidate** property to the field you want validated; ASP.NET will make sure that field is entered from the user's side. ASP.NET will check the target browser's capability, and if it can run JavaScript, it will write out client-side JavaScript to do the validation. If the target browser cannot support this functionality, ASP.NET will do the validation on the server side. ASP.NET is a great start toward eliminating browser-independent code. It is by no means perfect, but this is just the first version of great things to come.

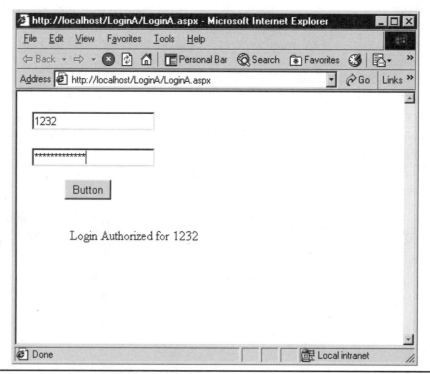

Figure 5-13   *Our login from Internet Explorer*

Creating a Simple Web Service

Microsoft, many other industry giants like IBM and Sun, and thousands of smaller independent software vendors are "hoping" that .NET will generate collaborative programming efforts around the world through the Internet. .NET applications can be run from anywhere on the Internet using Web services. But what is a Web service?

A Web service is a collection of methods (functions and procedures) that are published to a Web server and made available for use by consumers anywhere in the world. Based on evolving technologies that interoperate on the World Wide Web, Web services are fast becoming the building blocks for creating open-distributed systems that allow us to interchange information and functionality on a wide scale.

How does a Web service work? The following steps are considered the standard process for providing a Web service:

1. A provider creates and deploys a service using his or her platform of choice (we love VB.NET, VS.NET and IIS).

2. A provider defines the service in WSDL (Web Services Description Language), which is a standard for describing a Web service over the Internet.

3. The service is then registered in UDDI (one of the new standards that everyone is backing and which stands for Universal Discovery, Description and Integration). UDDI allows us to publish our service and allows our consumers to search for them over the Internet.

4. The consumer's application binds to the service and invokes its methods using the simple object access protocol (SOAP), which encapsulates XML arguments transmitted to our methods' parameters and caters to any return values that come back over HTTP.

From our viewpoint in Visual Studio.NET, we can think of a Web service as any reusable component that can be called from a Web Form or even a classic Windows Form. These Web services are discoverable in such a way that an organization can publish the service and anyone who wants to use it can automatically find out what the methods and properties are and use it when they need it.

Suppose that our engineer needs to log in to the system databases with his or her tricorder and download systems state information. You can do this now from anywhere in the universe—over the intergalactic Web—via a Web service.

1. Open a new project and select ASP.NET Web Service. Name the project **LoginWS**.

2. After the project completes the initial file creation, you will see a blank designer screen. In the Solution Explorer, you will see a file called

Service1.asmx. Rename this file **LoginWS.** The .asmx is the extension for Web services.

3. Double-click on the blank space in the designer screen to switch to the **LoginWS.asmx.vb** code page. Rename the **Service1** class **LoginWS.** Below that, you will see a Web service example code that is commented out. Delete the template and add the following code:

```
Imports System.Web.Services
Imports CrewClasses

Namespace CrewClasses.Webservice
Public Class LoginWS
    Inherits System.Web.Services.WebService

<WebMethod()> Public Function GetStatus(ByVal UID As String, _
    ByVal PWD As String, ByVal SystemID As String) As String
        Return (Status(UID, PWD, SystemID))
    End Function

    Private Function Status(ByVal UID As String, ByVal PWD _
        As String, ByVal SYS As String) As String
        Dim ItsAGo As Boolean
        Dim E1 As New CrewClasses.WarpEngineer()

        ItsAGo = E1.AuthUser(UID, PWD)
        If ItsAGo Then
            Select Case SYS
                Case "1000"
                    Return "Online"
                Case "1001"
                    Return "Online"
                Case "1002"
                    Return "Offline"
                Case "1003"
                    Return "Online"
                Case "1004"
                    Return "Online"
                Case "1005"
                    Return "Online"
            End Select
        End If
        If Not ItsAGo Then
            Return ("Authorization Failed")
        End If
    End Function
End Class
End Namespace
```

The **<WebMethod()>** that appears before the function name is what tells .NET to make this function available over the Web. This allows you to create a Web service that also has private internal functions that can be used in conjunction with the public Web method, but are not exposed to the outside world.

If you want to test to make sure that this works, you can right-click the **LoginWS.asmx** file in the Solution Explorer and click the Build And Browse button. The browser window will return with an informational page about the service and what methods it provides. Right now, only the **GetStatus** function appears, but it's easy to see that you could build a robust library of functions to allow the world to access all that functionality. Notice, at the top of the informational page, a link for the **GetStatus** function. If you click on this link, a new page (as illustrated in Figure 5-14) will appear with a box asking for the user ID, a password and a **System** number (the parameter we specified in the Web method). If any other parameters existed, these would have been listed as well. This built-in functionality gives a developer the information needed about the service and its use.

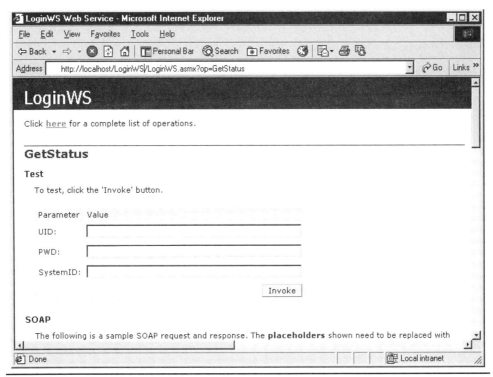

Figure 5-14   *Interacting with the support service for the Web service*

Now we have a service for clients to use. And any client (browser based, UNIX, or otherwise) can use your Web service. To use the service the client application or consumer needs to reference the Web service in the same fashion as referencing classes, components, and libraries (such as **CrewClasses**), just as we have done several times in this chapter. Visual Studio lets you create a Web reference to the Web service running on the Web server via its UDDI services as described earlier.

Observations

What did we set out to achieve in this chapter, you and I? We talked about VB.NET in action. Well what was the action? We saw how easy it is to create objects and work with object fields and data without the need for a Windows Form, or to tie the object to any specific container. This lets us create and work without objects with the extra baggage required of the form.

We also uncovered the rich and powerful support of the **System.IO** classes, which allow us to write any desirable file and data manipulation code for our applications.

We learned about the Serialization classes available to .NET and how easy it now is to persist data out to the hard disk. We also learned how the new ADO.NET classes allow us to work with data sources such as SQL Server in a disconnected state.

And finally, we investigated the new Windows Forms technology, ASP.NET, and Web services. But we also realized one thing—we do not need to have a form in the picture until it is absolutely necessary. I know, you'll say, "but we could do that before." Sure you could; VB 6 could create classes that could be used by any VB consumer and we even used them in ASP pages—just not with the same amount of power and flexibility. We can do everything we need to do in an object derived from a custom-made parent class.

Obviously there is still volumes more that we can explore, try out, develop; such is the magic of Visual Basic.NET. And much of what you have seen and tried here has been further extended and expanded in *Visual Basic.NET: The Complete Reference* (Osborne/McGraw-Hill, 2002.)

CHAPTER 6

Migration to and Interoperability of VB.NET

IN THIS CHAPTER:

Protecting Your Investments

VB to VB.NET Migration

COM/.NET Interoperability

ASP to ASP.NET Migration

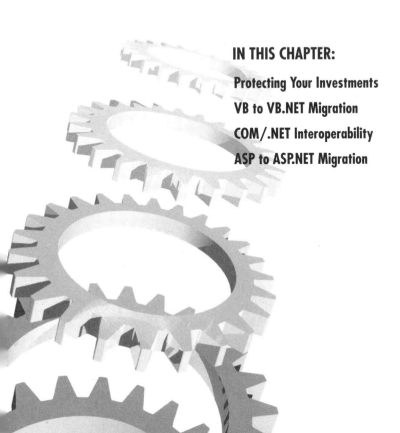

Every journey is a learning experience, and the past five chapters have no doubt taught you a couple of things. First and foremost, you know that developing for the .NET Framework is different from any VB development you have ever done, at least developing for the Windows platform. Except for the Java junkies, who have been coding to a managed, garbage-collected environment for many years now, most Windows programmers will find VB.NET a highly challenging, yet rewarding way to develop applications for the Web.

For Visual Basic programmers, you are in for a heavy transition period as you make the move to VB.NET on the one hand and protect your investment in classic VB code on the other. Consider the following food for thought:

▶ The move to a pure object-oriented (OO) language introduces tons of syntax and concept changes that will at first be difficult to grasp. Concepts like structure exception handling (SEH) and true inheritance introduce a new way of thinking when designing, modeling, and prototyping software.

▶ While there are some idiomatic similarities between VB and VB.NET, the migrating tool that ships with VB.NET is not a panacea for your migration or porting ills. For example, for a number of years, I worked on an extensive call-center application that was split across several tiers and included a number of utilities written in VB. After upgrading some of the applications, many sections needed to be hand-coded—so many, in fact, that it made more sense for me to write the application all over again.

▶ More than a decade has been invested in maintaining and improving classic VB code. Tons of code still reside in VB 3, 4, 5, and 6 applications. Although migration strategies are available, as you'll learn in this chapter, the options and the results are far from straightforward.

▶ VB programmers have been writing COM and reusing COM components for years. In the mid-1990s, most COM components were written as ActiveX controls, while the latter part of the decade saw tons of COM and COM+ components written for Web and Windows DNA (Distributed interNet Application) applications.

Because Microsoft knew the transition from VB to VB.NET wouldn't be easy, the company has provided extensive interoperability support as an alternative to migration. Seven-plus years of coding COM, DCOM, and COM+ components cannot simply be wished away, so the Microsoft .NET team has written migration wrappers that allow .NET-free passage into the COM world. Plus, COM citizens also enjoy the ability to visit the heart of .NET. Both of these alternatives are discussed in this chapter.

This chapter has been conceived as a guide and an introduction to the migration and interoperability support in VB and is food for thought as you begin to assess and plan how (or if) you want to attack adoption of the .NET Framework and Visual Basic.NET.

Protecting Your Investment in Existing Code

For as long as most of us remember, a new version of Visual Basic was released every 12 to 18 months. It was pretty common to be in the midst of writing an application and have another new VB version turn up. Usually, the new version would lie around the office for a few months while the current version of code in your application was finalized and shipped. If you are currently in such a situation and have made a substantial investment in classic VB code for applications currently in production, the best advice is to wait: don't integrate VB.NET into current applications for now. Put the compiler on the shelf. Become familiar with the VB.NET framework and language, but don't fall into the trap of thinking you can do better by changing from VB to VB.NET in the middle of a project and still meet target ship dates!

Finish what you are doing and forget that VB.NET exists for a while. When you return from a well-deserved vacation, you can install the new version, get up to speed, consult the references, and begin to assess how the next version of your product can be migrated to .NET, or if it should be. Often, migrating existing code to a new language, let alone a new and radically different version, can be a complex and risky business. Some companies' applications are so huge that incremental porting is the only feasible course of action.

As you consider migration, several options are open to you:

▶ You can stay in classic VB and pretend .NET doesn't exist (you won't be alone).

▶ You can rewrite your projects for VB.NET—in other words, port the existing code.

▶ You can support your old applications for a while, but start them all over again with VB.NET.

Each of these options has its pros and cons.

Stay in Classic VB

If maintenance is minimal, or a deadline is just around the corner, you should consider this option. VB versions 5 and 6 produced some great applications, and if they are functioning well, there's probably no reason to change them. This also applies to ASP applications in which you have a lot of VBScript working against COM and COM+ components written in VB. If it ain't broke, don't fix it!

While it can be cool to move to a new version of the software development language of your choice, it's often not practical, viable, or cost effective. This is truer today than it was a half-dozen years ago, when software development on the Windows platform was still in its "kindergarten" years. Customers were keen to move from 16-bit to 32-bit and from Windows 3 to Windows 95 and NT because what they needed just couldn't be done with those earlier versions. But today, upgrading and migrating is not as critical (and there's no Y2K issue to help fuel the effort). Only now (mid-2001) are companies starting to think about Windows 2000, and already we are seeing the new .NET enterprise operating systems that will ship with the Common Language Runtime.

Here are some good reasons for keeping applications in classic VB:

▶ The target environment cannot be readily or easily upgraded to be .NET compliant. Reasons include operating system upgrade costs; costs of additional hardware, such as memory and hard disk space; and legacy device driver considerations.

▶ Client machines cannot be readily or easily upgraded to .NET, for the same reasons.

▶ The applications work fine now, and users are not complaining (which, for many developers, is as likely as being able to dance on the head of a pin).

Migrate Code to VB.NET

VB.NET is definitely a new science, and while it might be more feasible to keep legacy applications and data sources in business, most of us still want to stay current and hate the thought of coding on an inferior platform (VB 6 was the best, but that was before lunch).

VB.NET options allow you to run the upgrade wizard to assess how much of your current applications need to be manually migrated to .NET. At best, your applications will run with little modifications, but, so far, the only application that migrates without much manual work is the "Hello World" demo you tried out when you started up VB 6 for the first time. In reality, you will need to look into the upgraded code and manually adjust it. The good news is that, many times, you will find algorithms that required you to write dozens of lines can achieve the same results in a single function call in VB.NET, which is 10 times faster. The upgrade wizard will not make such magical conversions to the new code for you, though; you'll have to code it yourself.

Rewrite

This is many a developer's dream. The project manager has come up with all the right reasons to rewrite the product in .NET from the ground up. So why would you want to start all over again?

Investing in OO technology has many advantages, including easier enhancements, code reuse, modeling, reusable patterns, self-documenting code, self-describing code, and on and on. Visual Basic.NET is a pure OO development environment. I know you've probably read this a thousand times already, not counting the number of times it appears in this book, but what does this mean really?

It means that your applications can be properly analyzed and designed using tried-and-tested OO techniques and tools, plus decades of analysts' experience. You saw a little of this type of design in Chapter 4. If you don't know how to model, design, and document in Unified Modeling Language (UML), your chances of becoming a VB.NET guru are as solid as Swiss cheese. But even so, don't let people tell you modeling in UML is a waste of time or has no practical value.

NOTE

See Visual Basic.NET: The Complete Reference *(Osborne/McGraw-Hill, 2002) for design guidelines.*

Object-oriented software development, as you saw in Chapters 4 and 5, centers on relationships—parents and children, inheritance and delegation, interfaces and polymorphism, *is a* relationships, *is a kind of* relationships, *roles,* composition, and on and on. Modeling languages like UML let you design your code according to these relationships, starting with how your users and processes interact with your software, in diagrams called *use cases.* You can further extrapolate these high-level abstractions into class diagrams, sequence diagrams, and other hierarchical elements.

Because OO principles and practices are standard across all modern computer languages, these solutions, or patterns, that work for one work for all. Patterns are reusable software solutions to the many common problems that developers encounter. In multiple inheritance, patterns can be easily adopted with a little creativity. They can be adopted in your VB.NET applications as if they were designed for VB.NET.

And as soon as CASE (Computer Aided Software Engineering) tools mature to include VB.NET code, you'll be able to model class diagrams visually and have much of the base classes and a lot of the standard code generated for you.

NOTE

UML has advanced far enough that it can even generate COM interfaces for you.

VB.NET is so different from VB that if you are ready to port to .NET, it would probably be better to maintain your existing applications on VB 6, and just start all over again with .NET. Many of the new features that .NET enables can then be provided to your installed base on the new software. Consider the following list of reasons:

▶ OO development requires a new approach to how you model and design your applications. The three amigos of OO—inheritance, encapsulation, and polymorphism—require that you think in terms of classes and objects from the first line of code you write. VB.NET software should be properly modeled before it is assigned and developed. With classic VB, it was often much harder to code to abstract guidelines because of VB's limitations, such as inheritance (or the lack thereof). But using .NET, you can design class diagrams and immediately reproduce the hierarchy (complete with method definitions) in code.

▶ Trying to retrofit code can be tedious and time-consuming. It gets worse if the code was not written by you, because not only do you have to read the documentation (if it exists), but you have to figure out what the original developer intended and how he or she achieved the result. Then you have to figure out how to repeat the effort using VB.NET. By the time you are done, you might have spent three days in the migration, when starting from the ground up would have taken only a day.

▶ Rewriting the application from the ground up usually produces a better application. How many times have you "iterated" through various versions of your software or algorithms and found that the rewrite was much improved? Rewriting for .NET will almost always achieve much better software design, software code, and software documentation—and happier clients.

What could be more rewarding for a dedicated and hungry software developer (like you) than rewriting a familiar system on a new platform? You already know the client's business needs and rules, so you can focus on design and implementation. If budget and time allow, you'll be able to take advantage of all the new features that VB.NET offers to create a state-of-the-art solution. (However, and unfortunately, this option usually looks less appealing to management than it does to developers and engineers!)

Is It Worth Porting?

Many VB 6 applications have their roots in older versions of Visual Basic (sometimes as far back as version 3, and believe it or not many still have reasons to code in Basic). Of course, it is pointless to upgrade an application if the effort to move to VB.NET yields little or no gain. But if you determine that migration of old code to new is wise and in your immediate future, factor the following questions into the migration plan:

▶ How old is the project? The older the system, the less the chance that it will lend itself to a useful upgrade. I would think seriously about abandoning the migration route if you are still working with code or modules developed in VB versions 3 and 4.

▶ How well is the system fragmented? If you wrote your system in well-defended sections (presentation, business, data, and so on), you could upgrade or rewrite one section at a time. VB.NET will interact with older COM objects very efficiently.

▶ How well versed are you and your team in VB.NET? Of course, by now, you are an expert (you *did* read this book, after all), but to take full advantage of VB.NET, it usually takes a little more than an upgrade wizard and reading the last 200 or so pages. You need to become proficient in *all* aspects of the .NET environment. The various aspects of the runtime environment, assemblies, namespaces, and so on have been covered in past chapters. While these new models are far better than the old ones, it takes a new skill set and a new way of thinking to exploit them. Becoming proficient in VB.NET might take several months.

If, after weighing all your options, you decide that it would be best to upgrade your existing project to Visual Basic.NET, start by taking a crack at the Upgrade Wizard.

Using the Visual Basic Upgrade Wizard

The easiest way to upgrade a VB 6 project to VB.NET is to open the project in Visual Studio.NET. VS.Net will recognize the old version and automatically pop up step 1 of the Upgrade Wizard, which is shown in Figure 6-1. The Upgrade Wizard is a five-step process with little user input required. And if you don't get to the first screen there is something wrong with your VB 6 project file.

The first page of the wizard requires no input from you. Just click Next, and then proceed to step 2, where you'll be asked whether the source project is an EXE or a DLL project. If you choose the DLL option, you will be asked some interface questions, as shown in Figure 6-2.

Step 3 of the wizard asks you for a new location for your project. The wizard upgrades your old project by creating a new up-to-date version of it in a new folder. Your old code remains unmodified in its current location.

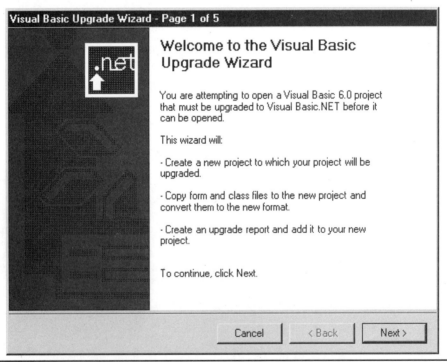

Figure 6-1   *The first page of the Visual Basic Upgrade Wizard*

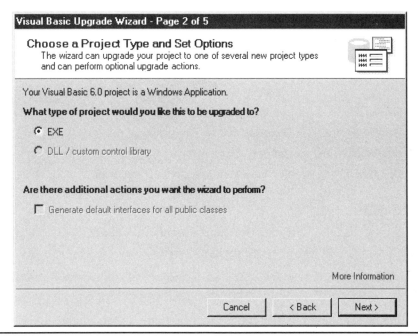

Figure 6-2   *Step 2 of the Visual Basic Upgrade Wizard needs to know the type of project being upgraded.*

In step 4, you are asked to confirm your intentions, and then in step 5 you'll see upgrade progress information with a time estimate. Large projects may take awhile to upgrade, possibly an hour or more because the process requires opening every file and inspecting the code.

Understanding the Upgrade Process

Once the Upgrade Wizard has done its work, it creates a new folder and stuffs the new project and source files into that folder. At the end of the process you will receive an upgrade report. The report is in HTML and will show up in the Solution Explorer. The report shows what the wizard did to the project, broken down to the individual component levels (forms, modules, classes, and so on), so you can see exactly what happened to each item in your project. It also lists any issues that may need to be resolved before the application can be compiled, with online help links that you can contact for assistance.

The wizard will make many changes to your code, and in some cases, where the conversion needs your attention, it will add comments with one of the prefixes shown in the following table:

Prefix	Meaning
UPGRADE_NOTE	An informational comment
UPGRADE_TODO	Requires that you finish something
UPGRADE_WARNING	Informs you of behavioral changes in the code
UPGRADE_ISSUE	Requires your attention; no automatic upgrade occurred

UPGRADE_NOTE

These notes can be left alone; they are simply common reminders, located above an object that you explicitly destroyed in your earlier code, as shown here:

```
'UPGRADE_NOTE: Object objConn may not be destroyed until it is garbage collected.
'Click for more: ms-help://MS.MSDNVS/vbcon/html/vbup1029.htm
```

This note does not require that you change anything, unless you explicitly terminated an object.

UPGRADE_TODO

The TODO comments require some intervention. These notes invite you to review and set the assembly attributes. In VB 6, this was accomplished under Project | Properties | Make. An example of this note is shown in the following code:

```
'UPGRADE_TODO: Review the values of the assembly attributes
```

UPGRADE_WARNING

These warnings are a little more involved, as shown in the following:

```
'UPGRADE_WARNING: Couldn't resolve default property of object Value1.
'Click for more: ms-help://MS.MSDNVS/vbcon/html/vbup1037.htm
```

During the upgrade process, any variant variables will become object variables. If your function expected two variants and returned their concatenated value, the upgraded function will now get two objects and will complain about VB's inability to resolve the default property of those objects. A simple fix could be to cast the object to strings with the **CStr()** conversion function.

Another warning could occur with upgrading arrays, as shown here. Arrays in VB.NET are all zero-based, and the following statement would yield an array of 11 elements:

```
Dim A (10) As Long
```

During the upgrade, VB.NET kindly adjusts all arrays with positive lower bounds to 0. It might look like a harmless change (just a little waste of memory), but it can change the way your code works in some situations. Consider the following VB 6 code:

```
Dim Codes(100 To 200) As Long
Dim x As Integer
Dim y As Integer
For x = LBound(Codes) To UBound(Codes)
  I = I + 1
  Codes(x) = I
Next
```

The upgraded code in VB.NET will look like this, and it will include the following warning attached above the declaration of the code's array:

```
'UPGRADE_WARNING: Lower bound of array Codes was changed from 100 to 0.
'Click for more: ms-help://MS.MSDNVS/vbcon/html/vbup1033.htm

Dim Codes(200) As Integer
Dim x As Short
Dim i As Short

For x = LBound(Codes) To UBound(Codes)
    i = i + 1
    Codes(x) = I
Next
```

While it seems that the only difference is that we now have 201 elements instead of 200, the problem is that X(100) now holds the value *101* instead of *1*, as it appeared in VB 6. These little problems are not always obvious, but they can lead to unexpected bugs in what was once working code.

UPGRADE_ISSUE

Continuing with the preceding array example, remember that in VB.NET, arrays with negative boundaries will fail to convert altogether, so your upgraded code will include a comment like this:

```
'UPGRADE_ISSUE: Declaration type not supported: Array with upper bound
'less than zero. Click for more:
'ms-help://MS.MSDNVS/vbcon/html/vbup1051.htm
```

Here, it would be necessary to modify the array declaration manually and retrofit the rest of your code to the new array dimensions.

Upgrading COM and COM+ Services Using the Wizard

If your old application used a COM DLL that made use of ADO or another DLL for which there is now a new .NET equivalent, use the .NET version, if you can, to make the code cleaner and faster. In some cases, dependencies preclude wrapping COM. For example, if you upgrade a project that uses the CDOSYS.DLL (the Windows 2000 Mail DLL), the wizard will create a new interoperable DLL for you called Interop.CDO_1_0.dll. Neat, huh? The only catch is that you will get burned with the version of ADODB that the Mail DLL is expecting. A cleaner solution would be to reference **System.Web.Mail** and modify your code to take advantage of this namespace and new functionality.

When you upgrade a project that made use of COM+ services, an interop DLL also gets created, and the code is converted to use the new DLL. Rather than using the interop layer, I recommend that you use the .NET framework's built-in **System.EnterpriseServices** class. Mark the class with the following attributes: **<Transaction(TransactionOption.Required)>** (or the appropriate transaction option). To make things simpler, VB.NET lets you mark a method with the **<AutoComplete(True)>** attribute, eliminating any need to add the **SetComplete** and **SetAbort** calls.

Upgrade Tools for Interop

Visual Basic.NET brings many new features to the table. But to understand them all will take some time. One of the biggest obstacles to overcome is the plethora of namespaces in the .NET Framework. And one of the most delightful utilities that Microsoft packaged with the framework is an executable called WinCV.exe.

This utility lets you specify a keyword for a search, and it lists all the classes with their corresponding namespaces and assembly names. This utility can be located in the **\FrameworkSDK\Bin** folder.

Accessing COM Components from VB.NET Clients

A large project that was partitioned into multiple tiers is a good candidate for conversion, but it is a challenge. You don't want to upgrade all the components at once; instead, you might want to upgrade each component of each tier, test it, and then move on to the next component.

The .NET Framework provides a callable wrapper for achieving interoperability between COM servers and .NET clients. Called the *Runtime Callable Wrapper (RCW)*, it allows your .NET objects to interoperate with COM servers as if they were .NET managed types. The wrapper wraps the COM object, which is instantiated inside the wrapper.

NOTE

The Runtime Callable Wrapper is actually the .NET Callable Wrapper, which is not really Microsoft nomenclature, but helps distinguish this wrapper from the COM Callable Wrapper discussed in the next section.

The wrapper exposes the interface to the .NET client transparently, which accesses the component as if it were just another .NET object. And all HRESULTS, return values, reference counting, and other COM intricacies are handled for you. .NET creates an assembly for the COM object, so you can reference the object as you do the assemblies for any .NET namespace.

NOTE

Adding interoperabilty tends to impact performance, so it is best to try and work with the new classes and leave COM interop to your "out of options" situations.

To wrap a COM object successfully, you need to import the type libraries of your COM objects so that VB.NET can make use of them. The best tool for the job is called TLBIMP.

Using the TLBIMP Utility

TLBImp.exe is a command-line utility that expects COM DLL as the input and emits a DLL that will act as a "bridge," or wrapper, between the original DLL and your new .NET code. You can run the utility using command-line arguments that follow:

```
TlbImp.exe VB6COM.DLL /out:INTEROP.VB6COM.DLL
```

Command-line arguments let you control the namespace of the assembly and set the assembly's version.

> **NOTE**
>
> *TLBIMP stands for type library import utility.*

Another way to create the interop DLL is to add a reference to a COM DLL from the project you are working on. If VB.NET cannot find an interop DLL, it will ask whether you want to create one. If you click Yes and then look in the project folder, you'll find that a new DLL, called Interop.VB6COM_1_3.dll, has been generated. The new interop DLL automatically gets the Interop prefix, and its version number (1.3 in this case) is appended with underscores to the original name. Once the interop DLL has been created, you can still use the old DLL, which will perform as a standard .NET DLL—in fact, you are using a .NET DLL that simply wraps your old COM library.

After you have a reference to the interop DLL, you can start using it in your code immediately:

```
Imports zxShared
Public Class Form1 :  Inherits System.Windows.Forms.Form
Private Sub ConfirmLogin()
  Dim objLogin As New cLogin()
'Call objLogin Methods Here:
'No need to explicitly dispose the object,
'GC will take care of it.
End Sub
End Class
```

As shown in this previous code snippet, there is no need to dispose of objects explicitly, as was the case with earlier versions of VB. This is correct for any object used from VB.NET, no matter whether it is a wrapper DLL or a native DLL. But you still may want to dispose of objects manually for the following reasons:

▶ It makes your code more readable.

▶ You can release your object to the garbage collector (GC) before it goes out of scope some time later.

▶ You can use finalize and dispose methods to perform maintenance.

▶ You are using the object with COM+ services.

The last reason in the list is the most important for you to understand. In your classic VB code, when you included a line such as this,

```
ObjQueuedComponent = Nothing
```

COM+ moved the object back to the pool. However, if the GC manages to grab the object first, because the order of terminating objects is indeterminable, it will dash your expectations of having an object in the queue when you expect it.

Calling .NET Objects from COM or Standard VB Clients

.NET interoperation is a two-way street, and just as it is possible to wrap a COM component for a .NET client it is also possible to wrap a .NET object for a COM client. This is one reason you might consider mixing and matching classic VB and VB.NET code. With all the legacy VB apps in the world, rewriting a COM component's functionality as a .NET component is just as easy as wrapping the COM component in the RCW.

The reverse procedure requires the architecture of the COM Callable Wrapper (CCW), which means the .NET objects can be called from COM, the antithesis of the Runtime Callable Wrapper (calling COM from the .NET runtime). To turn your .NET component into a COM object, you can use the TLBEXP tool to generate a COM-type library from your assembly. TLBEXP will also support both early binding and late binding or IDispatch functionality of COM components.

NOTE

TLBEXP stands for type library export utility.

Since we already created a .NET DLL in Chapters 4 and 5, let's go ahead and wrap them for our VB 6 (or Visual J++) client login requirements. To do this, run TLBEXP from the command line referencing your .NET assembly, as follows:

```
TLBEXP CrewClasses.dll
```

This command will generate a CrewClasses.tlb file, which is the type library needed for consumption by COM clients.

However, we are now back in COM world, so our DLLs need to be registered. You can do that with **REGASM** (register assembly). The following command will register the CrewClasses.tlb file:

```
c:\regasm CrewClasses.dll
```

To confirm the registration, take a peek at the registry…. Yup, it's in there, as you can see in Figure 6-3. And there is little to do to turn your .NET objects into COM components, but doesn't registration seem Neanderthal in comparison to XCOPY deployment and side-by-side execution?

NOTE

Further study on COM/.NET interoperability is beyond the scope of this book. However, the subject has been fully covered in Visual Basic.NET: The Complete Reference (Osborne/McGraw-Hill, 2002).

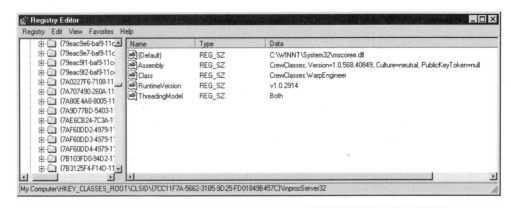

Figure 6-3   *The RegAsm utility that ships with the .NET Framework SDK registers your assemblies so that they can be called from COM clients.*

Understanding Object Lifetime and Deterministic Finalization

In the COM world, we were masters of our own domains, in charge of creating and terminating objects. While this was a powerful way to control our objects' retirement and free up resources, it was also the root of many nasty bugs and memory leaks. In addition, COM has a way of reference counting that makes it impossible to create circular references without a major hack and inevitable memory leaks. VB.NET, on the other hand, enlists the services of the GC to take care of all of those problems for us, as discussed in Chapter 2, and demonstrated everywhere by the absence of terminators and finalizers in our code.

It's important, however, to understand that, unlike COM objects, .NET objects can be terminated at any time and in any order when they get de-referenced and go out of scope. Finalization events will therefore occur just as randomly. If you have relied on the **Class Terminate** event to save data or to do other important work, you may run into problems with the GC. The best practice to prevent these problems is to create a new public method and call it explicitly from the same place where you terminated your COM objects originally.

Moving from ASP to ASP.NET

Moving from ASP to ASP.NET is an entirely different issue from VB migration for several reasons. First, just about any ASP page converts and works unmodified in the ASP.NET runtime, because the script is directly supported and there is no such thing as Visual Basic code for old ASP. VBScript and Visual Basic are not the same thing, just as JavaScript and Java are not the same thing. Second, if Web sites and intranets built on ASP are working, there's no need to change them. Third, if your ASP Web pages are producing dynamic content, interacting with the users and fetching and updating data, and being regularly updated, you can just redo the entire page in VB.NET if it makes sense.

If the Web site is a busy one, many of the ASP pages will likely be replaced or updated soon after the original versions. Some Web sites even go overboard. BellSouth, for example, changes so often and so dramatically that visitors get lost every time they return. A better idea is to build your new Web application in ASP.NET, and gradually replace ASP pages on old Web sites as required.

Observations

This chapter highlighted a number of issues you need to contend with while moving to Visual Basic.NET and the .NET Framework. For starters, as you know, you have to learn a new language and a new programming model.

If you have a heavy investment in classic VB code, you have a heavy decision to make—do nothing, migrate, or start all over with .NET. You now know the benefits of moving to .NET, but maintaining existing code in VB might be more feasible and less costly (for both you and your clients).

Making the Move to VB.NET

IN THIS CHAPTER:

Syntax and Idioms

Managed Execution and Managed Code

VB.NET and Java

VB.NET and Delphi

VB.NET and C#

VB.NET as a RAD Tool

Market Demand

Comparing languages feature for feature is an exercise in futility in today's marketplace. Saying that VB is better than Java or that C# is for pros and VB is for kids is also very immature. I have studied and worked with more than a dozen computer programming languages over the past 13 years, starting in 1988 with DBase and COBOL, and then C, C++, ObjectVision, PAL and Pascal, Delphi, SmallTalk, VB, Java, and countless scripting and interpreted languages. And now VB.NET and C#. If there is one thing that I have learned over the years, it's that you never learn a language because "it's what the pros use," or because it's more superior to something else. You use a language because it fits your programming needs.

The following list of criteria can help you in choosing the best programming language for your needs; it should be the criteria you use to decide whether moving to VB.NET is in your future:

- ► Does the language and its integrated development environment (IDE) do the job for you?

- ► How different from other languages is its syntax and idioms?

- ► Is it a managed environment or one that grants freedom of expression?

- ► Do you need to create rich or thick-client user interfaces, or will the browser or thin-client model suffice?

- ► What rapid application development (RAD) functionality do you need?

- ► How important is database support?

- ► What about backward compatibility?

- ► What market demand is there for the language?

- ► Is learning the language akin to studying ancient Egyptian, or is it straightforward?

- ► Is it object-oriented or structured?

The list could go on, and we would need many pages to drill down into these issues. If you are perplexed about the choice of .NET languages, this chapter provides some food for thought that might help in your decision making.

What Makes a Software Development Language

Language makers like Sun and Microsoft, although fiercely competitive, create computer languages to achieve the same goal of allowing you to write software, mainly for their platforms. You learn a particular computer language because it's the language you need to use to achieve certain objectives. Granted, some languages have more "desirable" features than others. If you desire those features, that language is the one you must use, plain and simple. Of course, choosing a .NET language is not too difficult, because they all support the Common Language Runtime (CLR); there are few differences among the .NET languages.

Consider Visual Basic. Over the years, the majority of programmers have learned VB not only because it was so easy to use, but also because it got the job done far quicker than anything else on the market did—at least for certain applications. As you read in Chapter 1, people chose VB in the mid-1990s because it supported Microsoft's database technologies better than many other tools on the market. And millions of small businesses use Microsoft's database technologies because they are not only affordable (like Microsoft Access) but they are also very powerful (like SQL Server).

Most of the world's developers chose VB because it is the best rapid application development (RAD) environment and because it supports the Active Data Objects better than any other tool. You could always argue that Delphi compiled faster and has easier deployment footprints—back in the days when VB was still sitting atop a p-code interpreter—and that it has always been an object-oriented language. But these features weren't helpful if you needed to develop for Microsoft Access or the earlier versions of SQL Server.

In 1995, Java arrived on the scene and became an overnight hit. It did well not because it was better or more powerful than VB or C++ or even Delphi, but because it was best suited to developing applications for the Internet. Now, seven years after its release, Java has become the de facto language that's taught in educational institutions, rapidly unseating Pascal and C++ as the student's language of choice. Why? The world is in love with object orientation (OO) because it makes software development a fun and much easier proposition. OO to software development is like chlorophyll to plant life, nighttime to bats, Beethoven to music. It just makes sense.

Java's rich and powerful OO model is a critical component of any learning institution's coursework because OO coding is a skill required by employers the world over. It has been predicted that the number of Java users will reach about 4 million by 2004. I believed that, when it was predicted in early 2000, but I now believe that C# and VB.NET will cut into that Java wave and ride alongside it at the next pass. Why? As popular as Java is, it is *not* the most suitable language for building traditional Windows-based applications or for Microsoft's Web and Internet solutions. VB.NET and C# are the current best contenders, and by using them, we can meet the demands of the Internet and the OO requirements of business.

The Way It Was

Back in the mid-90s, I chose Delphi because I was writing communications applications such as email servers and FTP servers that did not require any extensive database support. Back then, we needed small-footprint applications, slick libraries, and, of course, free threading.

In 1996, my Delphi multithreaded applications were so powerful that on several occasions I broke sockets. Winsock version 1.00 and the earlier releases of version 2.00 could not cope with the rapid opening and closing of sockets that led to memory leakage deep down in the operating system, where we had no access (Microsoft did fix that issue). Still, there was no other application development environment at the time that could do the job with the time to market required. Couple this with the needed power of multithreading and structured exception handling, and it's easy to see why I chose Delphi.

A little later, I adopted Java and Visual J++ for several reasons, some of which had to do with Internet development, and others which had to do with what Anders Hejlsberg and his team were doing with Visual J++. And like many other developers, I was unnerved by Borland's shenanigans in the 1990s. I believed it wise not to be too dependent on one modern language and one software development company. I chose to move to VJ++ primarily because I needed access and native support for the Windows platform and a RAD tool. I had also built up significant expertise in an OO language (Delphi) and found the two object models so similar that I was programming in Java within a day of moving from Delphi.

But the love affair with VJ++ ended with the bitter dispute between Sun and Microsoft, and without any sign of a future for VJ++, I moved to Borland JBuilder. When in 1998 I needed to build a call-center application and some banking applications for a large company, the language I chose was Visual Basic—for two reasons: I needed urgent access to an unshakable Microsoft database-development environment and nothing on the scene was better equipped than VB. I was also asked to generate a large number of reports, and they had to be supported in Crystal. Crystal Reports was practically built for Visual Basic.

VB was so at home with Crystal that reports could be turned out in days instead of weeks. VB was also ideal for asynchronous communications. A number of APIs were available to VB programmers and, like Crystal Reports, they were built for VB.

The Way It Is

The languages you choose today have a lot to do with the platforms you support, and of course with your alliances in the Cold War between Sun and Microsoft, which is going to get a lot colder. The Sun camp programs with Java and rallies around Corba (mainly) for the object model and componentware, Oracle for database (mainly), and UNIX or Linux for the operating system. The Microsoft alliance codes for the Windows platform (and probably will be for many more years to come); COM, and now .NET, for objects and components; and SQL Server (mainly) for database access.

Where the software Cold War will lead is anyone's guess, but the war has one positive aspect. We, the software developers, are going to see this competition generating some of the coolest and most powerful technologies ever, for years to come.

Let's go over some of the issues that play an important role in choosing a software development language today.

Syntax and Idioms

If you are a Visual Basic 6.0 developer, it definitely makes a lot of sense to learn VB.NET and none of the other .NET languages, especially C#. A number of VB bashers have suggested that VB programmers would be better off learning C# or going to Java because VB.NET is so different than classic VB. But this is bad advice.

If you intend to develop for .NET, be assured that—except for a few items that VB.NET has and C# does not, and vice versa—the only differences between C# and VB.NET (or VB.NET and the rest of .NET) is the syntax. C# gets its syntax from C and C++, and VB.NET gets its syntax from a decade's worth of Visual Basic versions.

To make VB.NET, however, a lot of wizardry went into overhauling the VB product, and while VB.NET is syntactically different from C# and the rest of .NET, it has also introduced a number of syntax changes that will require some diligence to master even on the part of VB 6.0 experts.

There is no discounting the importance of a language's syntax and idioms. If you are a VB programmer, here's a little test. Which syntax for constructors in the following code can you understand more easily, and which one do you recognize the quickest? This one?

```
Public Sub New()
 MyBase.New()
End Sub
```

Or this one?

```
Public MyBase():base(){
 }
```

Here's another example. Is this easier for you?

```
For (x=1; x<3; x++)
{}
```

Or is this one easier?

```
For x = 1 to 2
Next x
```

The two loop constructs are actually identical, and the evaluation of the values in the loop happens in the same order. Both elicit the same resources. If you needed to evaluate the expressions for the number of operations that each performs, they will come up the same. But as a VB programmer, you'll immediately recognize the VB syntax.

On the other hand, if you are a Java programmer and you need or want to code to .NET, you should come over to C#, because Java got its syntax from C/C++. Learning VB.NET would be more difficult for you as a Java programmer for the same reasons a VB programmer would find it more difficult to learn and become productive with Java or C# than VB.NET.

NOTE

If you're very good at programming in a certain language, it can be as familiar to you as your mother tongue.

I write in VB code every week, and I am writing a series of books on VB.NET. But every week I also write code in Java, and I evangelize Java to the thousands of subscribers of my Java newsletter (because Java is a great language). I can tell you that it takes a lot of effort on my part to break away from VB syntax to write Java code, and vice versa. Swinging both ways is not very productive.

Trying to maintain software in one language while learning and working in another is not conducive to making a good living as a developer. It is also much harder to debug software if you are not particularly familiar with the language or if you cannot recognize problems quickly. If you have to turn to documentation as your only means of figuring out what a developer was trying to do, you probably don't have sufficient command of a language to be productive and an asset to your employer or client.

Given that code written in VB.NET and C# compile to the same intermediate code, saying that one is better than the other is no reason for choosing one over the other. However, some features in C# make sense for certain algorithms, while some nuances available in VB.NET would thrill the C# people. But as I said earlier, it all depends on the job at hand.

Managed Execution, Managed Code . . . and Java

Only one managed code environment is in widespread use today: Java. But that monopoly will be short-lived if the .NET Framework catches on. Java applications compile to the so-called bytecode, while .NET applications compile to Microsoft Intermediate Language (MSIL, or IL). The Java environment is similar to the .NET CLR environment. Both runtimes compile their intermediate source code to machine code using just-in-time (JIT) compilation techniques. However, Java has primarily been an interpreted language, and JIT compilation is an option. On .NET, everything gets JIT compiled before it is executed.

Java has achieved a measure of cross-platform support with the widely available JVM, which runs on all modern operating systems. .NET's CLR is targeted to the Windows platforms, and the Common Language Infrastructure (CLI) targets non-Windows operating systems, an effort that is going to take a number of years before it gets anywhere close to the platform-agnostic nature of the JVM and its wide and varied deployment.

Both Java and .NET manage a garbage-collected heap. Java and .NET languages do not require deterministic finalization, and thus the purist in either camp will argue that neither language environment is suitable for high-end mission-critical and time-critical applications.

Both Java and .NET work extensively with metadata. Both environments thus allow you to access runtime type information through the *reflection* interface classes (they implement reflection differently, but they still achieve the same objective). The JVM and CLR execute all the code compiled to an intermediate language for their respective runtime environments. And both environments maintain strict access and tight security for accessing system resources.

The one big difference between .NET and Java, which is proving to be a major coup for Microsoft, is that the CLR and the Common Language Specification (CLS) encourage a language-agnostic platform and thus promote language interoperation.

While many COBOL and Eiffel programmers moved to Java to access the benefits of its runtime, many programmers found it difficult to move their expertise to the Java language. With .NET, these programmers now have a lot of leverage in coding, even in writing Web applications, in the languages they have been using all their lives. Who would have thought a mainframe programmer, out of a job, could make a living programming in ASP.NET? (The only problem, of course, is that not everyone wants a COBOL programmer to maintain their Web site.)

Delphi programmers who code for the Windows platform may opt to switch to a .NET language to support a number of projects. However, I have yet to see an object-oriented Pascal .NET environment that is as rich as that of Visual Studio, so

Delphi programmers adopting .NET will need to think about choosing a language supported by Visual Studio. Still, I firmly believe that VB is probably more suitable as a .NET language for Delphi programmers, because Delphi's syntax is more similar to VB than it is to C#.

Delphi, or Object Pascal, also enjoys the benefits of an object reference model. Delphi has a pure object-oriented heritage and similarly supports a single-inheritance hierarchy, starting with the root **Object.** Delphi also supports structured exception handling (SEH) and free threading, to name but two of the most important of the features of .NET. VB.NET now does everything Delphi (and Kylix) does, albeit under a managed code environment.

However, if you have expertise in Object Pascal and need to maintain that for developing fast and powerful applications for both Windows and Linux, at this writing, you would certainly be better off sticking with Delphi.

User Interfaces

If you are looking to build software products that do not require classic rich-client user interfaces and that need to be supported on a wide variety of operating systems, at the time of this writing, Java might be your best choice. However, the introduction of Web forms, Web services, and ASP.NET now allows you to create browser-based applications that support a rich user interaction experience as well.

If you are creating applications and rich user interfaces for Windows clients, any of the .NET languages will do the job for you. The new Windows forms technology on .NET is far more feature-rich than anything previously created for the Win32 platform.

VB.NET: The Best RAD Tool

Several features of VB.NET make it an excellent RAD tool choice. Coupled with the new power of VB.NET, the language and tool now offer compelling features that would make it your number one choice as a development environment. Although, admittedly, there is little difference between the RAD capabilities of C#.NET and VB.NET, thanks to the CLS and Visual Studio.NET, the following are some compelling, if not the most important, characteristics unique to VB.NET.

Late Binding

VB.NET comes with built-in late-binding support, an ability it inherited from its predecessor. *Early binding* means that in order to activate and access an object, such as calling its methods, the object first has to be implicitly declared and identified to the compiler. *Late binding* means that the code can dynamically work with the object at runtime. In other words you can call methods in your source code without the compiler having to perform compile-time discovery to verify the existence of the objects in which the methods reside. Late binding lets the compiler locate the objects that have those methods at runtime. *Early binding*, on the other hand, requires this at compile time. (See also the "Addition Operator" section in Chapter 3 and the "Polymorphism" section in Chapter 4.)

Late binding is a boon for VB.NET developers and can save a lot of time—which translates into quicker time to market—thanks to significant programmatic savings. This extra latitude in VB.NET results from the compiler's ability to perform background compiling as you type code. You might expect that this background work would drain resources (and you can switch it off), but it does not. C#, on the other hand, cannot "compile" while you code. Instead, it needs to parse code to check syntax, but it still relies on the compiler at compile time to resolve method calls.

VB.NET With Blocks

VB.NET also provides an interesting syntax convenience that C# and other .NET languages do not provide: **With** blocks. These constructs can cut code verbosity while simultaneously allowing you to code faster. While not a big deal to C# programmers, this feature has been inherited from classic VB and it is thus very much a style "gene" that many VB programmers would have missed if it were not present in VB.NET.

Basically, the **With** and **End With** construct is an inline shortcut to an object's reference variable. Here's an example:

```
If Not IsPostBack Then
  With Movies.Items
    .Add("Spy Kids")
    .Add("Star Trek 46")
    .Add("Planet of the Apes ")
    .Add("Jurassic Park III")
    .Add("Apocalypse Now")
    .Add("Grease")
  End With
End If
```

This is obviously a simple example, but the dot notation in the **With** section of the **WithTester** module can save a lot of extra code and time when you need to make a large number of references to an object. It will save you significant time coding database examples, as well as Web site code, as the ASP.NET example in Chapter 5 showed you.

Market Demand

You can make comparisons forever and sit in the office and marvel at how great a software development tool is, but after the work is done, you realize that bringing home the bacon is the most important thing. This brings us to a sensitive subject: market demand. When all is said and done and the comparisons are over, it's the person who has the job, not the person with the best development tool, who wins the day.

There are three languages in popular demand today, and if you know one of them well, it can pretty much guarantee job security: Visual Basic, Java, and C/C++. Specialize in anything else and you run the risk of finding yourself wishing you learned Visual Basic or Java or C++ long ago. How did I arrive at such a conclusion? Simple. I looked at jobs on the Internet. You need no independent auditor to verify the figures. All Web sites and Web programming jobs report the same story (at least in the USA).

As of this writing, in July 2001, the demand for pure Java programmers is roughly equal to that for Visual Basic programmers. There are still a lot of C/C++ jobs out there, but C/C++ is used to maintain a lot of "Model T" applications that were coded in the years of the flower children. Searching all of the main job-posting Web sites in the United States turns up about the same amount of Java references as Visual Basic references (excluding VBScript and JavaScript).

I also researched the demand for Delphi programmers, and while Borland claims a huge following, the Web sites clearly indicate that nobody wants to hire them. Even COBOL programmers have a better chance of finding employment! Table 7-1 represents the approximate number of jobs advertised for three of the most popular languages on the three main job-posting Web sites for software developers and IT professionals: Dice, Monster, and BrainBuzz.

Of course, the version of Visual Basic that everyone needs experts in is not VB.NET (at least not now). Still, it goes without saying that existing investment in VB code means that VB programmers will be required for a long time to come. As stated throughout this chapter, the natural migration path for a VB programmer will be to VB.NET.

Skills	BrainBuzz	Dice	Monster
C/C++	7	5498	1000+
Java	59	7763	1000+
Visual Basic	63	7231	1000+

Table 7-1   *Monster Does Not Return an Exact Amount. Dice Probably Has the Most Accurate Figures.*

NOTE

During the writing of this book (July 2001), the number of .NET jobs advertised had tripled.

In some parts of the US, Java and C++ programmers are earning a lot more money than VB programmers—although not that much more, save in some exclusive areas. Still, the significant learning curve to move from VB to Java is just too steep, especially with VB.NET around the corner. In my estimation, it would require a VB programmer at least six months (and probably a year or more) to become proficient in Java, C#, or C/C++, while it would take less than six months for a VB programmer to master VB.NET to achieve the same level of power offered by at least Java and C#.

Observations

This chapter took a quick sojourn into helping you consider making the move to VB.NET. Clearly, with the demand for VB programmers still brisk, it would make no sense for you to embark on a costly learning experience by moving to C# or Java. VB.NET is just as powerful as C# and has a number of conveniences that make it a great RAD development tool.

Making the move to VB.NET has some significant advantages for VB programmers. Market demand and the need to maintain a knowledge base and expertise in classic VB to service existing investments are very compelling reasons to stay with VB.

You need to make your decisions about learning VB.NET on several levels. The time you would spend learning Java is not a bad investment if the amount of money you can earn as a Java developer is what matters to you more than anything else (and it comes with a significant stress factor) and you are learning your first language. Plus, if you are studying a computer language at school, you will probably be required to take a course in Java.

But, especially if you've programmed in VB, there is little risk in learning VB.NET, and it's a great language. Even if you later decide to learn to program in C# and/or Java, what you learn in VB.NET can ease the transition, because the object models, runtime environments, class libraries, modeling approaches, patterns, and other features are very similar.

Index

Symbols
, (comma) as group separator, 98

A

abstract classes, 128
accessor methods, 104
Add Reference dialog box (Visual
   Basic.NET), 142
ADO
   ADO.NET vs., 173–174
   object model for, 173
   technology overview of, 173–174
ADO.NET, 173–179
   about, 173
   ADO vs., 173–174
   connection architecture for offline
     work, 176–177
   as database technology, 28–29

DataSet, DataAdapter, and Connection
   objects in, 174–176
implementing database integration
   with, 178–179
object model for, 175
serializing data with XML, 177
AndAlso short-circuit operator, 69–70
application design
   adding constructors to class, 138–140
   adding methods to class, 134–137
   application domains, 50–51
   creating classes in class library,
     129–132
   enabling application functions on Web,
     191–193
   evaluating class design, 123–124
   implementing interfaces, 180–182
   instantiating more than one object,
     143–144

modeling user authentication and login
for class, 125–127
object-oriented, 124–127
selecting software development
language for, 214–217
setting up class inheritance, 132–134
tips for exception handling, 156
using classes in console-based
applications, 141–143
See also building VB.NET
applications; object-oriented software
development
applications
maintaining in classic Visual Basic,
197, 198
porting to Visual Basic.NET, 198–199,
201
using classes in console-based,
141–143
See also building VB.NET
applications; migrating to Visual
Basic.NET
applying VB.NET capabilities, 148–194
ADO.NET, 173–179
ASP.NET, 187–190
creating Web service, 191–194
extending base class, 157–159
forms, 182–187
interfaces, 180–182
.NET exception handling, 148–156
object serialization and .NET I/O,
160–172
arithmetic operators, 70–71
arrays, 79–85
about, 79
cautions resizing with ReDim
statement, 83
declaring and initializing, 79–80
differences between collections and,
85, 86
finding size of with UBound and
LBound statements, 82

IsArray function, 85
join and split methods for, 101–102
releasing instance of with Erase
statement, 84–85
upper boundary of, 82–84
VB 6 syntax for lower- to upper-bound
elements unsupported, 80
working with, 80–82
ASP
migrating to ASP.NET, 211
VBScript and development in, 20–21
ASP.NET, 187–190
creating login application in, 188–190
features and advantages of, 29–30
migrating to, 211
Web application security, 53
ASP.NET Forms, 184–185
assemblies, 37–42
basic functions and features of, 37–40
defined, 38, 62
elements of, 42
names of in GAC, 55
PE files vs., 42
role of, 41–42
assembly metadata, 42
assignment operators, 66–67
automatic memory management, 51–53

B

base classes
extending, 157–159
synonyms for, 115
BCL (Base Class Library), 13
Bitwise operators, 69–70
Boolean operators, 69–70
branching statements, 71–73
GoTo, 71–72
On Error, 72–73
building VB.NET applications, 58–106
arrays, 79–85

coding in Notepad, 60–63
collections, 85–87
data type conversions, 63–64
execution control statements, 71–76
interation statements, 76–79
methods, 104–106
operators, 64–71
overview, 58
shifting from forms-based model to
   object-oriented programming, 58–60
strings, 87–104
using Option directives, 63
See also specific building components

C

C#
   coding similarities between VB.NET
     and, 217–218
   development of, 21–22
   value of True in, 64
C++
   competition with Visual Basic, 20
   market demand for C and, 222–223
callable wrappers, 207–209
cascading deletes and updates, 176
Choose function, 74–75
classes, 127–134
   adding constructors to, 138–140
   adding methods to parent, 134–137
   in console-based applications, 141–143
   creating exception, 155–156
   denoting encapsulation in UML,
     128–129
   designing in class library, 129–132
   differences between Collection and
     Array, 85
   evaluating design of object, 123–124
   extending base, 157–159
   inheritance for, 132–134

modeling user authentication and login
   for, 125–127
NET Class Library, 13
in object-oriented software
   development, 110
objects vs., 127
of operators and their precedence,
   65–66
referencing serialization, 163
StringBuilder, 104
supporting file I/O, 163–167
synonyms for base, 115
System.Array, 79
of System.Collections namespace,
   86–87
System.String base, 87
visibility and role of, 128
Clone method, 88–89
CLR (Common Language Runtime), 34–56
   assemblies, 37–42
   checking code prior to processing by
     JIT compiler, 48–49
   compliance of software development
     features to, 44, 45
   defined, 13, 34
   deployment scenarios for, 54–56
   generating MSIL, 43
   as hosted execution environment,
     35–36
   language interoperability, 44–46, 219
   layers of, 35, 36
   as managed code environment,
     219–220
   managed execution by, 36–37, 49–53
   metadata, 46–47
   .NET security levels, 53–54
   value of True in, 64
CLS (Common Language Specification)
   class visibility and role in, 128
   interoperability and, 219
code access security, 53

code reuse, 116
coding
    checking code prior to processing by
        JIT compiler, 48–49
    in Notepad, 60–63
    porting to Visual Basic.NET, 198–199,
        201
    similarities between VB.NET and C#,
        217–218
COFF (Common Object File Format)
    standards, 38
collections, 85–87
    about, 85–86
    differences between arrays and, 85, 86
    System.Collections namespace, 86–87
COM (Component Object Model)
    calling .NET objects from clients,
        209–210
    development of componentware with
        OLE and, 19
    evolution of, 3
    failures of, 11–12, 30–31
    programming goals of, 6–11
    upgrading with Visual Basic Upgrade
        Wizard, 206
COM interface
    defined, 6–7
    encapsulation and, 9
COM object, 6
comma group separator (,), 98
Common Language Runtime. *See* CLR
Common Language Specification. *See* CLS
Common Object Request Broker
    Architecture (CORBA), 6
Common Type System (CTS), 109
Compare method, 90
CompareTo method, 90–91
Component Object Model. *See* COM
componentware, 19
Concat method, 91
concatenation operators, 69

conditional errors, 150
connection architecture, 176–177
Connection objects, 174–176
console-based applications, 141–143
constants, making private, 120
constructors
    adding to base class, 138–140
    declaring private, 139
    omitting, 140
Copy method, 91–92
CopyTo method, 92
CORBA (Common Object Request Broker
    Architecture), 6
Crew class
    adding constructors to, 138–140
    adding methods to, 134–137
    extending base class, 157–159
    hierarchy of, 115–117
    modeling user authentication and login
        for, 125–127
    setting up inheritance for, 132–134
CryptoStream class, 165
CTS (Common Type System), 14, 109
currency formatting, 94–95
custom formatting, 97
    custom positioning of decimal
        points, 98

D

data
    hiding, 119–121
    serializing with XML, 177
    working with offline, 176–177
data type conversions, 63–64
DataAdapter object
    in ADO.NET, 174–176
    in SQL Server .NET, 177
databases
    ADO.NET technology for, 28–29
    integration with ADO.NET, 178–179

DataReader object, 178–179
DataSet object
    cascading deletes and updates, 176
    defined, 174–175
    illustrated, 175
DataTable object, 177
DCOM (Distributed Component Object Model)
    connecting through firewalls, 9
    programming evolution of, 3
decimal formatting, 95
decimal points, custom positioning of, 98
decision-making statements and switches, 71, 73–76
    If...Then...Else, 73–75
    Select Case, 75–76
declaring and initializing arrays, 79–80
delegation, 27
Delphi applications, 10
    market demand for, 222
    migrating to .NET Framework from, 219–220
deployment scenarios for CLR, 54–56
deserialization
    activating method at runtime, 172
    defined, 161
    reconstituting object with, 170–172
digital signing, 54
directives
    listing collection of, 61
    types of Option, 63
Distributed Component Object Model. *See* DCOM
Do...Loop statements, 76–77
dynamic assemblies, 42
dynamic linking in COM, 10, 12

E

encapsulation
    in COM, 8–10
    for object-oriented development, 119–121
    UML notation for class, 128–129
End While termination statements, 78, 79
EndsWith method, 93
enumerations, defined, 110
Equals method, 93
Erase statement, 84–85
exception classes, 155–156
exception handling
    breaking out of Try...Catch blocks, 153–154
    creating exception classes, 155–156
    example of structured, 151–153
    nesting exception handlers, 154–155
    tips for, 156
    in Visual Basic, 148
    Visual Basic.NET and structured, 149–151
    See also structured exception handling
execution control statements, 71–76
    branching statements, 71–73
    decision-making and switches, 71, 73–76
    GoTo, 71–72
    If...Then...Else, 73–75
    On Error, 72–73
    Select Case, 75–76
execution stack for CLR, 37
Exit Try keyword combination, 153–154
exponential formatting, 95

F

fields
    dangers of public, 121
    making private, 120
files
    assemblies vs. PE, 42
    PE/COFF, 38, 39
FileStream class, 164

finalization events, 211
Finally keyword, 153
fixed-point formatting, 95–96
For...Next statements, 77
For Each...Next statements, 78
foreign-key relationships, 174
Format method, 94–99
    currency formatting, 94–95
    custom formatting, 97
    decimal formatting, 95, 98
    exponential formatting, 95
    fixed-point formatting, 95–96
    general formatting, 96
    group separator, 98
    hexadecimal formatting, 96–97
    number formatting, 96
    percent notation, 98–99
    placeholder options, 97–98
forms, 182–187
    creating graphical login for new
        project, 185–187
    in object-oriented software
        development, 182–183
    Web (ASP.NET), 184–185
    Windows, 184
free threading, 27–28
functions
    of assemblies, 37–40
    enabling Web application, 191–193
    IsArray, 85
    legacy VB-style functions for strings,
        87–88
    of methods, 106

G

GAC (global assembly cache)
    about, 54, 55
    location of, 55
    names of assemblies in, 55
garbage collector
    about, 51–53

disposal of unused exception objects
    by, 149
    finalization events and, 211
global assembly cache (GAC), 54, 55
GoTo statements, 71–72
group separator, 98

H

Hejlsberg, Anders, 21
hexadecimal formatting, 96–97
hosted execution environment, CLR as,
    35–36

I

I/O, 160–172
    classes deriving from Stream class, 164
    file I/O and collateral support classes,
        165
    support for in .NET, 163–167
If...Then...Else statements, 73–75
IL (Microsoft Intermediate Language) code
    compilation to, 36
    generating, 43
    as part of assembly, 42
    in PE/COFF file, 38
ILDASM (IL disassembler application),
    39, 40
IndexOf method, 99
inheritance, 114–119
    by classes, 114–115
    of class implementation, 138–140
    hierarchy of class, 115–117
    interfaces and, 119
    multiple, 117–118
    setting up for class, 132–134
instance variable, 111–112
instantiating strings, 88
interation statements, 76–79
    Do...Loop statements, 76–77
    For...Next statements, 77

For Each...Next statements, 78
While statements, 78–79
interfaces, 27, 180–182
COM, 6–7, 9
creating, 180–181
defined, 180
implementing, 181–182
inheritance and, 119
of System.Collections namespace, 86, 87
Intern method, 100–101
Internet Explorer, creating login from, 190
interoperability
calling .NET objects from COM or VB clients, 209–210
CLS and, 219
between COM servers and .NET clients, 207–209
of language provided in CLR, 44–46
provided in CLR, 44–46
IsArray function, 85
IsInterned method, 100–101
IsolatedStorageFileStream class, 166
IsPostBack keyword, 189

J

Java
JVM and managed code environments, 219–220
market demand for skills in, 222–223
migrating to .NET Framework from, 217–218
similarities between NET framework and, 219–220
similarities to VB.NET, 15–17
user interfaces and, 220
JIT compiler. *See* .NET JIT compiler
job opportunities, for VB programmers, 22
join method, 101–102

L

languages
CLS, 128, 219
independence in COM, 8, 11–12
interoperability of CLR, 44–46
market demand for software, 222–223
popularity of Visual Basic, 20
selecting software development, 214–217
UML, 124, 125
LastIndexOf method, 99
late binding support of VB.NET, 220–221
layers of CLR, 35, 36
LBound statement, 82
Like operator, 68
logic errors, 150
logical operators, 69–70
Login dialog box (Visual Studio.NET designer), 185–186
login for new application, 125–127
LoginWS Web Service, 193
looping, interation statements for, 76–79

M

managed code environments, 13, 219–220
managed execution, 49–53
about, 28
application domains, 50–51
in CLR, 36–37
garbage collector, 51–53
side-by-side execution, 49–50
market demand for software languages, 222–223
metadata
CLR and, 46–47
Java and .NET applications use of, 219
methods, 104–106
accessor, 104
making public, 120

modification, 104
polymorphism and different
implementations of, 122
sub-procedures and functions, 106
in VB.NET, 104–105
migrating to Visual Basic.NET, 196–212,
214–223
callable wrappers for interoperability,
207–209
calling .NET objects from COM or VB
clients, 209–210
choosing when to migrate, 197
compatibility of syntax and idioms in
VB.NET, 217–218
deciding whether to migrate to
VB.NET, 214
keeping applications in classic Visual
Basic, 197, 198
late binding support of VB.NET,
220–221
market demand for software languages,
222–223
moving from ASP to ASP.NET, 211
object lifetime and finalization events,
211
overview, 196–197, 212, 223
porting existing code to VB.NET,
198–199
rewriting applications in .NET, 199–201
selecting managed code environments,
219–220
selecting software development
language, 214–217
TLBIMP utility, 208–209
user interfaces and, 220
using Visual Basic Upgrade Wizard,
202–207
weighing decision to port existing code,
201
With blocks in VB.NET, 221
mixin, 117
modification methods, 104

MSIL (Microsoft Intermediate Language).
See IL code
multi-file assemblies, 42–43
multiple inheritance, 117–118
multithreading, 27–28

N

names
of assemblies in GAC, 55
strong, 54
namespaces
defined, 62
searching for in upgraded VB.NET
projects, 206–207
serialization and, 162
System.Collections, 86–87
System.Collections.Specialized, 87
System.IO, 163
nesting exception handlers, 154–155
.NET Callable Wrapper, 207
.NET Class Library, 13
.NET Framework, 13
ADO.NET database technology,
28–29
application development in, 196
ASP.NET, 29–30
CLR as managed execution
environment for, 34, 35
CLS class visibility and role, 128
connection architecture for offline
work, 176–177
development of VB.NET and C#,
21–22
exception handling, 148–156
I/O in, 160–172
interfaces and inheritance, 119
interoperability between COM servers
and .NET clients, 207–209
object reference model for, 110–114
origins of, 2–12

rewriting applications in, 199–201
security levels, 53–54
System.Collections namespace, 86–87
value type reference model for, 109–110
.NET JIT compiler
  checking code prior to processing by, 48–49
  deployment scenarios for CLR, 54–56
NetworkStream class, 164
New Project dialog box (Visual Basic.NET), 141
New Project dialog box (Visual Studio.NET designer), 185–186
Next Generation Windows Services (NGWS), 2
NGWS (Next Generation Windows Services), 2
non-deterministic finalization, 16
Notepad, coding in, 60–63
number formats, 96

O

object graph, 160
object model
  for ADO, 173
  for ADO.NET, 175
object reference model, 110–114
object-oriented software development, 108–145
  adding constructors to class, 138–140
  adding methods to parent class, 134–137
  application design, 124–127
  classes in, 110
  creating classes, 127–134
  designing classes of objects, 123–124
  encapsulation, 119–121
  forms in, 182–183

inheritance, 114–119
instantiating more than one object, 143–144
overview, 108–109, 145
polymorphism, 121–123
shifting from forms-based model to, 58–60
types supported by CTS, 109–110
using classes in console-based applications, 141–143
VBScript in ASP development environment, 20–21
Visual Basic's weakness in, 18, 19
See also classes
objects
  in ADO, 173–174
  calling from COM or VB clients, 209–210
  classes vs., 127
  COM, 6
  Connection, 174–176
  connection architecture and, 176
  DataAdapter, 174–176, 177
  DataReader, 178–179
  DataSet, 174–175, 176
  DataTable, 177
  disposing of unused exception, 149
  evaluating class design for, 123–124
  instantiating more than one, 143–144
  lifetime of, 211
  multiple string, 104
  object lifetime and finalization events, 211
  object reference model for, 110–114
  polymorphism and, 122–123
  RecordSet, 176
  restoring data to current object, 170–172
  serialization and deserialization of, 160–172
  string, 87–89

wrapping COM, 207
See also object-oriented software
development; strings
OCX components, 10
OLE componentware, 19
On Error statements
Visual Basic, 148, 156
Visual Basic.NET, 72–73
operating system and CLR, 35, 36
operator overloading, 44
operator precedence, 65–66
operators, 64–71
arithmetic, 70–71
assignment, 66–67
concatenation, 69
logical and Bitwise, 69–70
operator precedence, 65–66
relational, 67–68
unary, 66
value of True for, 64–65
Option Compare directive, 63
Option directives, 63
Option Explicit directive, 63
Option Strict directive, 63, 64
OrElse short-circuit operator, 69–70

P

padding strings, 102
PadLeft method, 102
PadRight method, 102
PE (Portable Executable) files
assemblies vs., 42
standards for, 38
PE/COFF file, 38, 39
percent notation, 98–99
placeholders
digit and pound for, 97–98
digit or zero for, 97
polymorphic assignment, 123

polymorphism, 121–123, 145
defined, 122–123
methods and, 122
objects and, 122–123
porting existing code to VB.NET, 198–199,
201
precedence of operators, 65–66
primitives, 110
private modifier for encapsulation, 129
programming evolution, 2–17
development of Visual Basic.NET, 17
of Visual Basic, 17–18
of Windows DNA, 3–6
properties for methods, 136
protected modifier for encapsulation, 129
public classes, 128
public modifier for encapsulation, 129

R

RecordSet object, 176
ReDim statement
cautions resizing arrays with, 83
syntax of, 82–83
working with arrays, 84
reference types, 110–114
RegAsm utility, 210
relational operators, 67–68
Remove method, 102
Replace method, 102–103
role-based security, 53
Runtime Callable Wrapper, 207
runtime errors, 149–150

S

sealed classes, 128
security
assembly and, 41

dangers of public fields, 121
data hiding and, 120
levels of .NET, 53–54
SEH. *See* structured exception handling
Select Case statements, 75–76
serialization, 160–172
    activating at runtime, 169–170, 172
    of data from DataTable object, 177
    defined, 161
    marking classes for, 163
    namespaces and, 162
    reconstituting object with
        deserialization, 170–172
    serializing object and saving to disk,
        167–170
SerializeOut method, 169–170
side-by-side execution, 49–50
software development languages
    features and compliance to CLR, 44, 45
    market demand for, 222–223
    migrating to .NET Framework from,
        217–218
    selecting, 214–217
    user interface choices in, 220
split method, 101–102
SQL Server .NET, 177
StartsWith method, 93
static assemblies, 42
Stream class, 164
String class, 88–104
StringBuilder class, 104
strings, 87–104
    Clone method, 88–89
    Compare method, 90
    CompareTo method, 90–91
    Concat method, 91
    Copy method, 91–92
    CopyTo method, 92
    EndsWith and StartsWith methods, 93
    Equals method, 93
    Format method, 94–99

IndexOf and LastIndexOf methods, 99
    instantiating, 88
    Intern and IsInterned methods, 100–101
    join and split methods, 101–102
    legacy VB-style functions for, 87–88
    locating characters in, 99
    PadLeft and PadRight method, 102
    Remove method, 102
    Replace method, 102–103
    SubString method, 103
    ToCharArray method, 103
    ToLower and ToUpper methods,
        103–104
    Trim methods, 104
    working with multiple string objects,
        104
strong naming, 54
structured exception handling (SEH), 26,
    148–156
    about, 148–151
    breaking out of Try...Catch blocks,
        153–154
    creating exception classes, 155–156
    example of exception handler for,
        151–153
    nesting exception handlers, 154–155
structures, 110
sub-procedures of methods, 106
SubString method, 103
syntax
    errors in, 149
    of ReDim statement, 82–83
    for VB 6 lower- to upper-bound
        elements unsupported, 80
System.Array parent class, 79
System.Collections namespace, 86–87
System.Collections.Specialized
    namespace, 87
System.IO classes, 194
System.IO namespace, 163
System.String base class. *See* strings

T

TLBIMP (type library import) utility, 208–209
ToCharArray method, 103
ToLower method, 103–104
ToUpper method, 103–104
Trim methods, 104
True for operators, 64–65
true object orientation, 23–26
Try...Catch blocks
    breaking out of, 153–154
    in structured exception handling, 149
    tips for exception handling with, 156
    writing code within, 151–153
TypeOf operator, using with If...Then...Else statements, 74–75
types, 109–110
    reference, 110–114
    value, 109–110

U

UBound statement, 82
UML (Unified Modeling Language), 124, 125
    notation for class encapsulation, 128–129
    Visio UML diagrams, 124, 125
unary operators, 66
Unified Modeling Language. *See* UML
upgrade reports from Visual Basic Upgrade Wizard, 203–206
UPGRADE_ISSUE, 206
UPGRADE_NOTE, 204
UPGRADE_TODO, 204
UPGRADE_WARNING, 204–205
upper boundary of arrays, 82–84
user authentication, 125–127
user interfaces, 220

V

Validator controls, 190
value type reference model, 109–110
variables
    instance, 111–112
    making private, 120
    in object-oriented software development, 111
VBScript (Visual Basic Scripting Edition), 20–21
version control
    assemblies and, 41
    COM and, 10–11, 12
virtual classes, 128
virtual functions table (vtable), 7
Visio UML diagrams, 124, 125
Visual Basic
    C++ competition with, 20
    calling .NET objects from clients, 209–210
    development of componentware with OLE and COM, 19
    development of VB.NET and C#, 21–22
    evolution of, 17–18
    exception handling in, 148
    form-based application development of, 18
    keeping applications in, 197, 198
    legacy functions for strings, 87–88
    market demand for skills in, 222–223
    On Error statements, 148, 156
    popularity of, 20
    programming in, 59
    value of True in, 64
    VBScript and ASP development, 20–21
    See also migrating to Visual Basic.NET
Visual Basic Upgrade Wizard, 202–207
    interpreting upgrade reports from, 203–206

opening projects in Visual Studio.NET, 202

upgrading COM and COM+ services with, 206

Visual Basic.NET, 2–31

ADO.NET database technology, 28–29

compatibility of syntax and idioms in, 217–218

constructor and destructor methods for objects, 25–26

data type conversion in, 63–64

delegates, 27

development of, 17, 21–22

evaluating whether to migrate to, 214

exception handling in, 149–151

features of, 23

interfaces, 27

late binding support of, 220–221

managed execution, 28

market demand for skills in, 222–223

methods in, 104–105

multithreading, 27–28

nomenclature for class visibility and role in, 128

object-oriented programming in, 59–60

origins of, 2–12

overloading of properties and methods, 24

overriding, 25

overview of, 13–15

porting existing code to, 198–199, 201

rewriting applications in, 199–201

similarities to Java, 15–17

structured exception handling, 26

true object orientation, 23–26

value of True for, 64–65

With blocks in, 221

See also building VB.NET applications; migrating to Visual Basic.NET

Visual Studio.NET, 185–186, 202

W

Web Forms

creating login application in ASP.NET, 188–190

defined, 184–185

Web service, 191–194

defined, 191

enabling application functions on Web, 191–193

steps in, 191

Wend termination statements, 78, 79

While statements, 78–79

WinCV.exe, 206–207

Windows DNA (Distributed Internet Applications Architecture), 3–5

Windows Forms, 184

With blocks in VB.NET, 221

X

XML, serializing data in, 177

INTERNATIONAL CONTACT INFORMATION

AUSTRALIA
McGraw-Hill Book Company Australia Pty. Ltd.
TEL +61-2-9417-9899
FAX +61-2-9417-5687
http://www.mcgraw-hill.com.au
books-it_sydney@mcgraw-hill.com

CANADA
McGraw-Hill Ryerson Ltd.
TEL +905-430-5000
FAX +905-430-5020
http://www.mcgrawhill.ca

GREECE, MIDDLE EAST,
NORTHERN AFRICA
McGraw-Hill Hellas
TEL +30-1-656-0990-3-4
FAX +30-1-654-5525

MEXICO (Also serving Latin America)
McGraw-Hill Interamericana Editores S.A. de C.V.
TEL +525-117-1583
FAX +525-117-1589
http://www.mcgraw-hill.com.mx
fernando_castellanos@mcgraw-hill.com

SINGAPORE (Serving Asia)
McGraw-Hill Book Company
TEL +65-863-1580
FAX +65-862-3354
http://www.mcgraw-hill.com.sg
mghasia@mcgraw-hill.com

SOUTH AFRICA
McGraw-Hill South Africa
TEL +27-11-622-7512
FAX +27-11-622-9045
robyn_swanepoel@mcgraw-hill.com

UNITED KINGDOM & EUROPE
(Excluding Southern Europe)
McGraw-Hill Education Europe
TEL +44-1-628-502500
FAX +44-1-628-770224
http://www.mcgraw-hill.co.uk
computing_neurope@mcgraw-hill.com

ALL OTHER INQUIRIES Contact:
Osborne/McGraw-Hill
TEL +1-510-549-6600
FAX +1-510-883-7600
http://www.osborne.com
omg_international@mcgraw-hill.com